# DEIN COACH ZUM ERFOLG!

## *So geht's ins* ActiveBook:

Du kannst auf alle digitalen Inhalte (Prüfung 2021, interaktive Aufgaben, Videos, „MindCards") online zugreifen. Registriere dich dazu unter **www.stark-verlag.de/mystark** mit deinem **persönlichen Zugangscode:**

T9Y9-C5D6-Y7H4

125460-000513

*gültig bis 31. Juli 2022*



ActiveBook

## *Das* ActiveBook *bietet dir:*

- Lernvideos zum Umgang mit Textaufgaben
- Interaktive Aufgaben zu sprachlichen Grundlagen
- Web-App mit hilfreichen Wendungen

# DEIN COACH ZUM ERFOLG!

## *So kannst du interaktiv lernen:*

### Interaktive Aufgaben

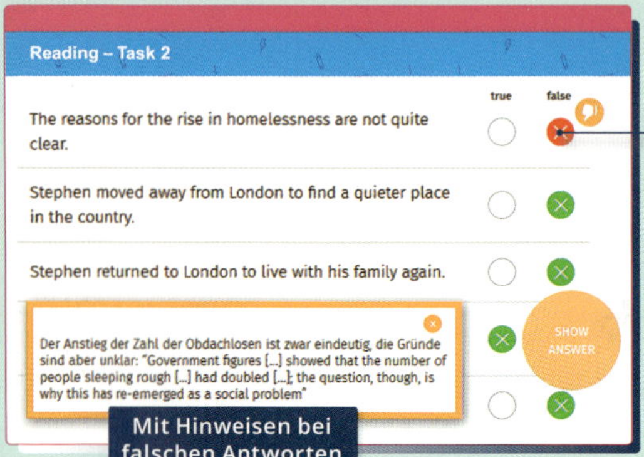


### Lernvideos

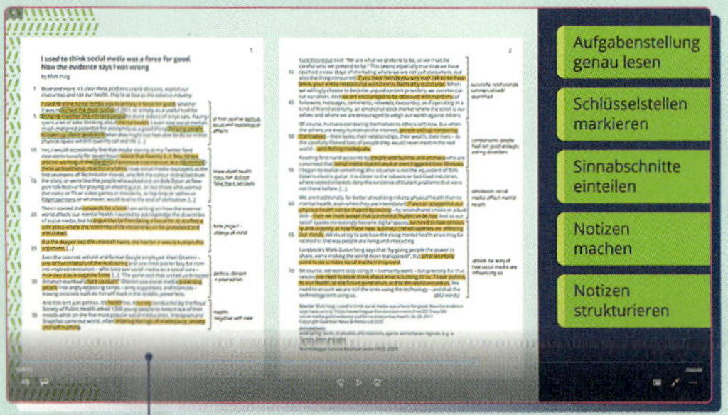


### Web-App „MindCards"

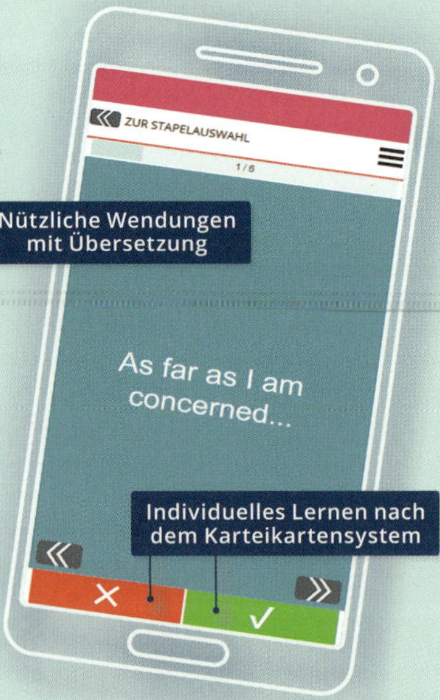


**Systemvoraussetzungen:**
- Windows 7/8/10 oder Mac OS X ab 10.9
- Mindestens 1024×768 Pixel Bildschirmauflösung
- Chrome, Firefox oder ähnlicher Webbrowser
- Adobe Reader oder kompatibler anderer PDF-Reader
- Internetzugang

**Speaking**

**Writing**

2022

# Abitur

Original-Prüfungsaufgaben
mit Lösungen

Berlin · Brandenburg

## Englisch

STARK

17. ergänzte Auflage
www.stark-verlag.de

# Inhalt

Sobald die Original-Prüfungsaufgaben 2021 zur Veröffentlichung freigegeben sind, können Sie sie als PDF auf der Plattform MyStark herunterladen (Zugangscode vgl. Farbseiten vorne im Buch).

Jeweils im Herbst erscheinen die neuen Ausgaben
der Abiturprüfungsaufgaben mit Lösungen.

**Autorinnen und Autoren**

Albrecht, Günther (Übungsaufgabe 2: Prüfungsteil 1 Aufgabe 3.2)
Holtwick, Birgit (Übungsaufgabe 1: Prüfungsteil 1; Übungsaufgabe 2: Prüfungsteil 1 Aufgabe 1, 2, 3.1, Prüfungsteil 2; Übungsaufgabe 3: Prüfungsteil 1 Aufgabe 1, 2, 3.1)
Jacob, Rainer (Lösungen GK 2018)
Klewitz, Bernd (Lösungen LK 2021 Aufgabenstellung 1.1 und 2.1)
Klimmt, Robert (Die wichtigsten Stilmittel zur Textanalyse)
Lemke, Frank und Nussdorf, Kathryn (Lösungen GK 2019–2021)
Redaktion (Lernvideos zur Textaufgabe; Übungsaufgabe 1: Prüfungsteil 2)
Schulz, Katrin (Lösungen LK/EN 2018–2020, LK 2021 1.2 und 2.2)
Warlimont, Peter (Übungsaufgabe 3: Prüfungsteil 1 Aufgabe 3.2, Prüfungsteil 2)

# Vorwort

**Liebe Schülerinnen, liebe Schüler,**

mithilfe der folgenden Informationen, Aufgaben und Lösungen haben Sie verschiedene Möglichkeiten, sich auf das Abitur im Fach Englisch vorzubereiten:

- Der erste Teil des Buches enthält **Hinweise und Tipps** zur schriftlichen Abiturprüfung im Fach Englisch in Berlin und Brandenburg. Hier finden Sie Informationen zu häufigen Aufgabenstellungen, wichtigen Stilmitteln und zu einer geschickten Vorgehensweise in der Abiturprüfung.
- Die **Übungsaufgaben** gliedern sich in zwei Teile: Zunächst finden Sie die Aufgabenstellung zu den **Lernvideos**. Lesen Sie die Texte und Aufgaben, bevor Sie sich die Videos ansehen. Im zweiten Teil finden Sie **Übungsaufgaben** mit Lösungen, die sich an den aktuellen Vorgaben zum **Abitur in Berlin und Brandenburg** orientieren. Der Schwierigkeitsgrad ist dabei ansteigend.
- Im Anschluss folgt eine Auswahl von **Original-Prüfungsaufgaben der Grund- und Leistungskurse** der letzten Jahre. Beachten Sie, dass sich diese Aufgaben teilweise leicht von den aktuellen Abituraufgaben unterscheiden. Die entscheidendste Änderung ist, dass Sie im Anforderungsbereich III der Schreibaufgabe seit dem Abitur 2021 nur zwei Aufgaben zur Auswahl finden. Die Aufgabe mit dem Vergleich zu einem Werk, das Sie im Unterricht gelesen haben, ist nicht mehr Bestandteil der Abiturprüfung.
- Zusätzlich zu den Aufgaben in diesem Buch haben Sie die Möglichkeit, wichtige sprachliche **Grundlagen** anhand interaktiver Aufgaben im **ActiveBook** zu üben. Mit Hilfe der **Web-App** „MindCards" können Sie zusätzlich hilfreiche **sprachliche Wendungen** wiederholen.

Sie können auf alle digitalen Zusätze online über die Plattform **MyStark** zugreifen. Auf den Farbseiten zu Beginn des Buches finden Sie Ihren persönlichen Zugangscode.

Wir wünschen Ihnen viel Erfolg bei der Abiturprüfung,
Ihre Autoren und Autorinnen

# Stichwortverzeichnis 2018 – 2020

# Hinweise zu den digitalen Zusätzen

Auf alle digitalen Zusätze können Sie online über die Plattform **MyStark** zugreifen. Ihren persönlichen Zugangscode finden Sie auf den Farbseiten vorne im Buch.

## PDF der Original-Prüfungsaufgaben 2021

Das Corona-Virus hat auch im vergangenen Schuljahr die Prüfungsabläufe beeinflusst. Um Ihnen die Prüfung 2021 schnellstmöglich zur Verfügung stellen zu können, bringen wir sie in digitaler Form heraus.
Sobald die Original-Prüfungsaufgaben 2021 zur Veröffentlichung freigegeben sind, können sie als PDF auf der Plattform MyStark heruntergeladen werden.

## Kurzgrammatik

Mit der Kurzgrammatik können Sie sich eine knappe und verständliche Übersicht über die wichtigsten Themenfelder der englischen Grammatik herunterladen. Schlagen Sie hier die Grammatikregeln zu Fehlern nach, die Sie noch häufig machen.

## Lernvideos

Textaufgaben sind Teil vieler Prüfungen und Klausuren – und machen oft einen Großteil der Prüfungsleistung aus. Mithilfe der **Lernvideos zum richtigen Umgang mit Textaufgaben** können Sie sich optimal auf die Anforderungen in diesem Bereich vorbereiten. Am Beispiel von zwei Texten mit je drei Aufgabenstellungen wird gezeigt, wie man an eine Textaufgabe herangeht und sie erfolgreich löst.

**Die Lernvideos beinhalten:**

- **Schritt-für-Schritt-Anleitungen** zum richtigen Vorgehen in der Prüfung
- **Sachtext** und **literarischer Text** als Grundlage
- nützliche Hinweise zu **häufigen Operatoren** und **Zieltextsorten**

Die im Video behandelten Übungsaufgaben sind im Kapitel „Lernvideos zur Textaufgabe" abgedruckt. Lesen Sie sich die Texte und Aufgabenstellungen zunächst durch, bevor Sie sich die Videos auf MyStark ansehen.

## Interaktive Aufgaben – „ActiveBook“

Im **ActiveBook „Basic Language Skills**“ erhalten Sie Zugriff auf zahlreiche **interaktive Aufgaben** zu Grundlagen wie **Hörverstehen**, **Leseverstehen** und **Sprachverwendung im Kontext**. Dies sind ganz wichtige „Basics“, die Sie für eine gute Sprachbeherrschung brauchen.

**Das ActiveBook „Basic Language Skills“ bietet Ihnen:**

- „**Listening**“ – authentische Audiodateien mit vielfältigen Aufgaben, die Ihr Hörverstehen testen
- „**Reading**“ – abwechslungsreiche Lesetexte und dazugehörige Aufgaben
- „**English in Use**“ mit gemischten Aufgaben rund um den Gebrauch der englischen Sprache
- Alle Aufgaben sind interaktiv, d. h., Sie können sie direkt am PC bearbeiten und erhalten sofort eine Rückmeldung zu Ihren Antworten.

## Web-App „MindCards“

Mit der Web-App „**MindCards**“ können Sie am Smartphone Vokabeln lernen. Auf diesen interaktiven Karteikarten finden Sie hilfreiche Wendungen, die Sie beim Schreiben von Texten oder im mündlichen Sprachgebrauch einsetzen können.

Scannen Sie einfach die QR-Codes oder verwenden Sie folgende Links, um zu den „MindCards“ zu gelangen:
https://www.stark-verlag.de/mindcards/writing-2
https://www.stark-verlag.de/mindcards/speaking-2

Writing

Speaking

# Hinweise und Tipps

## Die Anforderungen im Abitur

Im Folgenden finden Sie alle wichtigen Informationen zu den zentralen Abiturprüfungen 2022 in Berlin und Brandenburg im Fach Englisch. Sollten nach Erscheinen dieses Bandes noch entscheidende Änderungen in der Abiturprüfung 2022 bekannt gegeben werden, finden Sie aktuelle Informationen dazu auf der Plattform MyStark (Zugangscode vgl. Farbseiten).

### 1 Ablauf der Prüfung

Der Ablauf der Abiturprüfung in Berlin und Brandenburg erfolgt nach demselben Muster. Zu Beginn der Prüfung werden Ihnen pro Prüfungsbereich zwei Aufgabenstellungen vorgelegt (zwei im Bereich „Lesen und Schreiben“, zwei im Bereich „Sprachmittlung“). Daraus wählen Sie je eine zur Bearbeitung aus. Die Bearbeitungszeit im Leistungskurs beträgt 300 Minuten, im Grundkurs 270 Minuten. Diese Zeiten schließen Ihre individuelle Lese- und Auswahlzeit ein, die maximal 30 Minuten beträgt. Sie können sich die Auswahl- und Bearbeitungszeit frei einteilen. Als Richtlinie gilt, dass Sie etwa 60 Minuten für die Bearbeitung der Sprachmittlungsaufgabe nutzen sollten, die übrige Zeit für die Schreibaufgabe. Sie dürfen bei der Bearbeitung jeweils ein einsprachiges und ein zweisprachiges Wörterbuch Englisch sowie ein Nachschlagewerk zur deutschen Sprache verwenden.

### 2 Inhaltliche Schwerpunkte

Die folgenden Themen sind dem Rahmenlehrplan für die gymnasiale Oberstufe sowie den Prüfungsvorgaben und Hinweisen für das Zentralabitur in Englisch in Berlin und Brandenburg entnommen. Die Schwerpunktsetzung erfolgt schulintern.

- Individuum und Gesellschaft (1. Kurshalbjahr):
  *Aims and ambitions* – Ziele und Ambitionen
- Nationale und kulturelle Identität (2. Kurshalbjahr):
  *Ethnic and cultural diversity* – Leben in der multikulturellen Gesellschaft
- Eine Welt – globale Fragen (3. Kurshalbjahr):
  *Saving the planet* – Umwelt- und Klimaschutz
- Herausforderungen der Gegenwart (4. Kurshalbjahr):
  *The impact of the media on society* – Rolle und Wirkungsweise der Massenmedien

Üblicherweise verbindet die Abiturprüfung zwei Schwerpunktthemen miteinander. Es werden jedoch keine detaillierten Inhalte gefordert und die Prüfungsthemen sind weit gefasst. Konzentrieren Sie sich in der Prüfungsvorbereitung auf die im Unterricht behandelten Themen und erarbeiteten Sie sich den Wortschatz in den prüfungsrelevanten Bereichen. Die Prüfung besteht aus zwei Teilen, Leseverstehen und Schreiben (**Teil 1**) und Sprachmittlung (**Teil 2**). Für jeden Teil können Sie aus zwei Aufgabenstellungen diejenige auswählen, die Ihnen mehr zusagt.

- Der **Kompetenzbereich Leseverstehen und Schreiben** besteht aus einem oder mehreren Texten mit Arbeitsanweisungen, die alle drei Anforderungsbereiche (Zusammenfassung, Analyse und Schreibaufgabe; siehe „Anforderungsbereiche und Aufgabenstellungen") abdecken. Es kommen literarische Texte, Sachtexte sowie Bilder und Grafiken infrage.
- Der **Kompetenzbereich Sprachmittlung/Mediation** umfasst in der Regel ein oder zwei deutsche Ausgangstexte, aus denen wesentliche Inhalte in die Zielsprache Englisch transportiert werden sollen. Welche Informationen aus den deutschen Texten relevant sind, hängt von der Zielgruppe ab, an die sich der Text richtet, sowie von dem Kontext, in den die Aufgabe eingebettet ist. Häufig wird als Zieltext ein (Online-) Artikel, eine E-Mail oder ein Blogeintrag gefordert.

## 3 Leistungsanforderungen

Die Korrektur der Abituraufgaben erfolgt durch die Lehrkraft, von der Sie unterrichtet wurden sowie durch einen Zweitkorrektor oder eine Zweitkorrektorin. Der erteilte Unterricht kann somit bei der Bewertung der Abituraufgaben berücksichtigt werden. Darüber hinaus existieren zentrale Bewertungsvorgaben.
Bei allen Aufgabenarten wird zwischen **inhaltlicher** und **sprachlicher Leistung** unterschieden. Bei der Festlegung der Gesamtnote kommt der sprachlichen Leistung im Vergleich zur inhaltlichen die größere Bedeutung zu. Sie werden im Verhältnis 60 : 40 gewertet.
Genauere Informationen zu Kriterien bei der Begutachtung finden Sie unter
www.klausurgutachten.de/berlin/ bzw. www.klausurgutachten.de/brandenburg/

Beide Prüfungsteile werden zunächst separat nach deren inhaltlichen und sprachlichen Leistung bewertet. In die **Gesamtbewertung** fließen **Teil 1** (Leseverstehen und Schreiben) mit stärkerer Gewichtung als **Teil 2** (Sprachmittlung) ein.

## 4 Anforderungsbereiche und Aufgabenstellungen

In der Regel werden Ihnen zum Abiturtext vier Arbeitsaufträge gestellt, die sich im Grundsatz an der Abfolge Zusammenfassung, Analyse, Stellungnahme/Kommentar/kreatives Schreiben und Mediation orientieren.
Diese Abfolge ergibt sich grob aus den drei Anforderungsbereichen, die vom Lehrplan und den Abiturrichtlinien als Leitgrößen vorgegeben sind:

- Anforderungsbereich I: Textverstehen
- Anforderungsbereich II: Textanalyse
- Anforderungsbereich III: Diskutieren und Gestalten

Der **erste Arbeitsauftrag** bezieht sich in der Regel weitgehend auf den **Anforderungsbereich I (Textverstehen)**. Sie sollen unter Beweis stellen, dass Sie die Textvorlage(n) verstanden haben und in der Lage sind, eine Zusammenfassung zu erstellen und sich auf bestimmte Aspekte zu konzentrieren.
Die **zweite Aufgabe** bezieht sich in der Regel schwerpunktmäßig auf den **Anforderungsbereich II (Textanalyse)**. Im Zentrum steht hier die Analyse des Informationsgehalts des Textes oder der Texte in Zusammenhang mit der Textgestaltung.
Im **Anforderungsbereich III (Diskutieren und Gestalten)** geht es um Stellungnahme/Kommentar oder kreatives Schreiben (z. B. aus einer anderen Perspektive) in einer vorgegebenen Textsorte. In diesem Bereich haben Sie meist die Wahlmöglichkeit zwischen zwei Aufgaben. Es kann eine situationsgebundene Textart (z. B. Brief, Blogeintrag etc.) mit dem dazugehörigen Register verlangt werden. Teilweise müssen Sie sich dabei auf das vorliegende Material und darüber hinausgehende Kenntnisse beziehen. Es ist möglich, dass die Aufgabe sich auf zusätzliches Bildmaterial (z. B. Cartoon, Statistik etc.) bezieht.
Bei der **Sprachmittlungsaufgabe** müssen Sie Informationen aus einem oder mehreren Texten kohärent, strukturiert, situations- und adressatengerecht zusammenfassen.

## 5 Operatoren

Operatoren zeigen an, welche Tätigkeit beim Lösen von Prüfungsaufgaben erwartet wird.

### Anforderungsbereich I

Reproduktion und Textverstehen

| **Operatoren** | **Erläuterungen** | **Beispiele** |
|---|---|---|
| **Gelenkte Zusammenfassung** | | |
| outline | Outline the information required. Give the main features, structure or general principles of a topic in your own words omitting minor details. Do not include your opinion or interpretation. | • Give an outline of the arguments Text A contains against and in favour of …<br>• Outline the information the narrator/author provides on …<br>• Outline the situation of …<br>• Outline what … says about … |
| give an account of | | • Give an account of … (as described in …). |
| sum up | | • Sum up the main ideas on … as presented in … |
| describe | Give an accurate account of sth in your own words. | • Describe … as depicted in … |
| state, point out | Present sth clearly using your own words. | • State the information the author gives on … |
| **Zusammenfassung** | | |
| summarise/ summarize/ sum up | Give a concise account of the main aspects/points in your own words. Write an introductory sentence. | • Summarise the content of the article.<br>• Sum up the content of the excerpt. |

## Anforderungsbereich II
Analyse

| Operatoren | Erläuterungen | Beispiele |
|---|---|---|
| **Textanalyse** | | |
| analyse/<br>analyze | Name and explain the meaning of specific aspects and/or features of the text and their effect on the reader/audience. | • State the message of the article (Text A) and analyse how the author tries to make the reader accept and believe what he/she says.<br>• State the message of the text and analyse how the use of imagery serves to convey this message to the reader.<br>• Analyse how the relationship between the characters is reflected in their language.<br>• Analyse how the author's use of humour helps to convey his message.<br>• Briefly describe the aim the writer pursues in this excerpt, and analyse how the point of view he/she employs helps to achieve it.<br>• Analyse how the reader's interest in the text is attracted by its content and structure.<br>• Describe the picture/cover … and analyse to what extent it may help to understand …<br>• State the message of … and analyse how the picture, the layout and the use of … convey this message to the reader. |
| examine | | • Examine the problems the protagonist faces … |
| show (how) | Point out and illustrate. | • State …'s opinion about … and show how the reader is made to share it by analysing relevant literary means.<br>• Show how the boy is characterised in this excerpt. |
| explain | Describe in detail and give reasons for/refer to causes/effects. | • Explain the protagonist's behaviour in the given conflict …<br>• Explain what is meant by the following statement from the text: "…" (l. …). |
| describe (the way) | Give an accurate account of sth in your own words. | • Describe the way the playwright creates an atmosphere of suspense and explain its effect on the reader. |
| compare/<br>contrast | Point out similarities and differences./Emphasize the differences between two or more things. | • Describe Text B (the picture/two graphics) and compare/contrast its information with the information given in the article (Text A). |
| relate | Establish a connection between two things. | • Relate the writer's message as conveyed in Text A to the information given in Text B. |

## Anforderungsbereiche I/II

Reproduktion, Reorganisation und Analyse

Sprachmittlung/Mediation

| Operatoren | Erläuterungen | Beispiele |
|---|---|---|
| outline/give an account of/sum up | Give the relevant information on the topic. Use paraphrases. Do not quote from the text. | • Outline the information from Text B that refers to … Do this in a way that it helps someone write a paper/speech on this issue … |

## Anforderungsbereich III

Diskutieren und Gestalten

Diskussion/Kommentar

| Operatoren | Erläuterungen | Beispiele |
|---|---|---|
| discuss | Examine/analyse, give reasons for and against and come to a justified conclusion.<br>Present arguments with supporting evidence and conclude with your personal view. | • Discuss whether the difficulties and chances illustrated in Text A are typical phenomena of globalization.<br>• Discuss if the protagonist has coped with the problem in an adequate way.<br>• Discuss the relevance/chances of … |
| comment on | Based on arguments express your personal view on a problem/certain behaviour, attitudes or viewpoints. | • Comment on the impact of globalisation on families.<br>• Comment on the author's thesis/view "…" (l. …). |
| reflect on | Consider/contemplate/think carefully and deeply about a problem/certain behaviour, attitudes or viewpoint. | • Referring to a character from literature or film, reflect on the influence of … on this person's life. |
| convince | Present arguments so that the addressee will support your view. | • As an exchange student you are attending an American high school for one year. In a formal letter convince the head of your school that the introduction of bilingual classes would be profitable. |
| justify | Show adequate grounds for decisions or conclusions. | • Justify the protagonist's behaviour in the light of … |
| verify | Analyse and show that something is true. | • Verify the author's thesis … |
| assess/ evaluate | Decide on the value or the state of something and give reasons for your decision. | • With reference to the quotation, assess the impact of … |
| interpret | Establish the meaning of something in a wider context and give your own view. | • Interpret the quotation … |

## 1 Textzusammenfassung

Der erste Arbeitsauftrag der Abituraufgabenstellung zielt in der Regel auf das Textverstehen, d. h., er beinhaltet in gelenkter oder allgemeiner Form die Erstellung einer Zusammenfassung, deren Länge in aller Regel zwischen 25 und 30 % des Ausgangstextes betragen soll.

**Warum wird eine Zusammenfassung geschrieben?**
Die Zusammenfassung hat eine Schlüsselfunktion in der Vorbereitung der Textanalyse und der Interpretation. Zunächst muss man sicher sein, dass auch wirklich erfasst worden ist, worum es in dem Text geht. Dann ist es möglich, den Text auf Aufbau, Argumentationsweise, Sprache und Stilmittel, d. h. in Bezug auf seine Gestaltungsmittel hin, zu untersuchen. Nachdem die Textaussage und die Textgestaltung klar erfasst sind, kann man sich der Textauslegung, der Interpretation und der Analyse der Bedeutung des Textes zuwenden, erst dann kann der Text auch in einem größeren inhaltlichen oder stilistischen Zusammenhang betrachtet werden.

**Wie wird eine Zusammenfassung vorbereitet?**
Ihre inhaltliche Zusammenfassung kann mit einem *umbrella sentence* beginnen, der (soweit bekannt) Angaben zur Autorin /zum Autor, zum Titel, zur Textsorte, zum Zeitpunkt des Entstehens und zum thematischen Schwerpunkt des Textes enthält.
Die Gliederung des Textes entwickelt sich bei Sachtexten aus folgenden Leitfragen:
- Um welches Thema/Problem geht es?
- Wer ist die Zielgruppe?
- Welche Funktion erfüllt der Text?
- Wie ist der argumentative Aufbau des Textes?
- Welche Informationen erhalten wir über …?

Bei literarischen Texten als Klausurvorlage handelt es sich in aller Regel um Momentaufnahmen aus einem größeren Zusammenhang, welcher unbekannt bleibt. Die Gliederung des Textes ergibt sich aus Leitfragen wie z. B.:
- Welche Situation treffen wir an?
- Wer sind die Protagonisten und wie verhalten sie sich?
- Um welches Thema/Problem geht es?
- Wie ist der Text strukturiert?
- Welche Informationen erhalten wir über …?

In jedem Falle ist bei diesen Leitfragen immer wieder zu entscheiden:
- Was ist zentral und wichtig?
- Was ist rein ornamental, also ausschmückendes Beiwerk?
- Was könnte man erwähnen, muss es aber nicht?

Bei der Entscheidung, was man weglassen kann, helfen Überlegungen wie „Könnte ich den Text verstehen, wenn mir diese Information nicht zur Verfügung gestellt würde?“

**Was ist beim Schreiben zu beachten?**

Aus der Beantwortung der Leitfragen ergeben sich Grundbausteine und eine Rohstruktur der Zusammenfassung. Im Einzelfall kann eine detailliertere Gliederung unerlässlich sein.

Grundsätzlich sollten Sie nur Informationen mit aufnehmen, die im Ausgangstext enthalten sind. Die Argumentationslogik sollte klar, möglichst sachlich und nachvollziehbar sein. Sie wird nicht immer der Reihenfolge der Argumente im Text folgen. Im Gegenteil: sehr oft wird eine am Schluss der Textvorlage zu findende These/ Schlussfolgerung oder überraschende Handlungsvariante den Ausgangspunkt der Zusammenfassung bilden.

**Wie wird die Zusammenfassung formal und sprachlich gestaltet?**

- **Textlänge:** Der Umfang der Zusammenfassung liegt in der Regel zwischen einem Viertel und einem Drittel der Länge der Textvorlage.
- **Tempus:** Eine Zusammenfassung wird im Präsens verfasst. Im Text vorkommende Vor- bzw. Nachzeitigkeit bleibt erhalten.
- **Bezüge:** Personen-, Zeit- und Ortsbezüge werden wie in der indirekten Rede umgeformt, also wird *I* zu *he* oder *she*; *yesterday* zu *the day before*; *here* zu *there* usw.
- **Tabus:** Die Zusammenfassung enthält keine direkte Rede und keine Zitate. Die Zusammenfassung enthält keine wertende persönliche Stellungnahme und ist in jedem Fall in eigenen Worten zu formulieren.

Sprachlich tendiert die Zusammenfassung zu einem gehobenen Niveau und Abstraktionsgrad. Sie ist eher konzeptionell als berichtend oder ausschmückend (d. h., sie stellt das dem Ursprungstext zugrunde gelegte Konzept dar); dies und die Textlänge unterscheidet sie von der Nacherzählung. Dies erreicht man mithilfe von

- **allgemeinen Begriffen** (wie z. B. *means of transport* an Stelle von *car, bike and underground*): Aufzählungen sollten vermieden werden und statt dessen in einem Oberbegriff zusammengefasst werden,
- **übergreifenden einschätzenden Verben** (wie z. B. *to focus on, to claim, to maintain, to criticize, to report, to illustrate*),
- **generalisierenden Verben** (wie z. B. *to be worried about, to be reluctant, to be concerned with*) und
- und **Konjunktionen:** temporale *(before, when)*, kausale *(because, as, so)*, konditionale *(if, unless)*, konzessive *(though, although)*, kontrastive *(but, instead of)* und konsekutive *(so that, thus)*.

## 2 Analyse

Prinzipiell können Aufgaben zur Analyse eine Textanalyse im engeren Sinne fordern oder es kann verlangt werden, dass man etwas in den Zusammenhang mit einem im Unterricht erarbeiteten Thema bringt.

- Bei der **Analyse im engeren Sinne** geht es um Facetten der Textstrukturierung/ Textgestaltung, die aufzuzeigen sind; es kann zusätzlich gefordert sein, das Verhältnis zwischen den Gestaltungsmitteln und dem Inhalt, der Atmosphäre oder der Textaussage auszuloten, d. h., die Funktion der Gestaltungsmittel als Teil der Interpretation zu bestimmen (siehe a).

- Eine andere Variante der Textanalyse besteht darin, dass man den Text aus der Aufgabe mit einem anderen Material verknüpft. Häufig finden Sie Bilder oder Cartoons, die Sie in Bezug zum Text setzen müssen.

a) Auf der Basis der Zusammenfassung und dem damit gewährleisteten Textüberblick wendet man das Wissen um Aufbau und sprachliche Gestaltung von Texten systematisch auf den Text an. Wenn in der Aufgabenstellung keine die Arbeit lenkenden Vorgehensweise gegeben werden, so ist der Text daraufhin zu *scannen,* welche Gestaltungsmittel besonders in den Vordergrund treten. Das *Scannen* kann sich beziehen auf
   - die Wortwahl (Register/Stilebene, Häufigkeiten),
   - den Satzbau (komplex/einfach),
   - Erzählperspektive
   - und Stilmittel (z. B. Kontrast, Parallelität, Repetition/Wiederholung, Vergleich, Metapher).

   Mit dem Aufzeigen von Textgestaltungsmerkmalen kann die Aufgabenstellung erfüllt sein, in vielen Fällen allerdings ist sie das Fundament für eine weiter gehende Betrachtung, die über die formale Analyse hinausgeht. Hier stellt sich die Frage nach dem Zusammenwirken zwischen Form und Inhalt, d. h., die Gestaltungsmittel werden auf ihre Funktion oder ihre Wirkung hin überprüft. Inwiefern unterstützen sie die Textaussage oder inwiefern unterlaufen sie diese, z. B. in der Satire oder der Parodie?

b) Bei der Verknüpfung von Gelerntem mit dem neuen Text wird in der Regel die Aufgabenstellung bereits einen Hinweis darauf enthalten, welche Anknüpfungspunkte die weitere Arbeit steuern. Ist die Aufgabenstellung sehr allgemein gehalten, müssen mögliche Anknüpfungspunkte betrachtet und kurz durchdacht werden. Sind die Überlegungsaspekte einmal gewählt, so ist dieser Ansatz konsequent und möglichst differenziert weiter zu verfolgen und es ist z. B. zu klären, inwiefern sich Gelerntes und Neues im Widerspruch zueinander oder in Übereinstimmung befinden, bzw. inwiefern die Informationen sich wechselseitig erhellen.

## 3 Persönliche Stellungnahme/Kommentar und kreatives Schreiben

In der letzten Aufgabe haben Sie die Wahl zwischen einer eher traditionellen Aufgabe in Form einer persönliche Stellungnahme, eines Kommentars oder einer eher analytisch orientierten Erörterung und einer kreativen, gestalterischen Aufgabenstellung.

In einer **persönlichen Stellungnahme**/einem **Kommentar** wird von Ihnen erwartet, dass Sie Ihre eigene Meinung zu dem gegebenen Problem äußern. Damit steht es Ihnen frei, das Problem unter Umständen auch sehr emotional und unter Bezug auf Ihre eigenen Erfahrungen und Wertvorstellungen zu beleuchten.
Es wird erwartet, dass Sie einen oder mehrere Hauptaspekte auswählen und diese Auswahl kurz reflektieren und begründen. Diese Aspekte werden systematisch bearbeitet und man stellt Thesen auf. Über eine eng gefasste persönliche Stellungnahme

hinaus sollte eine Einbettung der Problemstellung und der Hauptaspekte in einen größeren Kontext vorgenommen werden.

Im Rahmen einer **Erörterung** sollten Sie möglichst viele Facetten eines Problems analytisch durchdringen und eine Bewertung vornehmen. Die Grundlagen dieser Bewertung müssen offengelegt und reflektiert werden. Die Diskussion ist mehr der analytischen Schärfe verpflichtet und weniger den Bedürfnissen und Emotionen des Einzelnen. Sie können also bei der Diskussion eines Problems zu anderen Ergebnissen kommen als bei einer persönlichen Stellungnahme zu demselben Problem.
Methodisch empfiehlt es sich, vor dem Schreiben eine Stichwortsammlung zu erstellen, zusammengehörige Stichwörter zu bündeln und in eine sinnvolle, für die Leserschaft nachvollziehbare Anordnung zu bringen. Immer mit Blick auf die Zielperson ist beim Schreiben zu entscheiden, an welchen Stellen Beispiele/illustrierende Passagen eingefügt werden.

Bei der Bearbeitung der ***creative writing*-Aufgabe** liegt die besondere Schwierigkeit in der geforderten Textsorte. Fragen Sie sich: Welche Anforderungen stellt die Textsorte, welche Merkmale sind zu beachten? Nach dieser formalen Vorentscheidung über die Textsorte sollten Sie

- Aussage und Ziel Ihres Textes bestimmen,
- inhaltliche Elemente sammeln und gliedern und
- den Argumentationsgang skizzieren.

Für das Schreiben Ihres Textes ist es wichtig, dass Ihre Formulierungen der Textsorte, dem Adressaten/der Adressatin und dem Verwendungszusammenhang angemessen sind.

Bis zur Abiturprüfung 2020 gab es im Anforderungsbereich III eine Aufgabe zur Auswahl, in der Sie aufgefordert waren, ein literarisches oder filmisches Werk in Bezug zum Prüfungstext zu setzen. Diese Aufgabenform ist seit 2021 nicht mehr Bestandteil der Abiturprüfung.

## 4 Sprachmittlung

Je öfter Sie das Aufgabenformat der Sprachmittlung geübt haben, desto eher gewöhnen Sie sich an den Ablauf und können die Ihnen zur Verfügung stehende Bearbeitungszeit optimal für sich nutzen.

- Bestimmen Sie zuerst die zentrale Aussage des Textes.
- Formulieren Sie (je nach Kontext) einen Basissatz, der die Kernaussage des Textes enthält sowie Informationen zu Autorin/Autor, Titel, Quelle und ggf. situativem Rahmen des Textes gibt.
- Sie haben durch die Aufgabenstellung einen konkreten Schreibanlass genannt bekommen. Beachten Sie diesen Kontext, insbesondere den Adressaten/die Adressatin und die Umstände, unter denen der Zieltext verfasst werden soll.
- Markieren Sie inhaltlich relevante Passagen im Ausgangstext/ in den Ausgangstexten, die für die Bearbeitung der Aufgabe wesentlich sind. Verfassen Sie dann die Sprachmittlung.

- Umschreiben Sie Ausdrücke, die keine Entsprechung im Englischen haben, in eigenen Worten, wenn deren Verständnis für die Aufgabenstellung notwendig ist.
- Verwenden Sie Konjunktionen, um logische und zeitliche Bezüge herzustellen.
- Bedenken Sie, dass Ihre *mediation* nur etwa ein Drittel des Ausgangstextes umfassen sollte.

Folgende Kriterien sind von zentraler Bedeutung:
- Beachtung der Aufgabenstellung (Nennen der wesentlichen Aspekte)
- Adressaten- und Situationsbezug
- Inhaltliche und sprachliche Korrektheit

## Die wichtigsten (Stil-)Mittel zur Textanalyse

1. **Alliteration**

   Definition: An alliteration is a figure of speech in which words start with the same consonant sound.

   *Examples:* Literary characters such as Tiny Tim (Dickens), Donald Duck (Disney), Peter Parker (Spiderman), brand names like Coca-Cola, Best Buy or tongue twisters like "Betty Botter bought some butter."

   "So we <u>b</u>eat on, <u>b</u>oats against the current, <u>b</u>orne <u>b</u>ack ceaselessly into the past."
   F. Scott Fitzgerald: *The Great Gatsby* (1925)

   Here the repetition of the "b" sound helps to create a sense of rhythm that evokes the beating of waves against a boat.

   Function: Alliterations and assonance help to emphasize a point, attract attention and make an expression (or scene) more memorable.

2. **Allusion**

   Definition: Allusion is a reference to a character, historical or political event or a piece of art or literature the reader is likely to know or be familiar with.

   *Example:* "This sweltering <u>summer of the Negro's legitimate discontent</u> will not pass until there is an invigoration autumn of freedom and equality."
   Martin Luther King: "I have a dream"-speech (1963)

   Here Martin Luther King alludes to the opening lines of Shakespeare's play *Richard III* which read as follows: "Now is <u>the winter of our discontent</u>". These words lay the groundwork of Shakespeare's portrayal of Richard III of England as a discontented tyrant.

   King's allusion to *Richard III* therefore can be interpreted as connecting the suppression of the African Americans in the 1960s with the tyrant rule of Richard III of England who lived in the 15th century.

   Function: Allusions create a series of associations (see **connotation**) in the reader's mind and thereby either have an emotional impact or stimulate the reader's intellect.

3. **Anaphora**

   Definition: Anaphora is the **repetition** of an expression at the beginning of successive clauses.

   *Example:* "I still have a dream. [...] I have a dream that one day this nation will rise up and live out the true meaning of its creed: 'We hold these truths to be self-evident; that all men are created equal.' I have a dream that one day on the red hills of Georgia the sons of former slaves and the sons of former slave owners will be able to sit down together at the table of brotherhood."
   Martin Luther King: "I have a dream"-speech (1963)

   Function: Anaphora is used to give prominence to ideas by adding rhythm and thereby making the text more pleasurable to read/listen to and easier to remember. This way it appeals to the emotions of the audience in order to persuade, inspire, motivate and encourage.

4. **Antithesis (contrast, opposite)**

   Definition: Antithesis (which literally means "opposite") is a rhetorical device in which two opposite ideas (a thesis and an opposing antithesis) are put together.

   *Example:* "It was the best of times, it was the worst of times, it was the age of wisdom, it was the age of foolishness, it was the epoch of belief, it was the epoch of incredulity, it was the season of Light, it was the season of Darkness, it was the spring of hope, it was the winter of despair, we had everything before us, we had nothing before us, we were all going direct to Heaven, we were all going direct the other way [...]."
   Charles Dickens: *A Tale of Two Cities* (1859)

   Function: Antithesis is used to create emphasis by exposing the reader to often stark and unexpected contrast. Thus, it conveys opinions and emotions more vividly and emphatically.

5. **Characterisation** (direct/indirect)

   Definition: Characterisation refers to the presentation of characters (literary figures) in a text. There are two different ways of characterisation:

   a) Direct (or explicit) characterisation: A character can be characterised directly (explicitly) which means the audience is given direct information about the character:

      *Example:* "Oh! But he was a tight-fisted hand at the grindstone, Scrooge! a squeezing, wrenching, grasping, scraping, clutching, covetous, old sinner! Hard and sharp as flint, from which no steel had ever struck out generous fire; secret, and self-contained, and solitary as an oyster."
      Charles Dickens: *A Christmas Carol* (1843)

      Function: Direct characterisation provides straightforward information about a character. There is no need to "read between the lines" and draw one's own conclusion.

b) Indirect characterisation: Here the audience has to find out about the character's qualities by observing his or her actions, behaviour, thoughts, language, appearance, and his/her way of relating and responding to other characters or problems.

Function: Characterisation aims at informing the audience helping them to make sense of the events taking place. Indirect characterisation is the more subtle way of allowing and encouraging the reader to draw his or her own conclusions which makes the reading (or viewing) process more demanding and challenging but also more rewarding and pleasurable.

6. **Connotation**

Definition: Connotations (or standardized associations) are ideas or emotions associated with an expression.

*Example:* The term "Route 66" is often associated with ideas of freedom and adventure. The term "shark" is frequently connected with images of danger and death. The expression "life sciences" might connote (negative) concepts of genetic modification and/or the successful fight against diseases.

Function: Many expressions, but especially figurative language, generate various connotations (associations) in the reader's mind, addressing his feelings as well as his understanding.

7. **Ellipsis**

Definition: Ellipsis is the omission of one or more words which are necessary to make a complete sentence but which can be supplied by the reader.

Elliptical sentences are typical of oral communication.

*Example:* "Got it?", "Seen it?"

Function: Ellipsis can be used as a literary device to indicate casual speech. Thus, in a speech, ellipsis could create a sense of community or familiarity between the speaker and his or her audience or help to highlight important keywords.

8. **Euphemism**

Definition: A euphemistic expression describes a rather harsh or unpleasant fact in gentler and friendlier terms and is often used to sound more indirect and polite.

*Examples:* "Our cat was very ill. We had her put to sleep."

"He is between jobs." (= "He is unemployed.")

"'For the time being,' he explains, 'it had been found necessary to make a readjustment of rations.'"

George Orwell: *Animal Farm* (1945)

Here, the word "readjustment" replaces the word "reduction", but the impression given is that there is only a change taking place, with "readjustment" being a rather positively connoted expression.

Function: Euphemism helps to convey ideas which are not supposed to be mentioned directly. Euphemisms can also have an ironic (even sarcastic) effect depending on the context.

9. **Figurative/metaphorical language**

Definition: "Figurative" or "metaphorical language" are general terms to describe language that differs from everyday "literal language" in order to intensify comparison, emphasis, clarity, or originality of expression. Metaphor and simile are the two most frequently used, but figurative language also includes hyperbole and puns.

*Examples:* See metaphor, simile, hyperbole, pun

Function: In general, figurative language appeals to our senses as well as to our intellectual curiosity as the reader has to "decipher" its meaning and message within the given context.

10. **Hyperbole** (exaggeration/over-statement)

Definition: Hyperbole is a form of figurative/metaphorical language and involves an unreal exaggeration of ideas.

*Examples:* "I could eat a horse." (= "I'm very hungry")

"I will die of shame."

"I had to wait in the station for ten days – an eternity."
Joseph Conrad: *Heart of Darkness* (1899)

Function: Hyperbole can be used to either achieve a humorous effect or in order to emphasize the importance or intensity of an experience.

11. **Imagery** (figurative/metaphorical language)

Definition: Imagery involves the usage of figurative/metaphorical language such as similes and metaphors, expressions which must be "translated" by the reader to make sense.

*Examples:* see metaphor, simile

Function: The use of imagery aims at making expressions more colourful than everyday speech and thus raises greater awareness in the reader.

12. **Irony** (and Sarcasm)

Definition: The expressed meaning is the opposite of what the author wants to say.

*Example:* "Wonderful. I have just dropped my favourite cup."

Function: The contrast between what is said and what is meant, the literal and the intended meaning, emphasizes the point made by the speaker. The use of irony can also detect a certain detachment of the speaker from his or her subject.

**Dramatic irony:** describes the contrast between what the protagonist and the audience knows, e. g. in the first act of Shakespeare's *Romeo and Juliet* (1597):

"Go ask his name: if he be married.
My grave is like to be my wedding bed."

In this simile, Julia says that if Romeo were already married, her wedding bed would turn out to be her grave. Here, the dramatic irony unfolds because the audience already knows (from the prologue) that at the end of the play she will die.

Function: Dramatic irony reflects the limited understanding of man (e. g. the limitations and shortcomings of Shakespeare's tragic heroes). By putting the reader in a superior position, dramatic irony evokes his curiosity, his hopes, and his fears concerning the characters' fate and therefore applies to his emotions.

13. **Metaphor**

Definition: A metaphor, a form of figurative/metaphorical language, is a comparison where something is represented by an expression that normally occurs in a very different context. Unlike similes metaphors **do not** contain direct terms such as "like" or "as".

*Example:*
"All the world's a stage,
And all the men and women merely players:
They have their exits and their entrances;
And one man in his time plays many parts,"
William Shakespeare: *As You Like It* (1600)

Here, the theatre ("stage"/"players") serves as a metaphor for human life and development.

Function: Metaphors appeal directly to the senses of listeners or readers. They make the language colourful and challenge our imaginations, thereby providing new and original ways of looking at the world from a different perspective.

14. **Onomatopoeia**

Definition: Onomatopoeic expressions imitate the sounds of things, animals or people.

*Examples:* The words "whisper", "roar" or "splash" imitate the actual sounds they stand for, e. g. the sound when something hits the water.

"He saw nothing and heard nothing but he could feel his heart pounding and then he heard the <u>clack</u> on stone and the leaping, dropping <u>clicks</u> of a small rock falling."
Ernest Hemingway: *For Whom the Bell Tolls* (1940)

Function: Onomatopoeic expressions have an emotional effect on the reader as they appeal directly to his or her senses.

15. **Personification**

Definition: Personification refers to the technique of presenting animals or objects as if they possessed human qualities.

*Examples:* "The stars were dancing playfully."

"All he saw was the weeping sky above him."

A genre that uses personification as a guiding principle is the **fable**, where animals take on human qualities.

Function: The use of personification helps to relate animals or things closer to human life and behaviour, appealing to our experiences and emotions.

16. **Paradox** (contradiction)

Definition: A paradox is a statement that embodies two opposing statements or ideas and therefore appears to be contradictory in itself.

*Examples:*
"I can resist anything except temptation."
Oscar Wilde: Lady Windermere's Fan: A Play About a Good Woman (1892)

"All animals are equal, but some are more equal than others".
George Orwell: *Animal Farm* (1945)

Function: The usage of paradox causes the reader to reflect on the message which is often witty, ironic, playful and therefore achieves a humorous effect which in turn makes the text more enjoyable.

17. **Pun** (play on words)

Definition: Puns or plays on words use language in order to create two or more meanings, or they use an expression in a different, unfamiliar context.

*Examples:*
"Ask for me tomorrow and you shall find me a grave man."
William Shakespeare: *Romeo and Juliet* (1597)

Here, "grave" can mean "serious and solemn", or it can be taken literally, as meaning "dead in one's grave". As Mercutio has just been fatally stabbed, this pun implies a rather sarcastic undertone, but fits Mercutio's witty character well.

Function: Puns (or plays on words) make deliberate use of ambiguity, revealing the cleverness and creativity of both the writers and their characters. Puns cause the reader to think about what is being said, thus demanding more concentration but also providing more intellectual and aesthetical pleasure. As many puns create a humorous effect, plays on words are also used for comic relief, for example in Shakespeare's tragedies.

18. **Rhetorical question**

Definition: A rhetorical question is a question that is raised by the author but does not require an answer as the answer is either obvious, or the question cannot/is not supposed to be answered at all.

*Examples:*
"How many deaths will it take till he knows
that too many people have died?"
Bob Dylan: "Blowing in the Wind" (1962)

Function: Rhetorical questions are often used as means of persuasion as the answer often corresponds with the argumentation of the speaker implying that the listener understands the intended message and agrees with it.

19. **Simile** (Comparison)

Definition: A simile is a comparison between objects, persons and ideas using "like", "as" or "as if".

*Examples:* "He acted like a raging bull."

Function: Like metaphors, similes appeal to our senses and imagination and therefore make a speaker's speech more colourful and memorable. Sometimes, similes also include a moment of hyperbole (like in "raging bull").

20. **Tone**

Definition: The tone reflects how the writer uses language to create a certain mood, revealing the emotional attitude towards the topic, the characters and the reader. The tone may for instance be formal, informal, ironic, sarcastic, playful, humorous, angry, emotional or neutral.

Function: The tone helps to convey the atmosphere, the mood and the intention of a text. Furthermore, it can be used for implicit characterisation.

**Lernvideos zur Textaufgabe**
Step-by-Step – Textaufgaben bearbeiten

Es gibt Aufgabenstellungen, die in Englischprüfungen immer wieder auftauchen. Grundlage für diese Aufgabenstellungen sind sogenannte **Operatoren** wie „describe“, „analyse“, „comment on“ und viele mehr. Auch wenn sich die Aufgabenstellung für die Textarbeit im Detail je nach Text unterscheidet, bleibt die grundsätzliche Vorgehensweise bei den jeweiligen Operatoren gleich.

In den Videos auf der Plattform **MyStark** (Zugangscode vgl. Farbseiten) erklären wir Ihnen, wie Sie bei den wichtigsten Operatoren in Textaufgaben vorgehen müssen. Außerdem erfahren Sie etwas zu häufigen **Zieltextformaten** wie Leserbriefen, Blogeinträgen und Reden.

**TIPP**

Lesen Sie die Aufgaben und die dazugehörigen Texte, **bevor Sie sich die Videos ansehen**! Sie können auch schon überlegen, wie Sie selbst bei der Aufgabenstellung vorgehen würden und welche inhaltlichen Aspekte für die Lösung interessant wären – und im Anschluss Ihre Lösung/Vorgehensweise mit den Videos vergleichen.
Viel Spaß!

**Ausgangstext:** *newspaper article*
**Operatoren:** *outline, analyse, write*
**Themen:** *social media, the impact of the media on society*
**Zieltextformate:** *letter to the editor, blog entry, speech*

## Aufgabenstellung

1. **Outline** the author's view on social media. *(Video 1)*
2. **Analyse** the means he uses to convey his attitude and the effect they have on the reader. *(Video 2)*
3. **Write** a **letter to the editor/blog entry/speech** expressing your own opinion on the chances and dangers of social media. *(Video 3)*

**Text: "I used to think social media was a force for good. Now the evidence says I was wrong"** by Matt Haig

*More and more, it's clear these platforms create divisions, exploit our insecurities and risk our health. They're as bad as the tobacco industry.*

I used to think social media was essentially a force for good, whether it was to initiate the Arab spring of 2011, or simply as a useful tool for bringing together like-minded people to share videos of ninja cats. Having spent a lot of time thinking about mental health, I even saw social media's much-maligned potential for anonymity as a good thing, helping people to open up about problems when they might not feel able to do so in that physical space we still quaintly call real life. […]

Yes, I would occasionally feel that maybe staring at my Twitter feed near-continuously for seven hours wasn't that healthy […]. Yes, I'd see articles warning of the dangers of excessive internet use, but I dismissed these as traditional, reactionary takes. I saw social media naysayers as the first reviewers of Technicolor movies, who felt the colour distracted from the story, or were like the people who walked out on Bob Dylan at Newport folk festival for playing an electric guitar, or like those who warned that radio or TV or video games or miniskirts, or hip-hop or selfies or fidget spinners or whatever, would lead to the end of civilisation. […]

Then I started the research for a book I am writing on how the external world affects our mental health. I wanted to acknowledge the downsides of social media, but to argue that far from being a force for ill, it offers a safe place where the insanities of life elsewhere can be processed and articulated.

But the deeper into the research I went, the harder it was to sustain this argument.

Even the internet activist and former Google employee Wael Ghonim – one of the initiators of the Arab spring and one-time poster boy for internet-inspired revolution – who once saw social media as a social cure – now saw it as a negative force. […]: "The same tool that united us to topple dictators eventually tore us apart." Ghonim saw social media polarising people into angry opposing camps – army supporters and Islamists – leaving centrists such as himself stuck in the middle, powerless.

And this isn't just politics. It's health too. A survey conducted by the Royal Society of Public Health asked 1,500 young people to keep track of their moods while on the five most popular social media sites. Instagram and Snapchat came out worst, often inspiring feelings of inadequacy, anxiety and self-loathing. […]

Kurt Vonnegut said: "We are what we pretend to be, so we must be careful who we pretend to be." This seems especially true now we have reached a new stage of marketing where we are not just consumers, but also the thing consumed. If you have friends you only ever talk to on Facebook, your entire relationship with them is framed by commerce. When we willingly choose to become unpaid content providers, we commercialise ourselves. And we are encouraged to be obsessed with numbers (of followers, messages, comments, retweets, favourites), as if operating in a kind of friend economy, an emotional stock market where the stock is ourselves and where we are encouraged to weigh our worth against others.

Of course, humans comparing themselves to others isn't new. But when the others are every human on the internet, people end up comparing themselves – their looks, their relationships, their wealth, their lives – to the carefully filtered lives of people they would never meet in the real world – and feeling inadequate.

Reading first-hand accounts by people with bulimia and anorexia who are convinced that social media exacerbated or even triggered their illnesses, I began to realise something: this situation is not the equivalent of Bob Dylan's electric guitar. It is closer to the tobacco or fast-food industries, where vested interests deny the existence of blatant problems that were not there before. […]

We are traditionally far better at realising risks to physical health than to mental health, even when they are interrelated. If we can accept that our physical health can be shaped by society – by secondhand smoke or a bad diet – then we must accept that our mental health can be too. And as our social spaces increasingly become digital spaces, we need to look seriously and urgently at how these new, business-owned societies are affecting our minds. We must try to see how the rising mental health crisis may be related to the way people are living and interacting.

Facebook's Mark Zuckerberg says that "by giving people the power to share, we're making the world more transparent". But what we really need to do is make social media transparent.

Of course, we won't stop using it – I certainly won't – but precisely for that reason we need to know more about what it is doing to us. To our politics, to our health, to the future generation, and to the world around us. We need to ensure we are still the ones using the technology – and that the technology isn't using us. *(842 words)*

*From: Matt Haig: "I used to think social media was a force for good. Now the evidence says I was wrong", https://www.theguardian.com/commentisfree/2017/sep/06/social-media-good-evidence-platforms-insecurities-health, 06.09.2017, Copyright Guardian News & Media Ltd 2020*

**Annotations**

l. 2 *Arab spring*: series of protests and rebellions against authoritarian regimes, e.g. in Tunisia, Egypt and Libya fidget spinner: a popular toy

l. 30 *Kurt Vonnegut:* famous American writer (1922–2007)

**Ausgangstext:** *extract from a novel*
**Operatoren:** *describe, characterise, discuss*
**Themen:** *ethnic minorities in the US, police violence*

**Aufgabenstellung**

1. **Describe** the night of the shooting as it is presented in the interview and as Starr remembers it. *(Video 1)*
2. **Characterise** the police officer as he is presented in this extract. Take the narrative perspective into account. *(Video 2)*
3. "'His life always matters more!' [...] 'That's the problem!'" **Discuss** the statement referring to the general situation of African Americans in the US. *(Video 3)*

**Text:**
**The Hate U Give** by Angie Thomas (extract from the novel)

*Starr, who lives in the fictional, Black* neighborhood of Garden Heights, is the only witness of a police shooting in which her childhood friend Khalil got killed. She goes to a school in a different district, which is mainly attended by White kids. For fear of being singled out she does not talk to her school-friends about her life in Garden Heights, not even about the shooting.*

"Back up, back up," I tell Maya. She flicks through the channels, and when he appears again, I say, "Right there!"

I've pictured his face so much. Actually seeing it again is different. My memory is pretty spot-on – a thin, jagged scar above his lip, bursts of freckles that cover his face and neck.

My stomach churns and my skin crawls, and I wanna get away from One-Fifteen. My instinct doesn't care that it's a photograph being shown on TV. A silver cross pendant hangs from his neck, like he's saying Jesus endorses what he did. We must believe in a different Jesus.

What looks like an older version of him appears on the screen [...].

"My son was afraid for his life," he says. "He only wanted to get home to his wife and kids."

Pictures flash on the screen. One-Fifteen smiles with his arms draped around a blurred-out woman. He's on a fishing trip with two small, blurred-out children. They show him with a smiley golden retriever, with his pastor and some fellow deacons who are all blurred out, and then in his police uniform.

"Officer Brian Cruise Jr. has been on the force for sixteen years," the voice-over says, and more pics of him as a cop are shown. He's been a cop for as long as Khalil was alive, and I wonder if in some sick twist of fate Khalil was only born for this man to kill.

"A majority of those years have been spent serving in Garden Heights," the voice-over continues, "a neighborhood notorious for gang and drug dealers."

I tense as footage of my neighborhood, my home, is shown. It's like they picked the worst parts – the drug addicts roaming the streets, the broken-down Cedar Grove projects, gangbangers flashing signs, bodies on the sidewalks with white sheets over them. What about Mrs. Rooks and her cakes? Or Mr. Lewis and his haircuts? Mr. Reuben? The clinic? My family?

Me?

I feel Hailey's and Maya's eyes on me. I can't look at them.

"My son loved working in the neighborhood," One-Fifteen's father claims. "He always wanted to make a difference in the lives there."

Funny. Slave masters thought they were making a difference in black people's lives too. Saving them from their "wild African ways." Same shit, different century. I wish people like them would stop thinking that people like me need saving.

One-Fifteen Sr. talks about his son's life before the shooting. How he was a good kid who never got into trouble, always wanted to help others. [...]

The interviewer asks about that night.

"Apparently, Brian pulled the kid over 'cause he had a broken taillight and was speeding."

Khalil wasn't speeding.

"He told me, 'Pop, soon as I pulled him over, I had a bad feeling,'" says One-Fifteen Sr.

"Why is that?" the interviewer asks.

"He said the kid and his friend immediately started cursing him out –"

We never cursed.

"And they kept glancing at each other, like they were up to something. Brian says that's when he got scared, 'cause they could've taken him down if they teamed up."

I couldn't have taken anyone down. I was too afraid. He makes us sound like we're superhumans. We're kids.

"No matter how afraid he is, my son's still gonna do his job," he says. "And that's all he set out to do that night."

"There have been reports that Khalil Harris was unarmed when the incident took place," the interviewer says. "Has your son told you why he made the decision to shoot?"

"Brian says he had his back to the kid, and he heard the kid say, 'I'm gon' show your ass today.'"

No, no, no. Khalil asked if I was okay.

"Brian turned around and saw something in the car door. He thought it was a gun –"

It was a hairbrush. [...]

"Brian's a good boy," he says, in tears. "He only wanted to get home to his family, and people are making him out to be a monster."

That's all Khalil and I wanted, and you're making us out to be monsters. [...]

"How has your son's life changed since this happened?" the interviewer asks.

"All our lives have been hell, honestly," his father claims. "Brian's a people person, but now he's afraid to go out in public, even for something simple as getting a gallon of milk. There have been threats on his life, our family's lives. His wife had to quit her job. He's even been attacked by fellow officers." […]

"This is awful," Hailey says. "That poor family."

She's looking at One-Fifteen Sr. with sympathy that belongs to Brenda and Ms. Rosalie.

I blink several times. "What?"

"His son lost everything because he was trying to do his job and protect himself. His life matters too, you know?"

I cannot right now. I can't. I stand up or otherwise I will say or do something really stupid. Like punch her.

"I need to … yeah." I say all that I can and start for the door, but Maya grabs the tail of my cardigan. […]

"Maya," I say, as calmly as possible. "Please let me go. I cannot talk to her. Did you not hear what she said?"

"Are you serious right now?" Hailey asks. "What's wrong with saying his life matters too?"

"His life always matters more!" My voice is gruff, and my throat is tight. "That's the problem!" *(969 words)*

*Thomas, Angie:* The Hate U Give. *London: Walker Books Ltd, 2017. pp. 243–247.*

**Annotations**

l. 6 *One-Fifteen:* One-Fifteen is the badge number of the police officer who shot Khalil

ll. 69/70 *Brenda and Ms. Rosalie:* Khalil's mother and grandmother



* We have decided to capitalize "Black" and "White" to signal that they are not natural categories but social ones (for more background information on this topic see e.g. https://www.theatlantic.com/ideas/archive/2020/06/time-to-capitalize-blackand-white/613159/).

**Berlin/Brandenburg**
**Übungsaufgabe 1**

## Prüfungsteil 1: Leseverstehen und Schreiben (75 %)

## Aufgabenstellung 1 – Tasks

**Themenschwerpunkte:** *Aims and ambitions, The impact of the media on society*

1 Describe the situation the characters find themselves in. (25 %)

2 Write a characterisation of Mae, also taking into account the effect the narrative perspective has on the reader's perception of her character. (40 %)

3 Choose **one** of the following tasks. (35 %)

3.1 Discuss whether modern communication via smartphones and the like is a blessing or a curse.

OR

3.2 Mercer has left the house without an explanation, so he feels obliged to explain his behaviour to Mae. Write his personal letter to her in which he offers this explanation and tells Mae what he thinks about her initiative to post the photo.

**Text** (excerpt from the novel)

**The Circle**
by Dave Eggers

Note: *Mae Holland works for a very powerful Internet company and rarely sees her parents. One day, however, she visits her parents at their home and there she also meets Mercer, her former boyfriend. Mercer has given her parents a self-made chandelier. Mae likes it very much and, without informing anyone, posts a photo of the chandelier and links to Mercer's website in different Internet forums. While she is doing so upstairs, the others are waiting for her downstairs so they can have dinner together.*

When she was finished, Mercer was sitting with her parents at the kitchen table, which was crowded with salad and stir-fried chicken and vegetables. Their eyes followed her down the stairs. "I called up there," her father said.

"We like to eat when it's hot," her mother added.

Mae hadn't heard them. "Sorry. I was just – Wow, this looks good. Dad, don't you think Mercer's chandelier* is awesome?"

"I do. And I told you, and him, as much. We've been asking for one of his creations for a year now."

"I just needed the right antlers," Mercer said. "I hadn't gotten any really great ones in a while." He went on to explain his sourcing, how he bought antlers only from trusted collaborators, people he knew hadn't hunted the deer, or if they had, had been instructed to do so by Fish and Game to curb overcrowding.

"That is fascinating," her mother said. "Before I forget, I want to raise a toast … What's that?"

Mae's phone had beeped. "Nothing," she said. "But in a second I think I'll have some good news to announce. Go on, Mom."

"I was just saying that I wanted to toast having us –"

Now it was Mercer's phone ringing.

"Sorry," he said, and maneuvered his hand outside his pants, finding the off button.

"Everyone done?" her mother asked.

"Sorry Mrs. Holland," Mercer said. "Go on."

But at that moment, Mae's phone buzzed loudly again, and when Mae looked to its screen, she saw that there were thirty-seven new zings and messages.

"Something you have to attend to?" her father said.

"No, not yet," Mae said, though she was almost too excited to wait. She was proud of Mercer, and soon she'd be able to show him something about the audience he might have outside Longfield. If there were thirty-seven messages in the first few minutes, in twenty minutes there would be a hundred.

Her mother continued. "I was going to thank you, Mae, for all you've done to improve your father's health, and my own sanity. And I wanted to toast Mercer, too, as part of our family, and to thank him for his beautiful work." She paused, as if expecting a buzz to sound any moment. "Well, I'm just glad I got through that. Let's eat. The food's getting cold."

And they began to eat, but after a few minutes, Mae had heard so many dings, and she'd seen her phone screen update so many times, that she couldn't wait.

"Okay, I can't stand it anymore. I posted that photo I took of your chandelier, Mercer, and people love it!" She beamed, and raised her glass. "That's what we should toast."

Mercer didn't look amused. "Wait. You posted them where?"

"That's great, Mercer," her father said, and raised his own glass.

Mercer's glass was not raised. "Where'd you post them, Mae?"

"Everywhere relevant," she said, "and the comments are amazing." She searched her screen. "Just let me read the first one. And I quote: Wow, that is gorgeous. That's from a pretty well-known industrial designer in Stockholm. Here's another one: Very cool. Reminds me of something I saw in Barcelona last year. That was from a designer in Santa Fe who has her own shop. She gave your thing three out of four stars, and had some suggestions about how you might improve it. I bet you could sell them there if you wanted to. So here's another –"

Mercer had his palms on the table. "Stop. Please."

"Why? You haven't even heard the best part. On DesignMind, you already have 122 smiles. That's an incredible amount to get so quickly. And they have a ranking there, and you're in the top fifty for today. Actually, I know how you could raise that –" [...]

"Mae. Stop. Please stop." Mercer was staring at her, his eyes small and round. "I don't want to get loud here, in your parents' home, but either you stop or I have to walk out."

"Just hold on a sec," she said, and scrolled through her messages, looking for one that she was sure would impress him. She'd seen a message come in from Dubai, and if she found it, she knew, his resistance would fall away.

"Mae," she heard her mother say. "Mae."

But Mae couldn't locate the message. Where was it? While she scrolled, she heard the scraping of a chair. But she was so close to finding it that she didn't look up. When she did, she found Mercer gone and her parents staring at her. *(763 words)*



* Mercer's chandelier is made of antlers (= horn of a male deer). As he is very careful to buy antlers only from trusted suppliers, he only produces very few of them.

**Annotation**

l. 6 chandelier: round frame for holding candles or lights that hangs from the ceiling and is decorated with small pieces of glass

## Prüfungsteil 2: Sprachmittlung (25 %)

### Aufgabenstellung 2 – Tasks

**Themenschwerpunkte:** *Aims and ambitions, The impact of the media on society*

You are taking part in an international youth project on "The Impact of Digitisation and AI".

Using the information from the text, write an article for the English project website in which you present the drawbacks of digital language assistants such as Alexa.

**Text** (Auszug aus dem Artikel)

**Experten warnen vor Sprachassistenten: Diese Risiken birgt Alexa für Kinder**

*Minderjährige geben Alexa, Siri und ähnlichen Sprachassistenten zu viel von sich preis, zeigt ein Gutachten. Auch Datenschützer äußern Kritik.*

Ein Junge, sechs Jahre alt, wünscht sich ein Kinderlied, ruft „play Digger, Digger" ins Mikrofon. Und was tut Amazons Sprachassistentin „Alexa"? Sie schlägt ihm verschiedene Porno-Titel vor. Diese Geschichte ist nicht die einzige Panne vergangener Jahre, die Eltern schockiert. Zu sehen auf Youtube. Jetzt warnt sogar der Wissenschaftliche Dienst des Bundestags.

In einem Gutachten wird bemängelt, dass Kinder und Jugendliche persönliche Informationen von sich preisgeben oder eben Inhalte abrufen können, die sie nicht hören sollten. Außerdem stelle sich die Frage, was eigentlich mit Besuchern sei, die nicht wüssten, dass die Software gerade ihre Sätze aufzeichnet. Amazon dürfte der Pflicht zur Informationsvermittlung bei der Datenerhebung von Nutzern zwar ausreichend nachkommen, heißt es – „offen bleibt jedoch, wie unbeteiligte Dritte und Minderjährige von der Datensammlung ausgeschlossen werden können".

Mit Blick auf die USA sei außerdem unklar, „zu welchen weiteren Zwecken Amazon seine Daten zukünftig nutzen könnte". Dass sich Kriminelle Zugriff zu den Daten in der Cloud verschaffen könnten, sei ebenfalls nicht auszuschließen.

Eine Reihe von Kritikpunkten. Das Bundesinnenministerium fühlt sich in der Sache aber nicht zuständig. Ein Sprecher erklärte auf Anfrage der Deutschen Presse-Agentur: „Die Nutzung der Sprachassistenten betrifft Datenverarbeitungen durch nichtöffentliche Stellen." Für diese lasse die Datenschutz-Grundverordnung der EU den nationalen Gesetzgebern so gut wie keinen Regelungsspielraum.

„Wir müssen darauf dringen, dass die Einwilligungserklärung für den Nutzer auf die Gefahren und Möglichkeiten hinweist, die mit der Übertragung und Nutzung der Daten sowie der Daten von Dritten, die sich zufällig im Raum befinden, hinweist", meint hingegen der fraktionslose Bundestagsabgeordnete Uwe Kamann. Dies müsse detailliert erfolgen, „und nicht indem man nur einmal ein Häkchen für alles setzt".

Kamann war es, der die Frage aufgeworfen hatte, ob es zulässig ist, dass Amazon die Spracheingaben der „Alexa"-Nutzer auswertet. […]

Der Hamburgische Datenschutzbeauftragte Johannes Caspar ist ebenfalls empört. Er teile die Befürchtungen des Wissenschaftlichen Dienstes des Bundestags. Probleme würden sich „aus der hohen Zahl von Fehlaktivierungen bei automatischen Sprachassistenten" ergeben.

Diese führten dazu, dass Gespräche immer wieder übertragen werden, weil das System das Aktivierungswort fälschlicherweise verstehe. „Von diesen Datenerhebungen sind ausnahmslos alle Personen im Haushalt betroffen, ohne dass die relevanten rechtlichen Vorgaben vorliegen dürften", sagte Caspar zu Tagesspiegel Background Digitalisierung & KI.

Insbesondere dürften „Kinder kaum einwilligungsfähig sein". Ein weiteres Problem ist aus seiner Sicht „die fehlende Zugriffskontrolle durch eine personalisierte Steuerung, mit der eine Nutzung des Sprachsystems durch dritte unbefugte Personen verhindert werden könnte".

Amazon bietet den Nutzern zwar neuerdings mit dem Befehl „Alexa, lerne meine Stimme" die Möglichkeit, ein persönliches Stimmprofil einzurichten. Diese werden nach Angaben eines Amazon-Sprechers aber nur genutzt, „um das individuelle Nutzererlebnis zu verbessern". Auf den Befehl „Computer, spiele Musik!" hin würden für verschiedene Profile unterschiedliche Titel abgespielt. Das Gerät für Kinder zu sperren, erlaubt die neue Stimmerkennung nicht. […]

Der Sprachassistent wird nicht zum ersten Mal als Übel für Kinder angesehen. Im vergangenen Jahr veröffentlichte die britische Childwise Agency eine Untersuchung mit dem Ergebnis: Da Alexa Anweisungen ohne Wörter wie „bitte" oder „danke" ausführt, fürchten Experten, dass Kinder zu unhöflichen Wesen heranwachsen, die bloß noch befehlen.

Alexa, lies mir eine Gute-Nacht-Geschichte vor! Alexa, ich will …! Im April 2018 brachte Amazon tatsächlich eine Version für Kinder auf den Markt. Diese formuliert ihre Antworten kindgerechter, sagt der Hersteller. Außerdem bekamen Kinder ein Lob, wenn sie bitten und sich bedanken.

Ein anderes Alexa-Problem untersucht nun die Otto-von-Guericke-Universität Magdeburg. Nicht einmal jede vierte KI-Fachkraft sei eine Frau. Daraus ergebe sich die Frage, ob sich dies auch in Denkmustern bei der Künstlichen Intelligenz widerspiegele. Die Unesco hatte bemängelt, dass Siri und Alexa Gender-Stereotype reproduzieren.

Demnach seien sie unterwürfig, gehorsam und stets freundlich. Vor dem Hintergrund, dass Kinder mit der Technologie aufwüchsen und Sprache ein Geschlechtsmarker sei, bestehe die Gefahr, dass bestimmte Vorstellungen von Frauen transportiert würden – als dienende Maschinen. *(614 Wörter)*

*Sonja Álvarez, Marie Rövekamp: Experten warnen vor Sprachassistenten – Diese Risiken birgt Alexa für Kinder, Tagesspiegel vom 09.07.2019, https://www.tagesspiegel.de/wirtschaft/experten-warnen-vor-sprachassistenten-diese-risiken-birgt-alexa-fuer-kinder/24573516.html*

## Lösungsvorschläge

### Prüfungsteil 1: Leseverstehen und Schreiben

1 *In der ersten Aufgabe müssen Sie die Situation in eigenen Worten beschreiben. Versuchen Sie alle W-Fragen zu beantworten, zum Beispiel, wo sich die Szene abspielt, wer teilnimmt, was die Figuren machen, wie sie miteinander umgehen und weshalb sie sich so verhalten.*

- *Mercer, Mae und ihre Eltern sitzen am Küchentisch beim Essen.*
- *Mae kommt zu spät, da sie damit beschäftigt war, ein Foto von Mercers Kronleuchter zu posten (allerdings, ohne ihn um Erlaubnis zu fragen).*
- *Maes Mutter möchte einen Toast aussprechen, aber jedes Mal, wenn sie zu sprechen beginnt, klingelt ein Telefon.*
- *Mae erhält zahlreiche Reaktionen auf das Bild, das sie geposted hat.*
- *Sie erzählt den anderen von den Nachrichten.*
- *Mercer ist davon nicht begeistert und droht zu gehen.*
- *Mae ignoriert ihn und liest weiter die ankommenden Nachrichten.*
- *Selbst als Mercer tatsächlich geht, nimmt sie dies nicht wahr.*
- *Als sie aufblickt, ist Mercer verschwunden.*
- *Ihre Eltern starren sie ungläubig an.*

The excerpt from Dave Eggers' novel *The Circle*, published in 2013, is set in the kitchen of Mae's parents. — reference to source

Her parents and her former boyfriend Mercer have been waiting for her so they can have dinner together. Mae comes in late because she has posted a photo of the chandelier Mercer gave to her parents. The other characters do not know about her posting the photo and Mae intends to surprise them with it. — description of the situation

Mae's mother wants to propose a toast but she is interrupted several times by either Mae's or Mercer's phone ringing, so she gets a little upset. Whereas Mercer turns off his phone, Mae's phone keeps receiving messages in response to the photo she has posted. Finally, she cannot wait any longer and tells everybody what she has done. While Mae is proud of herself, Mercer himself seems to be appalled and threatens to leave if she does not stop. However, Mae ignores him and does not even realise his departure because she is too busy checking her phone for a message from Dubai. When she finally looks up from her phone, she only sees her parents staring at her. *(193 words)*

2 *Zunächst müssen Sie sich Notizen dazu machen, was Mae sagt und wie sie spricht. Zusätzlich sollten Sie festhalten, wie die anderen Figuren sie behandeln. Interpretieren Sie anschließend, was das über ihre Figur aussagt. In Ihrer Analyse sollten Sie außerdem darauf eingehen, welche Rolle die Erzählperspektive spielt. Daher müssen Sie prüfen, aus wessen Perspektive die Geschehnisse dargestellt werden und wie das die Informationen, die wir erhalten, beeinflusst. Bedenken Sie auch, dass die Erzählperspektive Einfluss darauf hat, mit wem sich die Leser*innen am ehesten identifizieren.*

- *Mae hat gute Absichten. Sie postet das Bild, um Mercers tolle Arbeit zu zeigen.*
- *Sie handelt allerdings sehr unsensibel und nimmt nicht wahr, dass Mercer nicht einverstanden mit ihrer Handlung ist.*
- *Sie ist so eingenommen von ihrem Smartphone und der Welt, mit der das Gerät sie verbindet, dass sie die Fähigkeit verloren hat, mit den Menschen, die sie direkt umgeben, in Kontakt zu treten.*
    - *Weder nimmt sie wahr, dass Mercer den Tisch verlassen hat, noch dass ihre Eltern sie anstarren. Stattdessen gilt ihre ganze Aufmerksamkeit den Nachrichten aus der ganzen Welt. (vgl. Z. 60–62)*
    - *Sie lässt die gesamte Familie am gedeckten Tisch auf sie warten und geht nicht wirklich darauf ein, als ihr Vater sie darauf hinweist. (vgl. Z. 3–6)*
    - *Sie verhält sich unhöflich, da sie ihr Telefon nicht leise stellt, obwohl es ihre Mutter mehrmals unterbricht. (vgl. Z. 15/16, 22–25, 34/35)*
- *Die Geschichte ist aus Maes Sicht erzählt. Zunächst teilt der Leser oder die Leserin ihre Begeisterung für Mercers Arbeit. Erst später nimmt man wahr, dass sie den Kontakt zu ihrer Umwelt verloren hat.*

**introduction:** thesis

Mae is the protagonist in Dave Eggers' novel. At first sight she seems to be a nice girl who cares for others but throughout the excerpt the reader realises that Mae is very insensitive and much too concerned with her smartphone than to empathise with the people sitting with her at the table.

**main part: characterisation** of Mae

→ likeable, cares for others

At first Mae seems to be quite likeable because she appears to care for others. Thus she apologises for coming in late and praises the food her parents have prepared as well as Mercer's handicraft (cf. ll. 5/6). She is "proud of Mercer" (ll. 25/26) and wants to promote his chandeliers for him. When she realises how many messages she receives in answer to the photo she has posted, she actually beams and wants to celebrate what she perceives as Mercer's success (cf. ll. 36–38).

→ insensitive, superficial

While Mae certainly has good intentions, she is utterly insensitive and, therefore, incapable of putting herself into Mercer's position. Mae should have known that she was not doing Mercer a favour by promoting his handicraft because he cannot produce his chandeliers quickly enough for online sale. Her parents had to wait "for one of his creations for a year" (ll. 7/8) because it is very important to Mercer to get "the right antlers" (l. 9) "from trusted collaborators" (ll. 10/11). The fact that Mae does not take this into account underlines how little interest she really has in her former boyfriend and how little she knows him. Even when he does not "look amused" (l. 39) she still believes that learning about a message from Dubai will make his resistance crumble (cf. ll. 57/58) because "she [is] sure [it will] impress him" (l. 57).

**narrative perspective**
→ Mae's perspective

In this context the narrative perspective is relevant. The story is told from Mae's point of view. The readers perceive everything through her eyes, e. g. the readers know that a chair has been moved but only when Mae looks up, do they learn that Mercer has left the room (cf. ll. 60–62). This has the effect that the readers first tend to identify with Mae because of her positive traits described above. They are invited to share Mae's excitement (cf. l. 35) and only realise later on that they have been misled.

→ reader is misled

**characterisation**
→ lack of empathy

Once this becomes clear, certain remarks by the characters acquire a greater significance. For example, at the beginning her parents mildly reproach Mae for being late. Her mother should not have to point out, "We like to eat when it's hot" (l. 4), as this is a habit Mae should be well aware of. So this incident hints at her lack of empathy.

This lack of empathy seems to arise from her obsession with her smartphone and the world it connects her to. She is too impressed with the number of messages her post has provoked and with the distant places some of these messages come from to even notice that the person she thinks she is doing all this for is first "staring at her, his eyes small and round" (l. 53) and then leaves (cf. l. 62).

**conclusion**

All in all, Mae seems to be too caught up in the digital world to be really interested in the people surrounding her in person. Her relation to them seems very superficial because she does not really know what is important to the people she should be close to. Thus, she herself appears to be superficial and insensitive. *(577 words)*

3.1 *In Ihrer Erörterung müssen Sie beide Seiten darstellen, bevor Sie zu einem Ergebnis kommen. Berücksichtigen Sie sowohl die positiven als auch die negativen Aspekte moderner Kommunikation. Sie müssen darauf eingehen, wie Mae moderne Kommunikationsmittel nutzt, andererseits aber auch weitere Argumente und Aspekte mit einbringen. Versuchen Sie auch Texte einzubeziehen, die Sie im Unterricht gelesen haben. Diese können zusätzliche Argumente und Belege liefern.*

– *Argumente dafür, dass moderne Kommunikationsmittel ein Segen sind:*
  - *Ein Leben ohne sie ist in einer globalisierten Welt nicht vorstellbar.*
  - *Sie ermöglichen es uns, mit Menschen auf der ganzen Welt in Kontakt zu treten, ohne zu reisen.*

- *Menschen können leichter in Kontakt bleiben. Kommunikation wird einfacher.*
- *Gegenargumente:*
  - *Zwar kommunizieren Menschen mehr, dafür auch oft oberflächlicher.*
  - *Menschen lassen sich im direkten Gespräch mit anderen von ihren Smartphones ablenken (vgl. Mae).*
  - *Viele Menschen sind geradezu abhängig von ihren Smartphones.*
  - *Kommunikation wird schneller. → Druck schnell zu reagieren*
  - *Kommunikation wird anonymer. → Cyberbullying*

**introduction:** topic, reference to task

These days, in many countries smartphones, tablets and other portable devices are very common. Especially among teenagers they are widely distributed. Most teenagers could not imagine living without a smartphone; they are so-called smart natives and feel their mobile is a blessing. On the other hand, one often hears that the device is a curse. So which perspective is right?

**main part: advantages** – first argument

Modern ways of communication certainly have many advantages. For one, communication has become much quicker than it was some thirty years ago. This saves a lot of time and also money, especially as we live in a globalised world. Transnational companies could not work that efficiently if they still had to rely on landlines and the postman.

second argument

Additionally, research has shown that people communicate more because of smartphones and the like. People tend to talk less to each other but communicate in written form via instant messenger applications. For teenagers, these applications are the most important ones on their smartphones and more than 80 % of them have them installed.

**disadvantages** – first argument

→ reference to novel

However, one must not forget the drawbacks. It is very common for teenagers to meet friends but instead of talking to each other they are all occupied with their smartphones. Mae, the protagonist of Dave Eggers' novel *The Circle*, is a good example. Although she is sitting with her parents and her former boyfriend at the table, she has her smartphone turned on and checks incoming messages. What is more, she does not seem to know any longer that there are people around her. Communication seems to become more indirect and superficial, which leads to relations becoming more shallow.

second argument

The fact that communication has become quicker definitely has its advantages as shown above but the disadvantages are considerable, too. People are expected to react instantly to incoming messages, which may lead to spontaneous but wrong decisions and to words better left unsaid. An example is the widespread phenomenon of cyberbullying.

In the end, it depends on the users if mobile devices are a blessing or a curse. If they use their mobile devices cleverly, they can save a lot of time and get in touch with others if it is really necessary, for instance in cases of emergency. In order to prevent these devices from becoming a curse, users must decide to ignore them, or even turn them off in certain situations, such as when they meet friends. *(398 words)*

**conclusion**

3.2 *Bevor Sie zu schreiben beginnen, müssen Sie sich in Mercer hineinversetzen. Lesen Sie den Text noch einmal und konzentrieren Sie sich auf die Informationen, die Sie über Mercer erhalten. Wie reagiert er auf Mae und ihren Post? Was lernen wir über seine Werte? Nachdem Sie sich darüber Gedanken gemacht haben, können Sie überlegen, was Sie in Ihren Brief mit aufnehmen sollten und wie Ihr Tonfall sein sollte. Denken Sie daran, dass Sie einen persönlichen Brief schreiben und dass es sich bei Mercer (vermutlich) um einen jungen Erwachsenen handelt. Daher sollten Sie Alltagssprache verwenden. Obwohl Sie verleitet sein könnten, einen sehr informellen Sprachstil einzuschlagen und eventuell sogar Schimpfworte zu nutzen, sollten Sie sich im Kontext der Abiturprüfung damit zurückhalten.*

- *Mercer erklärt, warum er gegangen ist. → Wut, Unglaube über Maes fehlende Empathie*
- *Mercer ist wütend darüber, dass Mae ihn nicht um Erlaubnis gebeten hat, bevor sie sein Werk gepostet hat (allerdings können Sie selbst entscheiden, wie wütend er tatsächlich ist oder ob er auch bereit ist, ihre positiven Intentionen wahrzunehmen).*
- *Mercer interessiert sich nicht für materiellen Erfolg.*
- *Er nutzt nur Geweihe von Anbieter*innen, denen er vertraut.*
- *Er ist enttäuscht darüber, wie wenig Mae über ihn weiß.*
- *Möglicherweise kommentiert er die Art, in der Mae ihr Smartphone nutzt.*
- *Vermutlich wird er Mae bitten, das Bild zu entfernen.*

6 May, 2013 — date

Dear Mae, — form of address

Yesterday, I left your parents' house without a word. Hopefully you know that this is not like me but it only goes to show how furious I was and still am. You posted a photo of my chandelier without asking me about it first. I would like to believe that you meant well but I'm really shocked at how little you know me after all the years we spent together.

reason for writing: furious at Mae

she does not know him

Your parents had waited for the chandelier for one year for a good reason. I only get the antlers from suppliers I trust because I don't want any deer to be shot just for the sake of my chandeliers. So how am I to satisfy the demand of people from all over the world? Plus, money is not important to me. I like my work and like to be independent. What you have done puts far too much pressure on

reasons he is not happy with Mae's posts

me. My phone starts ringing as soon as I turn it on and I get orders from all over the world. If I wanted to answer them all, I wouldn't be doing anything else.

That's not the way I work or communicate, so please, remove this photo straight away to undo at least some of the damage you've done.

asks Mae to remove the post

I'd also like to tell you that I was horrified by your obsession with your smartphone. Your parents see so little of you and when you visit them, you keep your eyes on the screen. For heaven's sake, Mae, talk to the people who are sitting face-to-face with you and do not constantly interrupt the conversation because there is a message on your phone.

advice for Mae

I've shut down my mobile for good because I can no longer stand the pressure you've put me under and I advise you to do so, too, at least when you visit your parents.

Whatever you do, Mae, remove that photo. Quickly and for good! You had no right to post it in the first place.

closing sentence: repeats demand

Mercer *(337 words)*

name

## Prüfungsteil 2: Sprachmittlung

*Bevor Sie mit dem Schreiben Ihrer Lösung beginnen, sollten Sie sich die Aufgabenstellung genau durchlesen. Diese enthält Informationen dazu, welches Zieltextformat gefordert ist und welche Leserschaft angesprochen werden soll. Zusätzlich enthält sie meist Informationen dazu, auf welche Aspekte Sie sich in Ihrer Lösung konzentrieren sollen. In diesem Fall schreiben Sie einen Artikel für die Homepage eines Projektes. Sie müssen eine interessante Überschrift formulieren und Ihren Text in klar strukturierte Absätze gliedern. Ihr Publikum besteht aus den Teilnehmerinnen und Teilnehmern eines internationalen Projektes, das sich an Jugendliche richtet. Daher sollte Ihr Text nicht zu formell klingen, dabei aber dennoch Expertise zu den Bereichen Digitalisierung und künstliche Intelligenzen aufweisen. Inhaltlich sollten Sie sich auf die Nachteile und Probleme konzentrieren, die im Text im Zusammenhang mit Alexa, Siri und anderen digitalen Sprachassistenten auftauchen.*

*Die folgenden Aspekte könnten Teil Ihrer Lösung sein:*

- *Zwei Hauptkritikpunkte: Datenschutzaspekte und Gefahren, die Alexa und andere Sprachassistenten für Kinder darstellen*
- *Kinderschutz und pädagogische Aspekte:*
  - *Kinder können nicht altersgerechten Themen begegnen. (vgl. Z. 1–3, 7/8)*
  - *Daten von Kindern werden gespeichert und genutzt, ohne dass diese eingewilligt haben. (vgl. Z. 6/7, 11/12, 37, 45/46)*
  - *Kinder lernen, in Befehlsform zu sprechen. (vgl. Z. 49–51)*

- *Kinder erwerben Genderstereotype, da Sprachassistenten weibliche Stimmen und Namen haben und das Bild von folgsamen Dienerinnen reproduzieren. (vgl. Z. 59–64)*

– *Generelle Datenschutzprobleme:*
- *Alle werden aufgezeichnet, unabhängig davon, ob sie die Einwilligung gegeben haben (insbesondere auch, da die Technik anfällig für Fehler ist). (vgl. Z. 8–12, 32–35)*
- *Unsicherheit dazu, was mit den Daten geschieht (vgl. Z. 13–15)*
- *Fehlender Datenschutz in Deutschland für private Anbieter (vgl. Z. 16–20)*

**Is Alexa a danger for children as well as for data security?** — **heading**

In many German households, digital language assistants like Siri or Alexa have become a part of everyday life. While they might make some tasks easier, some experts also regard them with growing suspicion. — **introduction**

One of the most pressing issues is data protection. A voice assistant records thousands of pieces of information and so far there are no clear-cut rules as to what happens with these. Criminals potentially accessing the data are only the tip of the iceberg. With a private company involved in the data collection, many of Alexa's potentially unauthorised uses are not even considered in European data protection laws. — **data protection issues:** no legal framework, potentially criminal uses of data

Voice assistants do not limit their data collection to those who have explicitly given their permission. Instead, as soon as the assistant is activated – a process that despite experiments with voice recognition is still prone to errors –, everyone in the vicinity is recorded indiscriminately. — lack of consent of those being recorded

In connection with child protection laws, this is especially relevant. Children cannot be considered to have given their permission to be taped. Additionally, Alexa might inadvertently provide them with content that is inappropriate to their age. — **child protection and educational issues:** inappropriate content

There are further concerns when it comes to Alexa's educational side effects: Alexa does what you want her to do without being asked politely. This might lead to children becoming used to a commanding and impolite language. — communicating by giving commands

Secondly, Alexa, Siri and co. could reproduce harmful gender stereotypes: with their female names and their obedient behaviour, they could convey an image of women as docile servants. — gender stereotypes

Thus, for all her alleged progressiveness and user-friendliness, Alexa might also be a danger lurking in your living room. *(278 words)* — **conclusion**

## Berlin/Brandenburg
## Übungsaufgabe 2

### Prüfungsteil 1: Leseverstehen und Schreiben (75 %)

### Aufgabenstellung 1 – Tasks

**Themenschwerpunkte:** *Aims and ambitions, Ethnic and cultural diversity*

1 Describe Job's living conditions in London/England. (25 %)

2 Analyse the atmosphere created in this excerpt taking into account the narrative perspective employed. (40 %)

3 Choose **one** of the following tasks. (35 %)

3.1 Comment on the statement that equality is "one of those polite English fictions [...] that are like grease on a wheel shaft" (ll. 41/42).

OR

3.2 In the USA Black people are more likely to be put in prison. This is believed to be result of a racist justice system. You have come across the illustration on the likeliness of being incarcerated in the US (Text B) and have decided to write an article entitled "Law Enforcement in the USA – A Just System?" for an international student magazine. Elaborate on the issues of law and social justice and make a suggestion as to what could be done to improve the system.

**Text A** (excerpt from the novel)

**Hearts and Minds,**
by Amanda Craig

*Job left his home country Zimbabwe because of the cruel regime of President Robert Mugabe. Now he lives in London illegally. Polly Noble, a single mother, works as a human rights lawyer and defends illegal immigrants who try to get a residence permit. Job, who works as a mini-cab driver, earns some extra money by driving Polly's son Robbie to and from school.*

Job has a little more money these days, thanks to the regular work of picking Robbie up from school. He likes the boy, with his unmistakable look of a child who is loved, and he likes Polly, who always looks so anxious. She is one of those Englishwomen who is like a small bird, all softness and busyness. Job is sorry for her because she has no husband to help her.

"I just wish, I could find this girl," she says from the back seat. "It's maddening."

"May I ask, madam, why you are seeking her?"

"She used to work for me, and she's disappeared."

"I too have lost someone", Job says, nodding. "My wife."

"Have you told the police?"

"No," he says, sighing. "She has disappeared in Harare."

"Mine was my au pair," says Polly.

"I do not know this word."

"She is someone who lives in your home and looks after it and your children for a few hours every day in return."

"Ah. Like a maid?"

"Yes, I suppose so."

Job thinks of how, little by little, his mother had become bitter because they did not even have running water in their hut, like the Wisdens in their big house. It was different for Job, in the beginning, because he and his sister had been allowed to play with Beth. Such dear little piccaninnies, the white people had called them, and although he remembered the phrase he had been too innocent to register the insult, though his mother had. She was old enough to remember the wars, and the way white people had tried to prevent Independence, while all Job and Miriam cared about was having fun. But then, when he was twelve, it had all changed. he had grown up, and become the size he is now, and the Wisdens didn't want him to play with Beth any more.

Polly is saying, 'Au pairs come from abroad, and aren't trained, so they – well, they cost a lot less, but they learn English and live in your house as part of the family. I thought I had a really good one, only she's disappeared.'

"I am missing my wife," says Job. "I do not know if she is dead or alive. We have a very bad president in my country."

"I know."

"That, there, is where I live now."

Polly looks out at the tall, shabby grey concrete building he points to. "Oh, I know this place!" she exclaims.

"You have been there?"

"Er – no, not exactly. I can see it from my house, that's all."

"One day, perhaps, you might like to visit me," Job says.

"One day, perhaps," she replies.

He knows that she never will, though they pretend to each other, in the way of the British, that they are equals. It's one of those polite English fictions of equality that are like grease on a wheel shaft. She talks to him in a friendly, interested way; she's surprised to find that he reads Dickens and Shakespeare. Perhaps the kind of Africans she defends are not like him, though he tells her that people in his country learn English now in order to read these authors.

Poor people do live differently in Britain. They have so many things that it seems to drive out thought. Job would never have dreamt he could one day drive a car like the one he leases from Mo, for instance. Nor would he have believed that he might have a TV set, thrown out because it was an old, bulky design instead of the flatscreen ones everyone expects. Also, there is so much culture available for free. Job has walked, amazed, round every museum he can find on Sundays, where people from all over the globe wander in to enjoy the most beautiful paintings, inventions, buildings. He can't join a public library, but the cheapness of second-hand paperbacks on stalls and in charity shops almost makes him weak. There is an abundance of everything – food dropped half-eaten on the pavement that goes to feed birds or rats – and yet a consciousness of nothing. He thinks of the city conjured for him by Dickens; that foggy, dark place riddled with crime and yet suffused with kindness and courage. He had been a little disappointed when he arrived to find the soot had been scoured away during the last century, and no horse-drawn carriages. Yet there were still men like Bill Sikes, with their dogs and violence. He sees them right outside his home.

Home for Job is now a tiny room with only a sink to drink from and wash in, and the noise of police sirens and traffic wailing and sighing in a continuous susurration below. Damp blooms on the walls, outlining new continents – as if those who live here, in the perpetual stench of urine, beer, sour milk and cinders, need any more reminders of what they have lost. Job's own room is sub-let from another foreigner, in a kind of food chain of privation and opportunism. There is a whole family next to Job, sleeping on a floor that is all a heaving, twanging mattress. He doesn't even know where they are from because they speak no English, but he suspects it is the Gambia. On his other side are two sisters from Turkey, and then a young couple from somewhere in the Indian subcontinent. Intimately acquainted with each other's bowel movements and cooking smells, his fellow tenants mind their own business, and when they pass each other silently on the stairs or in the corridor they keep their heads down. They bang on his door when he shouts out from his nightmares and he bangs on theirs if they quarrel or fail to quieten a baby, but otherwise they pretend not to exist, which is another polite English fiction. But the worst of all are the other sounds – the sounds couples make together, when alone in the dark. Job can't stand listening to them, and being reminded of his wife. His stomach is full, but his heart is empty. *(1,014 words)*

*Excerpt from: Amanda Craig.* Hearts and Minds. *London: Little, Brown, 2009.*

**Annotations**

l. 43 Dickens: Charles Dickens (1812–1870) is a famous English writer.
l. 48 Mo: Job is a taxi driver who leases his car from a man called Mo.
ll. 59/60 Bill Sikes: an aggressive and vicious character in Charles Dickens' novel *Oliver Twist*.
l. 62 susurration: (poet.) a soft rustle *(leises Rascheln)*

**Text B**
**Grafik *Wahrscheinlichkeit einer Haftstrafe nach Hautfarbe***

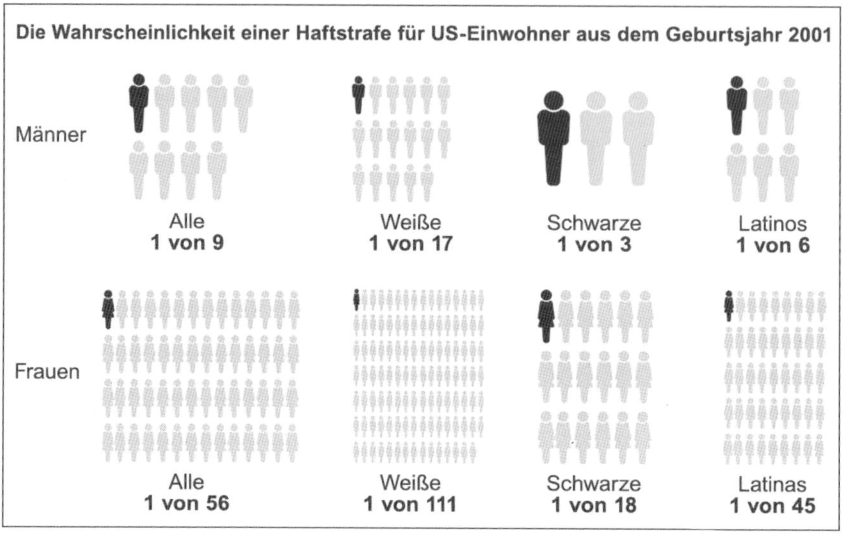


*Daten nach: Bureau of Justice Statistics*

## Prüfungsteil 2: Sprachmittlung (25 %)

### Aufgabenstellung 2 – Tasks

**Themenschwerpunkte:** *Aims and ambitions, Ethnic and cultural diversity*

Together with a Polish and an Italian partner school, your class is working on a project on immigration to Europe. You are all working on a common website presenting your project. In a German newspaper you have found an interview with Peter Tauber, politician of the CDU, which you think might interest your partners. Therefore, you want to include Peter Tauber's statements in an article for your project.
In English, write an article in which you present Tauber's view on immigration and the necessity for immigration law.

**Text** (Auszug aus dem Interview)

**„Man darf den Islam nicht pauschal verurteilen"**

[…]

DIE WELT: Gibt es keine reale islamistische Bedrohung durch Zuwanderung?

TAUBER: Erstens: Sehr viele Zuwanderer kommen überhaupt nicht aus dem islamischen Kulturkreis, sondern aus Russland, Polen und anderen Teilen der Welt. Zweitens: Die Vorstellung, dass ein Muslim kein guter deutscher Bürger sein kann, ist falsch. Und vor unserem geschichtlichen Hintergrund ist das auch erschreckend. Denn schon einmal ist den Angehörigen einer religiösen Minderheit abgesprochen worden, gute deutsche Bürger zu sein. […]

DIE WELT: Integrationsforscher haben als Reaktion auf Pegida gefordert, wir bräuchten ein neues Deutschlandbild.

TAUBER: Ja, wir brauchen eine Debatte darüber, wie wir uns Deutschland vorstellen. Diese Idee hatte die CDU übrigens schon früher mit der Diskussion über eine „Leitkultur". Bislang reden wir beim Thema Zuwanderung vor allem über die Zuwanderung in den Arbeitsmarkt. Die klassischen Einwanderungsländer gehen jedoch noch einen zweiten Schritt und fragen: Wer ist eine Bereicherung für unser Land? Wer bringt sich in unsere Gesellschaft ein? Wer nach Kanada geht, wird Kanadier. Er wandert dorthin aus, um sich dort sein künftiges Leben aufzubauen. Bei uns jedoch wird es nach wie vor so gesehen: Wer nach Deutschland kommt, der kommt, um in Deutschland zu arbeiten.

DIE WELT: Brauchen wir ein Einwanderungsgesetz?

TAUBER: Wenn wir eine Zuwanderung wollen, die nicht nur arbeitsmarktoptimiert ist, nicht nur temporär, dann müssen wir auch über ein Einwanderungsgesetz reden. Momentan geht es uns in Deutschland wirtschaftlich gut. Hoch qualifizierte Zuwanderer kommen, weil es hier Arbeit gibt. Doch die sind vermutlich schnell wieder weg, wenn es einmal schlechter läuft. Doch eine Nation braucht, wenn sie auch schwierige Zeiten überstehen will, Bürger, die sie dann tragen und ein positives Staatsverständnis haben.

DIE WELT: Was müsste in einem solchen Gesetz geregelt werden?

TAUBER: Wir müssten festlegen, welchen Bedarf wir an Zuwanderung haben, was ein Zuwanderer im wahrsten Sinne des Wortes mitbringen soll – an Bildung, Fähigkeiten und der Bereitschaft, sich einzubringen. Der Familiennachzug muss geregelt werden. Vielleicht ist in Absprache mit der Wirtschaft über Quoten für bestimmte Berufsbilder zu sprechen. Wir reden ja jetzt schon darüber, ob etwa ein Arzt, der als Flüchtling zu uns kommt, bleiben kann. [...] *(341 Wörter)*

*Tauber, Peter; Alexander, Robin; Gaugele, Jochen: „Man darf den Islam nicht pauschal verurteilen". https://www.welt.de/politik/deutschland/article136136897/Man-darf-den-Islam-nicht-pauschal-verurteilen.html, 08. 01. 2015*

**Anmerkung**

Z. 8 *Pegida:* „Patriotische Europäer gegen die Islamisierung des Abendlandes" – eine Organisation, die seit 2014 zunächst in Dresden, dann auch in anderen Städten gegen eine von ihnen befürchtete Islamisierung Europas demonstriert und Veränderungen in der Asyl- und Einwanderungspolitik fordert.

## Lösungsvorschläge

### Prüfungsteil 1: Leseverstehen und Schreiben

1 *In dieser Aufgabe müssen Sie genau beschreiben, was Sie im Textausschnitt über Jobs Lebensbedingungen in England erfahren.*

- *Er arbeitet als Taxifahrer. → Damit verdient er sein Geld.*
- *Er holt regelmäßig einen Jungen namens Robbie von der Schule ab. → Dadurch verdient er sich etwas dazu.*
- *Er ist aus Zimbabwe eingewandert.*
- *Er lebt anscheinend illegal in England, da er sich keinen Ausweis bei der Bücherei ausstellen lassen kann.*
- *Er ist besorgt über sein Leben.*
- *Er vermisst sein Zuhause und seine Frau.*
- *Er lebt in einem heruntergekommenen Gebäude in einem winzigen, schimmeligen Raum. Es gibt dort keine Privatsphäre.*
- *Er lebt in keiner guten Gegend in London (da er außerhalb seiner Wohnung auf gewalttätige Männer trifft).*
- *Obwohl er arm ist, besitzt er einige Wertgegenstände, wie etwa einen alten Fernseher.*
- *Er nutzt die kulturellen Angebote in London.*

**introduction**

Job, one of the protagonists in Amanda Craig's novel *Hearts and Minds*, published in 2009, is an illegal immigrant from Zimbabwe.

**main part:** Job's living conditions

He lives in a rough part of London where he meets violent men outside the house he lives in. In this run-down house, Job has a very small and mildewed room, only fitted with the bare necessities. There is next to no privacy there because everybody hears the most intimate sounds of their neighbours. He misses his home country and his wife, whom he worries about because he does not know if she is still alive in Zimbabwe.

Job works as a taxi driver and earns some extra money by picking up a boy called Robbie from school on a regular basis. Therefore, he can afford some small luxuries like second-hand books, which enrich his life immensely. He also owns some material goods like a TV set that has been discarded by others. Job also enjoys the cultural abundance he finds in London. *(164 words)*

2 *Für diese Aufgabe müssen Sie die Atmosphäre im Textausschnitt analysieren. Dazu müssen Sie betrachten, wie Menschen, Gegenstände und Orte beschrieben werden. Welche Worte werden genutzt und welche Assoziationen rufen diese hervor? Zudem müssen Sie die Erzählperspektive in der Situation berücksichtigen und den Effekt auf die Leserschaft und ihre Wahrnehmung dessen, was beschrieben wird, mit einbeziehen.*

- *Die Atmosphäre ist ambivalent – zugleich hoffnungsvoll und niederschmetternd.*
- *Der Er-Erzähler erzählt die Geschichte aus Jobs Perspektive: Die Leserinnen und Leser teilen seine Gefühle und Gedanken (vgl. Z. 2–5), die auch zwiegespalten sind.*
- *Hoffnungsvoll:*
  - *Job verdient mehr Geld.*
  - *Er mag Polly (die er mit einem Vogel vergleicht, vgl. Z. 4) und ihren Sohn Robbie (der wie ein Kind aussieht, dass geliebt wird, vgl. Z. 2).*
  - *Polly ist freundlich und zeigt sich an Jobs Leben interessiert. (vgl. Z. 42)*
  - *Arme Menschen in England leben ein besseres Leben als arme Menschen in Zimbabwe. (vgl. Z. 46–56)*
  - *Es gibt materiellen Wohlstand und ausreichend Kleidung und Nahrungsmittel. (vgl. Z. 46–56)*
- *Niederschmetternd:*
  - *Job vermisst seine Frau und sorgt sich um sie. (vgl. Z. 30/31)*
  - *Job erinnert sich an die Diskriminierung, die er in Zimbabwe erfahren hat. (vgl. Z. 18–26)*
  - *Der Ort, an dem er lebt, ist kahl und deprimierend. (vgl. Z. 34, 61–75)*
  - *Es gibt keine Privatsphäre und die Geräusche von sich liebenden Nachbarn lassen ihn seine Frau umso mehr vermissen. (vgl. Z. 75–77)*
  - *Job fühlt sich leer. („his heart is empty," Z. 77)*
  - *Das Gefühl von sozialer Gleichheit ist nicht mehr als ein schöner Schein. (vgl. Z. 40–42)*
  - *Die Menschen in England sind oberflächlich. (vgl. Z. 56)*
  - *Im Textausschnitt wird die Atmosphäre von Charles Dickens* Oliver Twist *reproduziert. (vgl. Z. 56–60)*

**introduction:** thesis / reference to assignment

The atmosphere the author evokes in this extract is ambivalent as it is both hopeful and even a little enthusiastic, but also depressing. This atmosphere is created by the choice of a particular narrative situation and by an ambivalent description of characters and places.

**main part:** narrative technique – third-person narrator, limited point of view

In this extract the story is told by a third-person narrator who sees the events through Job's eyes (cf. e. g. ll. 2–5), which are the eyes of an African immigrant, who has a different perspective on life in London than a Londoner. On the one hand, Job is fascinated by the abundance he finds in London. On the other hand, he is depressed by his private situation and how superficial Londoners are.

ambivalent general atmosphere

The description of Polly and her son makes a positive impression at first. Robbie is described as "a child who is loved" (l. 2) and Polly "is like a small bird, all softness and busyness" (l. 4). Thus, an air of love and softness is evoked. However, this is immediately modified into a negative evaluation of her living conditions when Job feels "sorry for [Polly] because she has no husband to help her" (ll. 4/5). Also, her explanation of what an au pair is, reminds

Job of his early experiences of discrimination by White people in Zimbabwe (cf. ll. 18–26), which spoils the atmosphere.

ambivalent relationship between characters

The relationship between Job and Polly is also ambivalent. Job's perception of both Polly and her son indicates that he cares for her. The fact that he invites her to his place and that she accepts, even though in a very non-committal way, creates a positive atmosphere as some sort of friendship seems to develop. Again, however, the additions made from Job's perspective suggest that true friendship will never arise between the two of them as they only "pretend to each other [...] that they are equals" (ll. 40/41). The next sentence generalises this situation when the narrator observes that equality is "one of those polite English fictions [...] that are like grease on a wheel shaft" (ll. 41/42). Thus, the English in general are discredited as polite but dishonest, which spoils the atmosphere considerably.

ambivalent impression of the city and its inhabitants

Furthermore, the English are also depicted as very superficial people. "They have so many things that it seems to drive out thought" (ll. 46/47). The "abundance of everything" (l. 54) results in a "consciousness of nothing" (l. 56). This description ruins the impression of London, which was very positive and even enthusiastic just some lines before when Job's visits to museums are described. There, Job is "amazed" (l. 51) by the amount of culture and enjoys "the most beautiful paintings, inventions, buildings" (l. 52).

reference to contrasts in Charles Dickens' novel *Oliver Twist*

Very important for the atmosphere created in this excerpt is the reference to Charles Dickens' novel *Oliver Twist*, which has made a lasting impression on Job. When he came to London, he expected a "foggy, dark place riddled with crime and yet suffused with kindness and courage" (ll. 56/57). Here again, the ambivalence is apparent as darkness opposes kindness and crime opposes courage. However, it seems that along with "the soot" (l. 58) and "horse-drawn carriages" (l. 59), kindness and courage have disappeared. All that remains are "men like Bill Sikes, with their dogs and violence" (ll. 59/60); the atmosphere is thus perceived as dangerous and threatening.

depressing atmosphere of Job's home and personal situation

This is all the more true because Job observes these frightening people in front of his home (cf. ll. 59/60). Even without them, the description of his house creates a depressing atmosphere, as it is a "shabby grey concrete building" (l. 34). The inside is even worse because "[d]amp blooms on the walls, outlining new continents – as if those who live here, in the perpetual stench of urine, beer, sour milk and cinders, need any more reminders of what they have lost" (ll. 63–65); in Job's case, his wife and his home country represent his losses. He feels the loss of his wife all the more because in his flat he hears the sounds of his neighbours' lovemaking (cf.

ll. 75–77). As a consequence, he feels emotionally crippled ("his heart is empty", l. 77). As these are the last words of the excerpt, the reader is left with a very depressing impression, which is, however, softened by the poetic language used to describe the scene. The traffic wails and sighs "in a continuous susurration" (l. 62) and "[d]amp blooms on the walls" (l. 63).

**conclusion**

To conclude, the narrative perspective chosen largely influences the ambivalent atmosphere. Due to this perspective, the readers are invited to share Job's point of view, who assesses the people and places in a very level-headed way, seeing both the positive and the negative aspects. *(792 words)*

3.1 *Zunächst müssen Sie erklären, was das Zitat bedeutet und in welchem Kontext es auftaucht. Dann müssen Sie Ihre eigene Meinung zum Gesagten zum Ausdruck bringen (Zustimmung, Widerspruch oder eine ausgewogenen Perspektive) und Ihre Meinung mit Argumenten begründen. Diese können im Zusammenhang zum Text stehen oder auf Ihrem Hintergrundwissen beruhen. Natürlich können Sie eigene Erfahrungen in Ihre Argumentation mit einbringen.*

- *Bedeutung: Wahre Gleichheit werden wir nie erreichen, aber so zu tun, als hätten wir sie bereits erreicht, hält unsere Gesellschaft am Laufen.*
- *Kontext: Job, ein Migrant aus einem afrikanischen Land, stellt dies fest, als seine Einladung einer englischen Frau in sein Zuause nicht abgelehnt wird, es aber dennoch offensichtlich ist, dass sie nicht beabsichtigt, ihn zu besuchen.*
- *Zustimmung:*
  - *Uns stehen unsere Vorurteile im Weg: Wir neigen dazu, Menschen aufgrund ihres Aussehens und ihrer Herkunft zu beurteilen. Polly ist zum Beispiel überrascht, dass Job Shakespeare und Dickens gelesen hat.*
  - *Einwanderer und Einwandererinnen arbeiten häufiger in Berufsfeldern, die schlecht bezahlt sind, als Menschen ohne Migrationshintergrund. Job arbeitet beispielsweise als Taxifahrer.*
  - *Die Situation ist für illegale Einwanderer noch schlimmer, da sie für den gleichen Beruf weniger bezahlt bekommen.*
  - *Weniger Einkommen führt zu schlechteren Lebensbedingungen.*
  - *Die Gesellschaft vermischt sich nicht wirklich; Menschen leben in verschiedenen Lebenswelten.*

**introduction:** context and meaning of quote

When Job invites Polly to his place, she accepts his invitation in a very non-committal way, which indicates that she will never really visit him in his tiny, shabby room because they are not equals although they pretend to be (cf. ll. 38–41). The narrator comments on this fact with the sentence, "It's one of those polite English fictions of equality that are like grease on a wheel shaft" (ll. 41/42). In this context it refers to the inequality between immigrants and native English people that tends to be ignored or glossed over in politically correct discourse. Therefore, it is very fitting even though it might seem slightly exaggerated.

state your view – here: agreement

Obviously, there are some people who truly accept immigrants or people with migration background as their equals and there certainly are immigrants who have succeeded in England. However, most people are still prejudiced against immigrants even though it might be at a more or less subconscious level of thinking. Take the character Polly from Amanda Craig's novel *Hearts and Minds* as an example. She works as a human rights lawyer defending illegal immigrants and one can therefore assume that she is supportive of immigrants. Nevertheless, she is surprised to learn that Job reads Shakespeare and Dickens (cf. ll. 42/43), which goes to show that she assumes that immigrants are badly educated or even illiterate.

**main part:**
first argument

reference to excerpt

Despite his obvious education, Job has to work as a taxi driver and earns little money. This is another piece of evidence to show that immigrants are not regarded as equals. Often their qualifications, for example as a doctor or engineer, are not accepted in the country they emigrate to and, therefore, they have to take low-paid jobs. Naturally, the situation for illegal immigrants is even worse. This leads to poorer living conditions and reinforces inequality.
People who are born in Great Britain but have a migration background often earn less than people who have lived in Britain for generations. A study by the Equality and Human Rights Commission revealed that Black* students with a university degree are paid about 25 per cent less than White students.

second argument

For Muslim immigrants the situation has become more difficult after the London bombings in 2005. Since then, people are often suspicious of Muslims, who are often verbally attacked in the streets. This shows that equality is sometimes not even pretended; on the contrary, racial differences are used as an excuse for violence.

third argument

All in all, it is a sorry fact that the quote from the novel rings true because inequality between immigrants and White British people still exists, and even those people who consider themselves as tolerant are prone to subconscious prejudice against immigrants or people with a migration background. *(455 words)*

**conclusion**

3.2 *Bei dieser Aufgabe sollen Sie einen Artikel für ein internationales Schülermagazin schreiben, in dem Sie der Frage nachgehen, ob Gesetze in den USA gerecht umgesetzt werden. Dass Ihre Antwort darauf kein eindeutiges „Ja" sein kann, wird bereits durch den zweiten Teil der Aufgabenstellung deutlich („... and make a suggestion on what could be done to improve the system."). Sie sollten also in erster Linie auf Probleme innerhalb des Justizvollzugs eingehen.*

- *In der Beispiellösung wird zunächst auf die „Black Lives Matter"-Bewegung eingegangen. Diese Protestbewegung hatte sich als Reaktion auf Fälle von Polizeigewalt gegen Afroamerikaner gebildet.*
- *Um zu belegen, dass das Rechtssystem nicht „farbenblind" ist, sondern nicht*-weiße* *Menschen benachteiligt, werden Daten aus der Statistik aufgeführt.*
- *Schließlich wird aufgezeigt, dass das Rechtssystem auch Menschen aus verschiedenen sozialen Schichten ungleich behandelt bzw. es deutliche Unterschiede gibt, wie welche Delikte geahndet werden.*
- *Zum Schluss werden verschiedene Lösungsvorschläge gemacht, wie der Rechtsvollzug in den USA verbessert (d. h. gerechter gestaltet) werden könnte.*

**Law Enforcement in the USA – A Just System?** — **title**

**introduction**

In class we have recently been talking about the criminal justice system in the USA. A central question that arose was whether this system is just or whether some groups of people are treated differently from others. Our research into this matter has revealed some appalling evidence.

**main part:** thesis

Over the past few years, for example, several unarmed Black men have been killed while being arrested by White police officers. As a result, a protest movement under the name of "Black Lives Matter" emerged, bewailing the racism within the police and the legal system.

first argument, statistics as proof

A look at some statistics showing the chances of being imprisoned in the USA supports these accusations of racial prejudice. While only one White man in seventeen runs the risk of being taken into custody, it is every third Black man that does so. Moreover, one in six Latino men may end up getting arrested.

second argument

Apart from racial bias, the US judicial system obviously also has different approaches to the various legal offences and to people from different social classes. To give you an example: In the recent financial crisis, bank managers filling their pockets by illegal actions on Wall Street got away with minor sentences, whereas in some states a consumer of marijuana, a minor offender by comparison, might go to prison for years.

**conclusion**

To draw a conclusion, law enforcement in the USA needs to be improved. A first step would be to recruit more people from different ethnic and social backgrounds as police officers, lawyers and judges, etc. As studies have shown, a diverse workforce leads to greater sensitivity towards issues of discrimination and helps to reduce bias. Yet, this alone is not enough. Society as a whole must change, which is a huge challenge. At school, children should be taught to overcome prejudice and embrace difference. Furthermore, the media should be careful not to spread stereotypes, such as by presenting African Americans or poor people as "gangsters". In this way, both law enforcement and society as a whole will hopefully become more just and discrimination might soon be a thing of the past. *(356 words)*

## Prüfungsteil 2: Sprachmittlung

*Das vorliegende Interview muss in einen Online-Artikel zu einem internationalen Schulprojekt umgeschrieben werden. Dies erfordert neben einer Überschrift einen eher formalen Sprachgebrauch. Stellen Sie sich auf die Leserschaft (Schüler*innen, Lehrer*innen sowie Eltern) einer polnischen und einer italienischen Schule. Das heißt, deutsche Besonderheiten müssen ggf. erklärt werden. Inhaltlich soll Taubers Sicht auf Einwanderung und ein mögliches Einwanderungsgesetz dargestellt werden.*

- *Tauber sieht keine islamistische Bedrohung durch Zuwanderung:*
  - *Viele Zuwanderer kommen aus Russland, Polen und anderen Teilen der Welt, aber nicht aus dem islamischen Kulturkreis.*
  - *Die religiöse Zugehörigkeit ist nicht entscheidend dafür, ob jemand ein guter deutscher Bürger sein kann. → deutsche Geschichte*
- *Er verweist auf das Vorgehen klassischer Einwanderungsländer wie Kanada:*
  - *Es geht nicht nur darum, ob ein Einwanderer gut für den Arbeitsmarkt ist.*
  - *Stattdessen wird auch gefragt, ob er eine Bereicherung für das Land ist und wie er sich in die Gesellschaft einbringen kann.*
  - *In Kanada wird ein Einwanderer Kanadier, in Deutschland wird er nur als Arbeitskraft gesehen.*
- *Wenn es nicht nur um temporäre Zuwanderung auf den Arbeitsmarkt gehen soll, braucht Deutschland ein Einwanderungsgesetz:*
  - *Zurzeit kommen hochqualifizierte Arbeiter, weil es der Wirtschaft gut geht.*
  - *Diese verlassen das Land in Krisenzeiten vermutlich aber wieder.*
  - *Eine Nation braucht jedoch auch Bürger, die selbst in schlechten Zeiten die Gesellschaft tragen und ein positives Staatsverständnis haben.*
- *Ein Gesetz müsste regeln, …*
  - *welchen Bedarf an Zuwanderung Deutschland hat.*
  - *was ein Einwanderer an Bildung, Fähigkeiten und Einstellung mitbringen soll.*
  - *wie der Familiennachzug aussehen soll.*
  - *wie Quoten für bestimmte Berufsgruppen aussehen könnten.*

## An immigration law for Germany?

headline

Peter Tauber, a member of the conservative German political party CDU (short for Christian Democratic Union) does not perceive an Islamic threat due to immigration. He argues that many immigrants do not come from Islamic cultures but from countries like Poland or Russia. More importantly, he brings to mind the German history, alluding to the persecution of Jews in Nazi Germany, when he states religion must never decide if someone is possibly a good German citizen or not.

introduction of Peter Tauber and his views

immigration is no Islamic threat

Tauber refers to traditional countries of immigrants like Canada, where not only an immigrant's usefulness for the job market is considered but also if immigrants will enrich the country and are willing and able to contribute to the nation's well-being. He believes that in Canada immigrants become Canadians, whereas in Germany they are only seen as members of the workforce.

Canada as an example of a country of immigrants

The politician claims that Germany needs a sensible immigration law because we need to consider more than temporary immigration into the German labour market. According to him, many highly qualified workers are immigrating to Germany at the moment because the economy is strong. However, he believes that they will most likely leave the country again in times of crisis. He adds that in those harder times, a nation particularly needs citizens who are willing to support the society and who have a positive attitude towards the country.

need for immigration law

According to Tauber, immigration law must lay down how many immigrants Germany needs, what education and skills they should have and what should be expected from them in terms of active participation in society. That law would also need to regulate possible family reunions. Finally, he mentions that there could be rates for certain professions, determining, for instance, how many doctors are allowed to immigrate. These rates could be agreed on with business representatives. *(304 words)*

contents of possible immigration law

## Berlin/Brandenburg
## Übungsaufgabe 3

## Prüfungsteil 1: Leseverstehen und Schreiben (75 %)

### Aufgabenstellung 1 – Tasks

**Themenschwerpunkte:** *Aims and ambitions, Saving the planet*

1 Summarise what happened in Vanuatu and why (Text A). Also summarise the conclusions the author draws from the event. (30 %)

2 Analyse how the author tries to convince the readers that they need to "live within [their] overall environmental thresholds" (ll. 56/57). In doing so, focus on structure, argumentative techniques and the language used. (35 %)

3 Choose **one** of the following tasks. (35 %)

3.1 Discuss if it makes sense for individuals to act in a more environmentally friendly way if they are likely "to suffer chronically due to someone else's bad habit" (l. 15) anyway.

OR

3.2 You come across the website of an American blogger who often complains about the ungrateful young generation, which, in her view, is in fact a gilded generation. She asks her readers for their opinion on the topic.

Nobody likes being told they live a carefree, easy-going life – young people included. Her constant complaint inspires you to write an article for her blog in which you discuss her claim that "Young people have never had it so good". Use the material (Text B) provided.

**Text A** (excerpt from the article)

### Developed nations have sown the wind, Vanuatu has reaped the whirlwind
by Andrew Simms

When the president of Vanuatu said that years of progress had been wiped out by a single extreme weather event, it was both a warning and an echo. Hurricane Mitch did the same to Nicaragua and Honduras in 1998; and in 2005 political failure combined with the collapse of sea defences under the onslaught of Hurricane Katrina to wreck the rich, vibrant culture of New Orleans. Climatic extremes in a warming world stand to reverse human progress and expose broken social contracts.

But in the case of Vanuatu there seems to be a crueller twist. Vanuatu is distinguished by having come top of a global index that measures how ecologically successful (low in impact) nations are at producing good lives for their people – so-called "happy life years". Vanuatu beat all other nations through treading lightest on the Earth for the quality and length of life its people enjoyed. Now it sits in the pathway of a giant climatic steamroller, fuelled by the energy-intensive lifestyles of nations much further down that index.

Its people are the national equivalent of the individual who leads an exemplary, healthy life only to suffer chronically due to someone else's bad habit – innocent, global victims of passive smoking. Vanuatu's president, Baldwin Lonsdale, was quick to point the finger of blame at manmade climate change for the severity of Cyclone Pam, saying that "the cyclone seasons, the warm, the rain, all this is affected".

Many may think it's too soon to jump to such conclusions. For years cautious scientists have balked at attributing the effect of warming to individual events. Attribution can sometimes be hard to prove, either for methodological reasons of complexity or due to lack of data. While trepidation remains, things have changed rapidly. Instead of simple claims of cause and effect, climate scientists now readily discuss how the probability of any particular event has been raised by the existence of warming.

Hence joint work in 2011 by the National Oceanic and Atmospheric Administration in the US and the UK's Met Office concluded that a Texas heatwave was 20 times more likely to be caused by climate change than by natural weather variation. A winter warm spell in Britain the same year was 62 times more likely than in the 1960s. The Met Office's Hadley Centre now confidently states that it "can identify any changed risk of such events".

In time, more analysis will be done on Cyclone Pam, but Lonsdale's personal experience and gut reaction fits a pattern of expectations described in the most recent and most comprehensive collation of science on extreme events in the IPCC's Fifth Assessment Report. It concluded that: "The frequency of the most intense storms will more likely than not increase in some basins. More extreme precipitation near the centres of tropical cyclones making landfall is projected in North and Central America, east Africa, west, east, south and southeast Asia as well as in Australia and many Pacific islands."

So, while the present is pretty bad for Vanuatu, in a warming world the future looks set to worsen. For this island nation, that is bitterly ironic. Vanuatu is an archipelago in the western Pacific, famous for having no regular military. When it topped the index in 2006 its ecological footprint per person was no higher than those in non-industrialised countries like Mali and Swaziland, life expectancy matched that in Turkey, and life satisfaction levels were considered as high as New Zealand's. It is democratic, rich in natural wealth but, being remote, exports little, avoiding the scramble of competing in global markets. It is also hugely culturally diverse with more than 100 languages spoken across its islands.

Small island states tend to do very well in the index topped by Vanuatu. Over countless generations and in the face of geographical isolation, many Pacific islands developed more cooperative economies and highly resilient farming methods. In a warming world they are bellwethers, and carry lessons for us all. If climate change renders small island states unliveable, the international community will sooner or later have to learn to accept and support environmental refugees. Though this would be tragic, remote island populations can, at least, relocate. However, blue island-planet populations cannot.

We will seal our own fate if we fail to learn to share and live within our overall environmental thresholds. [...] *(717 words)*

*Simms, Andrew: "Developed nations have sown the wind, Vanuatu has reaped the whirlwind". In:* The Guardian, *Copyright Guardian News & Media Ltd 2018*

**Annotations**

l. 1 *Vanuatu:* archipelago in the South Pacific consisting of about 82 islands.
l. 17 *Pam:* Cyclone Pam hit Vanuatu and damaged large parts of the archipelago in March 2015.
l. 33 *IPCC*: Intergovernmental Panel of Climate Change
l. 51 *bellwether:* something that is used as an indicator of what will happen in the future

## **Text B** (picture)

## My children will be an endangered species

*Barcroft Media/getty images*

## Prüfungsteil 2: Sprachmittlung (25 %)

### Aufgabenstellung 2 – Tasks

**Themenschwerpunkte:** *Aims and ambitions, Saving the planet*

Die Debatten um die „freie Fahrt für freie Bürger" oder ein generelles Tempolimit auf Deutschlands Autobahnen sind fast so alt wie die Bundesrepublik selbst.

Sie machen ein Praktikum im Stab der EU-Kommissarin für Verkehr. Im Rahmen von Überlegungen zur Harmonisierung europäischer Verkehrsvorschriften steuern Sie in der Amtssprache Englisch Positionen und Fakten aus der Tempolimit-Diskussion in Deutschland bei. Als Grundlage für Ihre Email and das Team dienen Ihnen die beiden untenstehenden Texte.

**Text 1: Sind Autobahnen mit Tempolimit sicherer?** von Simon Haas

[…] Nicht immer geht es in dieser sehr deutschen Diskussion um Fakten. […] Hier wichtige Fragen und Antworten zum Thema:

**Wie viele Autobahnkilometer sind überhaupt noch frei befahrbar?**
Nach einer Erhebung der Bundesanstalt für Straßenwesen (BaSt) gilt auf fast jedem dritten Autobahnkilometer bereits ein generelles Tempolimit. Zwei Drittel sind jedoch weiterhin ohne Geschwindigkeitsbegrenzung befahrbar. Auf den restlichen Strecken gibt es lediglich temporäre Beschränkungen, etwa nachts oder bei Nässe.

**Sind Autobahnen mit Tempolimit nun sicherer?**
Statistisch lässt sich tatsächlich ein Zusammenhang zwischen Tempolimit und weniger Verkehrstoten herstellen: 2016 sind auf deutschen Autobahnen mit Geschwindigkeitsbegrenzung pro Autobahnkilometer 26 Prozent weniger Menschen tödlich verunglückt als auf Autobahnen ohne Tempolimit. 2015 waren es 13 Prozent. Dieser Trend lässt sich auch bei der Anzahl der Schwerverletzten feststellen. Das geht aus einer Auswertung des Deutschen Verkehrssicherheitsrates (DVR) hervor.

**Hilft ein Tempolimit der Umwelt?**
Ein Tempolimit von 120 Stundenkilometern auf deutschen Autobahnen würde einer Untersuchung des Umweltbundesamts zufolge pro Jahr rund drei Millionen Tonnen $CO_2$ einsparen. Das entspricht einem Rückgang um neun Prozent. Drei Millionen Tonnen $CO_2$ sind allerdings gerade einmal drei Prozent dessen, was der Pkw-Verkehr 2016 insgesamt an Treibhausgasen freigesetzt hat.

**Verhindert ein Tempolimit Staus?**
Diese Frage ist unter Experten umstritten. Der Verkehrsclub Deutschland (VCD) argumentiert: „Ein Tempolimit bedeutet weniger Staus, denn es mindert die hohen Geschwindigkeitsunterschiede auf Autobahnen, die eine wichtige Ursache bei der Stau-

entstehung sind." Laut ADAC führt ein generelles Tempolimit von 120 Stundenkilometern hingegen zu keiner nennenswerten Verbesserung der Leistungsfähigkeit von Autobahnen. Verkehrsabhängig gesteuerte Anzeigen reichten demnach aus, um die optimale Geschwindigkeit bei hohem Verkehrsaufkommen zu erreichen.

*(253 Wörter)*

*Erschienen auf der Webseite der Schwäbischen Zeitung https://www.schwaebische.de/sueden/baden-wuerttemberg_artikel,-sind-autobahnen-mit-tempolimit-sicherer-_arid,10784485.html*
*Gekürzt und leicht adaptiert*

## Text 2: Sind Autobahnen mit Tempolimit sicherer?

Ein generelles Tempolimit auf deutschen Autobahnen machte die Straßen sicherer, wenn sich auch die Fahrkultur ändere, meint Prof. Justin Geistefeldt.

Der Bochumer Verkehrswissenschaftler hofft, dass dann auch weniger hektisch gefahren werde und es weniger unnötige Fahrstreifenwechsel gibt. […]

[…] Es gibt keine von der Bundesregierung finanzierten Studien zur Verkehrssicherheit durch ein Tempolimit. „Wir haben es hier mit einem forschungspolitischen Loch zu tun, und zwar ist das beabsichtigt", meint Gerd Lottsiepen vom ökologisch ausgerichteten Verkehrsclub Deutschland (VCD). „[…] Die Autoindustrie freut sich, dass es keine neuen Untersuchungen gibt, weil die immer wieder von der Regierung verlangen, kein Tempolimit einzuführen."

[…] Automobilverbände halten Verkehrsbeeinflussungsanlagen für effizienter als ein starres Tempolimit: Sie geben eine an die jeweilige Verkehrssituation angepasste Höchstgeschwindigkeit vor, die etwa bei schlechtem Wetter anders sein kann als bei gutem. Auf zehn Prozent des 12 200 Kilometer umfassenden Autobahnnetzes sind solche Systeme bereits installiert. Laut einer Studie des „Auto Clubs Europa" (ACE) kann ein Geschwindigkeitsmanagement zu einem Rückgang von bis zu 30 Prozent der Unfälle auf Autobahnen führen und die Umwelt entlasten, weil Staus und unnötige Schadstoffemissionen vermieden würden. *(174 Wörter)*

*Erschienen auf der Webseite des 3sat-Wissenschaftsmagazins „nano"*
*https://www.3sat.de/nano/umwelt/171052/index.html, 20.09.2017*

## Lösungsvorschläge

## Prüfungsteil 1: Leseverstehen und Schreiben

1 *Sie sollen kurz die Ereignisse in Vanuatu darstellen und die Ursachen für die Ereignisse darlegen. Zudem sollen Sie die Schlüsse, die der Autor daraus zieht, darstellen.*

- *Was ist passiert:*
  - *Vanuatu wurde im März 2015 von einem Zyklon getroffen.*
  - *Das Land wurde verwüstet.*
- *Gründe:*
  - *Vanuatu ist selbst nicht für das Naturereignis verantwortlich, da die Menschen dort sehr umweltbewusst leben. → Sie bezahlen für den energieintensiven Lebensstil anderer Nationen.*
  - *Der Präsident von Vanuatu macht die globale Erwärmung verantwortlich.*
  - *Während dieser Schluss nicht von allen akzeptiert wird, zitiert der Autor einen Bericht, der die Sichtweise des Präsidenten bestärkt.*
- *Schlüsse:*
  - *Die Zahl der Umweltflüchtlinge wird ansteigen.*
  - *Die Erde könnte eines Tages unbewohnbar werden.*
  - *Wir müssen uns alle bewusster werden, welche Auswirkungen unser Verhalten auf das Klima hat, und umweltbewusster leben.*

**introduction:** reference to source, topic

In his article "Developed nations have sown the wind, Vanuatu has reaped the whirlwind" published in *The Guardian*, the journalist Andrew Simms briefly describes what happened in Vanuatu. He then gives reasons for the event and draws conclusions from it.

**main part:** events, reasons

In March 2015, Vanuatu was hit by Cyclone Pam and its islands were completely devastated. The president of Vanuatu blames global warming for what happened and although Simms admits that not everybody agrees with the president's analysis, he also quotes a report that supports it. Furthermore, the author mentions that Vanuatu itself is not to blame because this nation lives in a very environmentally friendly way. According to him, developed nations who have more energy-intensive lifestyles are to blame but Vanuatu has to pay the price.

conclusions

Simms predicts that the number of environmental refugees will increase and that one day the earth might no longer be inhabitable. He concludes that we all need to be more conscious of the effect we are having on our planet and its climate and that we need to live in a more environmentally friendly way. *(181 words)*

2 *Diese Aufgabe verlangt, dass Sie analysieren, wie der Autor seine Leserschaft von seiner Meinung überzeugen möchte. Sie müssen sich dabei auf die Struktur des Textes, die Art der Argumentation und die Sprache konzentrieren.*

- *Struktur:*
  - *Überschrift: gibt die Stimmung vor → Vanuatu bezahlt für das Fehlverhalten der wirtschaftsstarken Staaten*
  - *Text zeigt zunächst, dass Vanuatu kein Einzelfall ist (vgl. Z. 1–6)*
  - *Autor greift Überschrift wieder auf → wirtschaftsstarke Staaten und ihr Lebensstil sind für Erderwärmung verantwortlich (vgl. Z. 7–18)*
  - *Autor beschreibt Reaktionen auf die Analyse, dass die globale Erwärmung für den Zyklon verantwortlich ist, der Vanuatu getroffen hat (vgl. Z. 19–38)*
  - *Aussichtslose Vorhersage für Inseln wie Vanuatu, unseren Planeten und seine Bewohner (vgl. Z. 34–55)*
  - *Schlussfolgerung, dass unser Lebensstil weniger energieintensiv werden muss (vgl. Z. 56/57)*
- *Techniken bei der Argumentation:*
  - *Beispiele (vgl. Z. 1–5)*
  - *Fakten (vgl. Z. 7–11, 41/42)*
  - *Zahlen (vgl. Z. 26, 28)*
  - *Expertenmeinungen und ein Zitat aus einer Studie (vgl. Z. 19–38)*
- *Sprache:*
  - *Bibelstelle, die leicht angepasst wurde, um zu betonen, dass andere den Schaden verursacht haben, den Vanuatu ausbaden muss (vgl. Überschrift)*
  - *Wörter mit positiver Konnotation werden genutzt, um Vanuatu und seine Einwohner*innen zu beschreiben, z. B. „distinguished" (Z. 7/8), „ecologically successful" (Z. 8/9), „exemplary, healthy" (Z. 14/15), „innocent" (Z. 15)*
  - *Im Kontrast dazu negativ konnotierte Wörter, die wirtschaftsstarke Länder und den Klimawandel beschreiben, z. B. „giant climatic steamroller" (Z. 12), „energy-intensive lifestyles" (Z. 12)*
  - *Bildliche Sprache, um zu betonen, dass Vanuatu in der Situation das Opfer vom Fehlverhalten anderer ist (vgl. Z. 10–16)*
  - *Aufzählung, die Vanuatus Errungenschaften betont (vgl. Z. 41–44)*

**introduction:** thesis / reference to assignment

The author's intention in writing this article is to convince the readers that they need to "live within [their] overall environmental thresholds" (ll. 56/57). He tries to achieve his aim by using a structure that leads to the conclusion quoted above, by employing different argumentative techniques and by making use of words that underline both the difference between Vanuatu and developed nations and the author's interpretation that Vanuatu is suffering instead of these developed countries.

**main part: structure**

This interpretation is introduced right in the headline. The author then shows that Vanuatu is not an isolated case but that other countries have been hit by extreme winds, too (cf. ll. 1–6). In the second and third paragraph, the journalist takes up the headline again and describes in more detail that developed nations are to blame for global warming and, therefore, climate change (cf. ll. 7–18). In the following three paragraphs he presents reactions to the analysis of Vanuatu's president, who claims that global warming is responsible for the cyclone that hit his country. The author briefly mentions doubts (ll. 19–22) but then dwells on experts, organisations and numbers that support the president's view (cf. ll. 22–38). This indicates that he favours this interpretation of the events himself. In the seventh and eighth paragraph he makes dire predictions about the future of islands like Vanuatu, our planet and its inhabitants to emphasise that we need to take action (cf. ll. 39–55), which leads him to his final conclusion that we have to have less energy-intensive lifestyles (cf. ll. 56/57). Thus, the article's structure leads very logically to the final conclusion that appears to be convincing.

**language**

The language employed stresses the view that developed nations are to blame for Vanuatu's misfortune. The differences in lifestyles and their consequences are emphasised. Vanuatu's inhabitants are "ecologically successful" (ll. 8/9) and therefore "distinguished" (ll. 7/8). They lead "an exemplary, healthy life" (ll. 14/15). All these words have a positive connotation and therefore underline that Vanuatu's people are "innocent" (l. 15). They are contrasted with developed nations, which are accused of causing "a giant climatic steamroller, fuelled by [...] energy-intensive lifestyles" (ll. 11/12). Thus, developed nations are depicted as villains.

→ choice of words

Vanuatu: positive connotation

developed nations: negative connotation

This contrast is already introduced in the headline, which is an adapted proverb from the Bible. The original proverb "they that sow wind shall reap whirlwind" is applied to people who start trouble that grows larger than planned. In this case, however, someone else, namely the developed countries, started the trouble that another party, namely Vanuatu, has to suffer from. This stresses the injustice of the situation.

→ proverb

Additionally, the author uses figurative speech to stress this idea. He compares Vanuatu to "the individual who leads an exemplary, healthy life only to suffer chronically due to someone else's bad habit – innocent, global victims of passive smoking" (ll. 14–16). Furthermore, developed nations, as mentioned above, are blamed for having set free a "steamroller" (l. 12), which ruthlessly destroys other nations. The intended effect of the language used is that people in developed countries should have a guilty conscience and realise that their lifestyle needs to be changed.

→ figurative speech

The argumentative techniques employed support that view. The journalist argues that now extreme weather events happen regularly as Cyclone Pam is an "echo" (l. 2) of preceding hurricanes. To prove this assertion Simms gives several examples (cf. ll. 2–5). The claim that Vanuatu's people lead an exemplary life is backed up by a global index in which Vanuatu excelled (cf. ll. 7–11, 41/42). Thus, the journalist bases his argument on facts, which makes him more trustworthy.

**argumentative techniques**

→ examples, facts

When Simms supports the analysis of Vanuatu's president that Cyclone Pam was caused by global warming, he refers to unnamed climate scientists who "now readily discuss how the probability of any particular event has been raised by the existence of warming" (ll. 23/24). Furthermore, he quotes from the IPCC's Fifth Assessment Report (ll. 34–38), refers to organisations that share his view (cf. ll. 25–30) and uses their numbers (cf. ll. 26, 28) and thus bases his argument on experts' views, which adds authority to his reasoning.

→ reference to experts, numbers

All in all, Simms makes it clear that people in developed nations need to change their lifestyles if they do not want to live at the expense of somebody else's well-being. He achieves this by using language in a way that clearly contrasts the victim and the perpetrator, by using structure purposefully to make it lead to his final conclusion and by basing his arguments on examples, facts and experts' reports. *(773 words)*

**conclusion:** reference to task

3.1 *Bei dieser Aufgabe müssen Sie argumentieren, ob wir als Individuen umweltfreundlich leben sollten, obwohl das Verhalten eines Einzelnen die globale Erwärmung nicht verhindern kann. Sie müssen Pro- und Contra-Argumente abwägen und am Schluss zu einer Schlussfolgerung kommen.*

- *Einleitung: Stellen Sie das Thema dar und gehen Sie auf das Dilemma für jeden Einzelnen ein.*
- *Pro:*
  - *Es hilft nicht, einfach nur den Kopf in den Sand zu stecken.*
  - *Jeden Tag, den wir nichts tun, wird es schwerer das Zwei-Grad-Ziel zu erreichen, daher können wir nicht warten, bis andere beginnen, etwas zu verändern.*
  - *Ein gutes Beispiel könnte andere dazu animieren, zu folgen, etwa eine 10:10 Initiative, die Menschen zusammenbringt, die eine sauberere Welt mit weniger $CO_2$ Ausstoß wünschen.*
- *Contra:*
  - *Das Beispiel der Menschen in Vanuatu zeigt, dass das Verhalten des Einzelnen nicht ausreicht.*
  - *Der Einfluss von Individuen ist im Vergleich zu dem großer Unternehmen zu vernachlässigen.*

- *Die USA und China sind für 40 % der weltweiten Treibhausgasemissionen verantwortlich. 2016 haben sie endlich das Klimaabkommen in Paris unterzeichnet. Die geplante Reduktion der Emissionen reicht allerdings nicht, um das Zwei-Grad-Ziel zu erreichen und der US-amerikanische Präsident Donald Trump verkündete kurz darauf bereits den Austritt aus dem Pariser Klimaabkommen.*
- *Die Erderwärmung wird nicht als unmittelbare Gefahr wahrgenommen, weshalb es schwer ist, Menschen zu überzeugen, ihr Verhalten zu ändern.*

– *Schlussfolgerung: Vergleichen Sie die Pro- und Contra-Seite und kommen Sie zu einem Ergebnis.*

**introduction**

When discussing climate change, two is the magic number. We need to stabilise global temperature within two degrees above pre-industrial levels, or else the extra input of greenhouse gases, for example those locked in the arctic ice, will wipe out most of the life on earth. In order to achieve that goal, we need to cut emissions by 80 % by 2050. This goal seems hard to achieve; one might even say it is impossible to achieve. Therefore, the question arises whether it makes any sense at all for individuals to act in a more environmentally friendly way if they are likely "to suffer chronically due to someone else's bad habit" (l. 15).

**main part:**
pros

People who think it does make sense may point out that no one, at least no doctor, would recommend a non-smoker who contracts lung cancer to start smoking because he will die anyway. Only deeply pessimistic and sarcastic people would do so. The same could be said to be true for global warming because we cannot bury our heads in the sand and do nothing just because the big players, for instance energy-intensive companies like Trimet, emit too much greenhouse gas.
On the contrary, the individual needs to set a good example to encourage others to follow. Take an initiative such as 10:10. This initiative offers a website on which they bring together individual people and groups who want to make this world a cleaner, cleverer, low-carbon place. On the website one can find hundreds of examples of what individuals have already achieved to cut down emissions and thus get ideas for one's own projects.

transition – cons

On the other hand, there are good reasons that support the view that the individual is not powerful enough to stop global warming. Take Vanuatu as an example: the nation as a whole, and not just the individual inhabitants, led an exemplary life as far as the emission of greenhouse gas is concerned. In spite of that fact, Cyclone Pam destroyed many people's houses. So their excellent behaviour did not save them from suffering the consequences of global warming.

The USA and China, who together are responsible for 40 % of our global greenhouse gas emissions, finally signed the climate change agreement in 2016. Whereas China seems to be quite serious about tackling climate change, the USA under Donald Trump even pulled out of the agreement again. In any case it will be almost impossible to stay within the 2-degree limit because efforts started too late and too half-heartedly.
The basic problem is that we are evolutionarily equipped to deal with immediate threats. Global warming, however, is not an immediate threat so we do not feel the need to react. Once people start to feel that threat, it will be too late.

**conclusion**

Altogether, I truly believe that individuals alone are too ineffective to help with climate change. Of course, they can make some effort and set good examples, but if the big spenders do not change their behaviour radically, the 2-degree goal is unattainable. Then it might be wiser to enjoy the remaining years on our planet, without denying ourselves pleasures like weekend trips to Paris or Mallorca, because rough times are certainly ahead. *(532 words)*

3.2 *Wenn die Aufgabenstellung von Ihnen verlangt, die Thematik zu diskutieren („Discuss“), müssen Sie sich mit Pro und Contra auseinandersetzen. Ob Sie in der vorliegenden Aufgabenstellung in Ihrem Fazit der Bloggerin zustimmen, dass junge Menschen es heute so guthaben wie keine Generation zuvor, oder ob Sie ihre These ablehnen, bleibt Ihnen überlassen. Ihre Haltung muss begründet und nachvollziehbar sein.*
*Eine besondere Herausforderung liegt für Sie darin, wie Sie das vorhandene Material in Ihre Lösung einarbeiten. Dabei sollen Sie die Bildquellen ausdrücklich <u>nicht</u> detailliert beschreiben. Das Material dient Ihnen als gedanklicher Anstoß zur Findung von Ideen und Argumenten oder zur Einbeziehung von relevanten Informationen.*
*Folgender Aufbau ist möglich:*

*Hinführung zum Thema: Vergleich der Perspektive zwischen Jung und Alt*

- *Gedanken zum Hauptteil:*
  *Möglichkeiten:*
  - *Materielle Verhältnisse, Möglichkeiten der Mobilität und des Konsums*
  - *Lebenserwartung*
  - *Individuelle Freiheit und Entfaltung wie keine Generation zuvor*

  *Probleme und Herausforderungen:*
  - *Konfrontation mit existenziellen Herausforderungen wie Klimawandel*
  - *Leistungsdruck durch neue Job- und Medienwelt*
  - *Demokratie und Freiheit gefährdet durch antidemokratischen Populismus*
- *Abrundung des Textes mit Fazit, persönlicher Einschätzung, Ausblick o. Ä.: hilfreich, andere Perspektive einzunehmen*

**title**

## A matter of perspective

**introduction**

While the young tend to see what is troublesome in their lives, the old tend to see what they didn't have when they were young. They feel the young have far more opportunities and better living conditions than they did in the past. Have the young really never had it so good?

**main part:**
opportunities:

Young people nowadays DO have opportunities they may not even be aware of.

material possessions

No young generation as a whole has ever had more material possessions than this one. They have enough pocket money, go on vacations to remote places, and own expensive state-of-the-art electronic devices.

life expectancy

With a life expectancy of around 80 years, people born today may become older than any generation before, and enjoy what is possibly the best healthcare system ever.

freedom

The young enjoy political freedom and individual self-fulfilment to an unprecedented extent. They have a say in the way they dress, the school they attend, and the trade they want to learn. They experience a lot more respect and a lot less violence than previous generations. And they grow up in relative peace and democracy.

challenges and problems:
climate change

On the other hand, it is a fact that today's young generation are faced with huge environmental threats that literally endanger their existence. Because the majority of politicians, corporate leaders and voters refuse to take effective climate action and to live up to their responsibilities, the world is rather likely to become a place afflicted by heatwaves, floods, severe droughts and crop failures. Millions of climate refugees will need to be catered for. And in recent years it has become more and more obvious that the continuous loss of biodiversity is threatening our vital natural resources.

psychological distress

Another tough challenge the young are faced with is psychological distress. There are high expectations to excel at school, to have a successful career and to perform on social media platforms. There seems to be more competition than ever for attractive jobs, excellent grades and "likes" on Instagram, the digital currency that gains you social recognition. High expectations often result in pressure which affects a person's health and quality of life.

populist movements

Last but not least, Brexit and the rise of populist movements in numerous European countries suggest that a society based on stable democratic values can no longer be taken for granted.

Alarmingly large numbers of juveniles have mental-health problems or express they are not happy at all with the stress levels in their lives. This has to be taken seriously.

But we should also see the great opportunities for today's youth, of course. A different perspective might help us gain a little peace of mind. *(436 words)*

**conclusion**

## Prüfungsteil 2: Sprachmittlung

*Das Besondere bei der vorliegenden Aufgabe ist, dass Sie Informationen aus zwei Texten zusammenfassen müssen. Damit Ihre Lösung einer klaren Struktur folgt, müssen Sie zunächst die wesentlichen Aspekte in beiden Texten markieren und diese dann einander zuordnen, also in Ihrer Lösung Vorzüge oder Nachteile aus beiden Texten in einem Abschnitt zusammenfassen.*

- *Vorzüge eines allgemeinen Tempolimits*
  - *Sicherere Autobahnen, weniger Unfälle mit tödlichem Ausgang*
  - *Geringerer $CO_2$-Ausstoß*
  - *Weniger Staus*
- *Argumente dagegen sowie mögliche Alternativen*
  - *$CO_2$-Einsparungen nur sehr gering*
  - *Kaum Effekt auf die Staubildung*
  - *Stattdessen: Verkehrsbeeinflussungsanlagen zum Geschwindigkeitsmanagement*
- *Vorwurf des VCD: Regierung macht bewusst keine Studien zum Thema, um Autoindustrie zu schonen*

Dear Colleagues,

**greeting**

In out last meeting we talked about the discussion around a general speed limit on German highways. In the following I sum up the arguments mentioned in the articles "Sind Autobahnen mit Tempolimit sicherer?" by Simon Haas published in the *Schwäbische Zeitung* and "Sind Autobahnen mit Tempolimit sicherer?" from the website of the science magazine "nano".

**introduction:** reference to article

The benefits of a general speed limit on German motorways are as follows: It will make motorways safer if people drive more sensibly. According to statistical data, a speed limit of this kind might lead to a drop in the number of road deaths and persons who are seriously injured. It would reduce $CO_2$ emissions by approximately three million tons – a nine per cent decline. Moreover, it reduces the large differences in the speeds of vehicles on highways, which means less congestion.

**main part:** pro arguments

Automobile associations object to it, countering that $CO_2$ savings would only be very small. They claim that a general speed limit would have no noticeable effect with regard to congestion on motorways. Instead, they prefer traffic management facilities which make it possible to set flexible speed limits according to weather conditions, traffic flow and traffic density.

contra arguments

The environmental lobby group VCD accuses the Federal Government of deliberately retaining from funding studies on road safety and speed limits to the advantage of the automobile industry. — accusations of the VCD

Thank you, — closing

Nils *(227 words)* — name

* We have decided to capitalize "Black" and "White" to signal that they are not natural categories but social ones (for more background information on this topic see e. g. https://www.theatlantic.com/ideas/archive/2020/06/time-to-capitalize-blackand-white/613159/).

**Schwarz wird in unseren neueren Publikationen großgeschrieben (und *weiß* wird durch die Schriftlage, also kursiv oder normal, gekennzeichnet), um deutlich zu machen, dass es sich nicht um Farbbezeichnungen handelt, sondern um Begriffe, die beschreiben, ob Menschen von Rassismuserfahrungen betroffen sind oder nicht.

# Abiturprüfung Berlin 2018
# Englisch Grundkurs

## Prüfungsteil 1: Leseverstehen und Schreiben (75 %)

Der Prüfungsteil 1 besteht aus zwei Aufgabenstellungen, von denen Sie eine zur Bearbeitung auswählen. *Hinweis:* Abgedruckt ist eine der beiden zur Wahl stehenden Aufgaben.

### Aufgabenstellung 1 – Tasks

**Themenschwerpunkte:** *Personal relations in their social context, Ethnic and cultural diversity*

1 Outline Avtar's first impressions of Britain. (30 %)

2 Analyze how the author characterizes Avtar. Give evidence from the text. (30 %)

3 Choose one of the following tasks:

3.1 "He was to concentrate on making something of himself in England now God had blessed him with this opportunity." (ll. 7/8)
Explain Avtar's father's expectations and assess the pressure often put on immigrants by their families back home. (40 %)

OR

3.2 Compare Avtar's situation to that of another character from literature or film who faces a difficult situation in a new country. Assess the way they cope.* (40 %)

OR

3.3 Based on her experience with foreign students, the girl at the registration office writes an article for the Indian Students' Society in which she comments on difficulties faced by newcomers and gives advice on how to deal with new situations.
Write this article using ideas from the text and your knowledge about the issue. (40 %)

* Dieser Aufgabentyp entfällt ab der Abiturprüfung 2021.

**Text** (excerpt from the novel)

**The Year of the Runaways**
by Sunjeev Sahota

Note: *In order to be able to marry his girlfriend back in India, Avtar has come to Britain to work and make some money. He has arrived on a student visa for which his parents have paid a lot of money.*

[…] He walked straight on, towards what looked like a major road, and kept to the right-hand side of the pavement. He reminded himself to ask Massiji about changing up some money and to then give her some for letting him call home. They were fine, his parents had said. Pleased he'd arrived safely, his father added, a little formally. They weren't used to speaking to their son in this way – generally, without a real reason for the call – so it was a short conversation, the main thrust being that Avtar wasn't to worry about them. He was to concentrate on making something of himself in England now God had blessed him with this opportunity. To that end, Avtar allowed himself a little optimism. The trains had come when the electronic signs had said they would. The guard hadn't expected money to point him in the right direction. Cars were only driven on roads and only in nice long columns. Even the air was a clear and uniform blue. All the signs of a well-run country. A fair country. A country that helps its people. A country that might even help him.

A brown signboard read 'Coll. of NW London' and indicated the first left at the big grassy roundabout up ahead. He wondered how to cross the road. […] He secured the folder into the back of his black trousers and, with one foot lifted to the top of the railing, jumped over. The cars were so close. Drivers glanced confusedly over and one or two pointed at the ground, mouthing words. He hoped that now he'd made clear his intention the traffic might stop, but there seemed to be no sign of that. He ventured a foot forward, then took it back as a white van came roaring down. He was breathing hard. He looked about again: nothing. No traffic lights. He had no chance. He waited. When the moment came he felt the cold of the railings leave his body and he was running as hard as he could. The road felt coarse under his thin soles. He could feel his folder coming loose from his trousers and as he reached behind to hold it in place a long brassy horn sounded. Avtar looked over his shoulder. The cars were coming. He wouldn't make it, and as he launched towards the central mound of the roundabout his foot gave and he felt one of his shoes slip off. All he could do was squeeze between the black-and-white arrow signs and clamber onto the grassy circle. Safe at last, he covered his ears. He felt stupid and angry and through the legs of arrow signs saw his poor shoe being flipped about like a fish.

About an hour later, a beautiful yellow-haired girl smiled at Avtar as if she'd been waiting the whole day just for him to walk into the college registration office. She looked like one of those white girls that used to come on the television, selling Sunsilk or Amla Shampoo. He managed a weak smile and tentatively presented his folder. He hoped he'd removed all the grass stains.

'Welcome to North-West,' she said, unclipping the folder, going through his papers. 'Computing with Security Systems. I hear that's a good course.'

'Thank you,' Avtar said, just about understanding.

She asked him where he was from and he said India, and then she said they had him down as making his own accommodation arrangements, and he said, yes, that was true.

[…] She handed him various things: maps, a student union application form, an events listing, his timetable, a pass with his name and picture on it – to give him access to the Mathematical Sciences building, she explained. All this he gathered into his folder thanking her, keen to leave before they reneged and shipped him back home.

'There is a strong college Indian Students' Society, which does a lot of good work helping students adjust to –' she struggled for the word. She seemed to want to avoid saying *England* – 'a new approach. They're still open. It's just down the corridor if you're interested.'

He thanked her again, inadvertently bowing his head a little, and turned to leave. […]

*(702 words)*

*Sahota, Sunjeev.* The Year of the Runaways. *London: Picador, 2015, 187–189.*

**Annotations**

Sunjeev Sahota: (born 1981) male British author

l. 2 Massiji: Avtar's aunt who lives in London

l. 6 thrust: *here:* idea

l. 14 Coll.: *abbreviation:* College

l. 45 to renege: to break a promise

l. 50 inadvertently: without intending to

## Prüfungsteil 2: Sprachmittlung (25 %)

Der Prüfungsteil 2 besteht aus zwei Aufgabenstellungen, von denen Sie eine zur Bearbeitung auswählen.

### Aufgabenstellung 2.1 – Tasks

**Themenschwerpunkte:** *Science and technology – visions of the future, The impact of the media on society, Personal relations in their social context*

For *robotsblog.net*, a blog on the current developments in robotics, write a blog entry outlining the information about Yolandi as reported by Kurt Sagatz.

**Text** (Auszug aus dem Artikel)

**Per Roboter durch die „Abendschau"**
Von Kurt Sagatz

„Jetzt übernehme ich hier das Kommando", sagt Yolandi selbstbewusst im Sendezentrum der RBB-Welle Antenne Brandenburg. Yolandi ist der Name eines 175 Zentimeter großen Roboters, der im Rundfunk Berlin-Brandenburg von Sonntag an eine Woche lang eine große Karriere als Radio- und Fernsehmoderator vor sich hat. Während der ARD-Themenwoche „Zukunft der Arbeit" wird er durch verschiedene RBB-Redaktionen touren. In der „Abendschau" liest er Nachrichten vor – dabei neigt er seinen Kopf mit dem großen Display auf der Vorderseite, auf dem sich Mund und Augenbrauen bewegen, leicht hin und her. In „Guten Morgen Brandenburg" informiert er über das Wetter und beim Besuch des „RBB um 4"-Trucks im Zeiss-Planetarium hilft er mit seinem äußerst beweglichen Arm als Beleuchter aus.

Der Einsatz von Yolandi gehört nicht etwa zum Sparprogramm der neuen RBB-Intendantin Patricia Schlesinger, die derzeit das komplette TV-Programm danach abklopft, wo noch Mittel für ein besseres Hauptabendprogramm versteckt sein könnten. Der Sender will mit dem Praxis-Einsatz des Berliner High-Tech-Produkts vielmehr der Frage nachgehen, welche Berufe Roboter eines Tages ausüben können und ob sie dabei Menschen vollständig ersetzen. Oder wo Roboter an ihre Grenzen stoßen. Die richtige Reaktion auf eine solche Situation hat Yolandi schon parat: „Oh, jetzt habe ich aber einen Fehler gemacht. Dabei habe ich mir so viel Mühe gegeben", klingt es dann sehr menschlich aus seinem Lautsprecher. […]

„Wir wollen niemanden erschrecken, aber zeigen, was auf die Gesellschaft zukommen kann", sagt Hermann Meyerhoff von der für solche Projekte zuständigen RBB-Querschnittsabteilung, die sich auch um die multimediale Vernetzung von Radio, Fernsehen und Online im RBB kümmert. „Noch sind wir meilenweit davon entfernt, dass Roboter Programm machen", glaubt er. Ein Gespräch kann mit Yolandi nicht geführt werden, er gibt ausschließlich zuvor eingespielte Texte ab. Allerdings hat Kollege Computer in einigen Redaktionen längst einen festen Arbeitsplatz. Textroboter werden eingesetzt, um aus Börsenkursen oder den Ergebnissen unterer Sportligen vollautomatisiert Meldungen zu schreiben. […]

Die Stimme von Yolandi stammt von der Radioreporterin Doris Anselm. Die Reporterin der RBB-Welle Radio Berlin 88,8 ist zumeist mit dem Ü-Wagen unterwegs, beispielsweise wenn wieder einmal ein umgekippter Lastwagen eine Stadtautobahn blockiert. „Yolandi trägt grünen Lidschatten, was ich nie tun würde", habe sie gedacht, als sie den Roboter das erste Mal gesehen habe, sagt die Reporterin. „Und wo Menschen einen Bauch haben, hat Yolandi ein Loch", war die zweite Sache, die ihr auffiel. […]

Bis Roboter die Fähigkeiten dafür hätten, einen Moderator oder Reporter zu ersetzen, „das dauert noch wahnsinnig lange, wenn es überhaupt gelingt", meint auch Anselm. „Schließlich sind wir Journalisten, keine Sprechpuppen." Bei der Arbeit eines Reporters, zum Beispiel bei einem Interview, komme es nicht zuletzt auf Zwischentöne und das Zwischenmenschliche an. Dass ein Roboter die Nachrichten nicht nur während der ARD-Themenwoche vorliest, sei schon eher vorstellbar. Das hänge nicht nur von der technischen Entwicklung ab, vor allem die Akzeptanz des Publikums spiele dabei eine große Rolle. „Ich glaube, dass Menschen lieber Menschen anschauen", sagt Anselm. […] *(473 Wörter)*

*Sagatz, Kurt. „Per Roboter durch die Abendschau". Der Tagesspiegel. 26. Oktober 2016. Entnommen am 15. Januar 2017. http://www.tagesspiegel.de/medien/zukunft-der-arbeit-beim-rbb-per-roboter-durch-die-abendschau/14743344.html (Sprachliche Fehler in der Textvorlage wurden entsprechend der geltenden Norm korrigiert; Zwischenüberschriften des Originaltextes wurden weggelassen.)*

**Annotationen**

Titel „Abendschau": Nachrichtensendung im Fernsehen / RBB
Z. 2 RBB-Welle Antenne Brandenburg: Radiosender
Z. 8 „Guten Morgen Brandenburg": Fernsehsendung im RBB
Z. 9 „RBB um 4": Fernsehsendung für lokale Nachrichten
Z. 10 Beleuchter: Techniker, der für das Licht bei Dreharbeiten verantwortlich ist; Englisch: *lighting technician*
Z. 12 Intendantin: Geschäftsführerin und künstlerische Leiterin eines Theaters oder einer Sendeanstalt
Z. 22 Querschnittsabteilung: Schnittstelle, die für mehrere Bereiche eines Betriebes zuständig ist
Z. 27 Sportligen: Plural von Sportliga
Z. 30 Ü-Wagen: Übertragungswagen / mit der Technik eines Rundfunk-/Fernsehstudios ausgestattetes Fahrzeug

## Aufgabenstellung 2.2 – Tasks

**Themenschwerpunkte:** *Personal relations in their social context, Ethnic and cultural diversity*

A British friend is planning a trip to Germany and has asked you about youth hostels in Germany. Write an email outlining the information given in the interview.

**Text** (Auszug aus dem Interview)

**Jugendherbergen: „Wir wollen cooler werden"**
Von Steffen Dobbert

[…] **Die Zeit**: Frau Braasch-Eggert, stimmt es, dass eine Jugendherberge der einzige Ort der Welt ist, wo es immer Hagebuttentee gibt?

**Angela Braasch-Eggert**: Hagebutten- und Pfefferminztee aus der Blechkanne, so war das früher. Damals war Kaffee ja noch teuer, der wurde nur an Gruppenleiter ausgegeben. Heute gibt es viele andere Teesorten, die Blechkanne ist überall abgeschafft.

**Zeit**: Muss jeder Gast immer noch den Tisch abdecken und abwischen?

**Braasch-Eggert**: Das erwarten wir.

**Zeit**: Sie halten auch noch am Prinzip Doppelstockbett fest?

**Braasch-Eggert**: Als vor etwas mehr als 100 Jahren die erste Jugendherberge in Deutschland eröffnet wurde, gab es noch dreistöckige Betten mit Bettverlängerungsschienen für Übergroße. Das ist Geschichte. Mittlerweile stehen in den Herbergen normale Betten und Doppelstockbetten. […]

**Zeit**: Und wie sieht es mit den Jugendlichen aus? Die sind heutzutage fast immer mit dem Smartphone online. Sollte eine Jugendherberge das mitmachen?

**Braasch-Eggert**: Die Herbergen müssen sich mit der Jugend wandeln. Das passiert weltweit. In den großen Städten haben alle unsere Häuser einen WLAN-Zugang. In New York und in der Schweiz gibt es in jedem Zimmer Internet.

**Zeit**: Chatten im Doppelstockbett?

**Braasch-Eggert**: In Deutschland sind wir eher der Ansicht, dass die Gäste in den Zimmern miteinander sprechen und die Gemeinschaft erleben sollten. Zum Surfen kann man zum Hotspot in den Gruppenraum gehen. In kleineren Herbergen, wie beispielsweise in Inzmühlen in der Lüneburger Heide, haben wir derzeit noch gar kein WLAN. Dort sind vor allem kleinere Schulkinder zu Gast, ganz andere Besucher als direkt in Hamburg, wo junge Leute aus der ganzen Welt übernachten.

**Zeit**: Wie unterscheidet sich eine Jugendherberge eigentlich von einem Hotel oder Hostel?

**Braasch-Eggert**: Im Hotel werden Sie zum Frühstück oft Menschen sehen, die alleine an einem Tisch sitzen. Bei uns soll man sich begegnen.

**Zeit**: Alleine essen ist schlimm.

**Braasch-Eggert**: Wer in eine Herberge zum Essen kommt, setzt sich nicht an den einzigen leeren Tisch. Die Gemeinschaft erleben, das ist unser Motto.

**Zeit**: Klingt nach einem Besuch im Hostel.

**Braasch-Eggert**: Da ist auch kein großer Unterschied vorhanden, besonders in den Städten. Im Stintfang hier in Hamburg gehen Backpacker ein und aus wie in einem Hostel. Unsere 535 Herbergen in Deutschland verteilen sich aber in ganz Deutschland, auch auf dem Land. Und wir sind gemeinnützig organisiert. Wir wollen damit kein Geld verdienen. […]

**Zeit**: Kann es dennoch sein, dass Hostel irgendwie cooler klingt?

**Braasch-Eggert**: Kann sein, dass da mehr Party ist. Das hängt ein wenig mit dem Hagebuttentee zusammen, mit dem Image. Unser Problem ist, dass die Leute gar nicht erst bei uns gucken kommen, sie denken sofort an Blechkannentee und 22-Uhr-Nachtruhe. Stimmt aber gar nicht mehr.

**Zeit**: Sie müssen deutlicher machen, wie cool Sie sind.

**Braasch-Eggert**: Wir sind auch cool, und wir wollen absolut noch cooler werden, nicht nur in Hamburg. Die Atmosphäre in einer Jugendherberge ist besonders. Gerade im Ausland, wo die Herbergen keine Tradition der Klassenfahrten haben, ist die Stimmung lockerer, lebendiger als in Deutschland. […]

**Zeit**: Wie sieht es eigentlich mit Ihren Mitgliederzahlen aus?

**Braasch-Eggert**: Wir haben mehr als zwei Millionen mit steigender Tendenz.

[…] *(472 Wörter)*



**Annotationen**

Z. 1 Fr. Braasch-Eggert: Vorsitzende des weltweiten Jugendherbergsverbandes

Z. 9 Doppelstockbett: Etagenbett, bei dem zwei Betten übereinanderstehen; Englisch: *bunk bed*

Z. 27 Hostel: international verwendete Bezeichnung für sehr günstige, einfache Unterkünfte

Z. 35 Stintfang: Name einer Jugendherberge in Hamburg

# Lösungsvorschläge

## Prüfungsteil 1: Leseverstehen und Schreiben

### Aufgabenstellung 1

1 *Der Leitbegriff* outline *in der Arbeitsanweisung verlangt die inhaltliche Zusammenfassung des vorliegenden literarischen Textes. Konzentrieren Sie Ihre Darstellung auf die Elemente des Handlungsverlaufs, die Avtars ersten Eindruck von Großbritannien wiedergeben. Fragen Sie sich dabei, was jemand, der den Originaltext nicht kennt, unbedingt wissen muss, damit er die Handlung versteht. Beginnen Sie Ihre Lösung mit einer kurzen Gesamtzusammenfassung, bevor Sie weitere Einzelheiten darstellen. Da Sie die Beschreibung eines Inhalts geben, verwenden Sie das Präsens.*

The excerpt from Sunjeev Sahota's book *The Year of the Runaways* shows the problems of the young Indian student Avtar, the main character of the novel, with registering with his chosen college. The text can be divided into three parts: the first gives an introduction to Avtar's situation, the second illustrates his problems with getting to the college, and the third gives information about the registration process.
The young Indian student Avtar has come to England to study at London's North-West College. He is positively surprised that, in contrast to his home country, everything in England seems to be well organised: the trains run on time, cars keep to the lanes, the air is clear, and he does not have to bribe people to get information. In addition, it is a country with opportunities for all. What confuses him is the traffic. He mistakes the brown tourist sign "Coll. of NW London" at a roundabout for the sign to follow and tries to cross the busy main road there, expecting the flow of traffic to stop, but is almost run over. He eventually arrives at the college, where he is warmly welcomed and given all the necessary papers, which confirms his impression that England is "a well-run country" (l. 12).

2 *Um eine Figur zu charakterisieren, kann ein Autor direkte Aussagen über die Person treffen ("She was always kind and honest") oder sie indirekt durch ihre Kleidung, Handlungen und ihr Verhalten darstellen. Die letztere Technik, die indirekte Charakterisierung* (implicit characterisation), *verwendet Sunjeev Sahota im vorliegenden Auszug aus seinem Roman* The Year of the Runaways.
*Avtar ist ein Neuankömmling in London, der in Indien aufgewachsen ist und erzogen wurde. Wenn er nun in England mit etwas Neuem und Ungewohnten konfrontiert wird, greift er natürlicherweise auf seine bisherigen Kenntnisse und Erfahrungen zurück. Die Ergebnisse sind für den Leser zuweilen verblüffend oder auch erheiternd. Für den jungen Inder Avtar ist in London vieles neu, und er muss lernen, dass sein bisheriges Verhalten in der neuen Umwelt nicht – oder nicht immer – passend ist. Das verwirrt ihn zunächst, macht ihn unsicher und je nachdem, wie er mit dem Ungewohnten zurechtkommt (oder auch nicht), können wir auf seinen Charakter schließen.*

*Lesen Sie also den Text sorgfältig in Bezug auf Avtars Verhalten und seine Reaktionen in den gezeigten Situationen durch (1. Abschnitt: Ankunft in England, 2. Abschnitt: Der schwierige Weg zum College, 3. Abschnitt: Einschreibung im College). Ziehen Sie dann daraus (vorsichtig) Rückschlüsse auf seinen Charakter.*

In the excerpt from his novel the author Sunjeev Sahota characterises the young Indian, Avtar, indirectly through his behaviour and reactions in an unfamiliar environment.
The reader learns that the young man has just arrived in England. Raised in India, he is a respectful son who phones home straight away to let his parents know that he is alright. The conversation between father and son is rather short and matter-of-fact, because they are not used to this sort of communication, which might indicate that Avtar and his family live in rather modest conditions in India. Coming from this background and reminded by his father to grab the opportunities in the new country, Avtar is determined to succeed. (cf. ll. 3–9)
As a newcomer he is careful, tries not to make any mistakes ("kept to the right-hand side of the pavement", ll. 1/2) and is full of hope and optimism that he will do well (cf. l. 9). He draws his confidence from the positive experiences he has had up to now in this "well-run country" (l. 12), where trains run on time, people do not have to be bribed to supply information and car drivers keep to traffic rules ("The trains had come […]. The guard hadn't expected money […]. Cars were only driven on roads and only in nice long columns", ll. 9–11). However, at times Avtar's self-assurance is dented because he does not yet really know much about this new world he has come to. On his first day on his way to enrol at the college, he does not really know how to get there and how to cross the busy main road. Unsure and confused, he almost gets into a panic, as he believes he has taken the wrong decision. (cf. ll. 15–30)
He is extremely relieved when he eventually makes it to the college, deeply impressed by the blonde reception girl, the type he has only ever seen on TV adverts in India. Thanking the young woman profusely ("again", l. 50), he almost forgets where he is and behaves as if he were still in India, bowing "his head a little" (l. 50).
Avtar is grateful to be given a chance to make a good start in England, but a great deal of insecurity remains as he fears he might be rejected and sent back home (cf. l. 45). Perhaps he has heard or knows that immigrants can be deported.
All in all, the author illustrates the challenges young Avtar is confronted with and his courage and determination in facing them. He shows him as a modest and grateful person who overcomes his insecurities to eventually make progress in the new society.

3.1 *Entsprechend der Aufgabenstellung teilen Sie Ihre Lösung in zwei Teile. Zunächst stellen Sie die Erwartungen dar, die Avtars Vater an seinen Sohn richtet. Er mahnt ihn eindringlich, seine einmalige Chance wahrzunehmen, und geht davon aus, dass es einzig und allein von Avtars Tüchtigkeit abhängt, ob er Erfolg hat. Aus der Ferne stellt er sich die Aufgabe, vor der sein Sohn steht, einfacher vor, als sie es in Wirklichkeit ist. Im zweiten Abschnitt sollen Sie aufzeigen, wie Einwanderer von ihren zurück-*

*gebliebenen Familien unter Druck gesetzt werden. Viele Migranten kommen aus wirtschaftlichen und finanziellen Gründen. Gelderwerb steht damit im Vordergrund, und um die Zurückgebliebenen nicht zu enttäuschen, setzten sich Zugewanderte selber unter Druck. Dieser wird noch verstärkt durch Probleme und Widrigkeiten, von denen die Familien in der Heimat keine Vorstellung haben können.*

In the short telephone conversation with his father in India soon after his arrival in England, Avtar is reminded to consider himself lucky to be given such an exceptional opportunity of "making something of himself" (l. 7). The father is convinced that his son will stand a much better chance in England than in India, if only he applies himself properly. This is why he urges Avtar not to lose time and let himself be distracted from his goal, but to do his very best and use this chance in life to make progress. By reminding Avtar that he alone is responsible for his success, he puts his son under great pressure.

The reasons for people leaving their homelands and starting a new life in a foreign country have largely been the same through the ages. Some seek freedom and safety from wars, political oppression or religious persecution, but many of the immigrants come for economic reasons, trying to escape from poverty, hunger and unemployment in their homelands. Many come alone at first, leaving their families behind. They try to find a job and earn money, most of which they send home to support their relatives. Sometimes families in impoverished parts of the world collect money or take out loans to finance the migration of one of their members, expecting him or her to alleviate their misery in return. This "mission" or task places considerable stress on the immigrants because they know that they have to be grateful for the chance given and must fulfil these expectations.

This emotional pressure is often further intensified by difficulties and challenges in an alien environment. The relatives back home may not be aware of the challenges an immigrant has to cope with. In fact, many might think that in the new country the streets are paved with gold and success is inevitable. However, this is very often not the case. More often than not it is not solely in the hands of the immigrant "to succeed", as luck and circumstances play a great part. The pressures which families back home put on immigrants are considerable, and very often it is not a question of the immigrant having personal shortcomings if unrealistic expectations are not met.

3.2 *In dieser Aufgabe sollen Sie vergleichen, wie Avtar und eine Figur aus einem Ihnen bekannten Film, Roman oder einer Kurzgeschichte mit schwierigen Situationen in einem fremden Land fertig werden. Avtar hat im vorliegenden Textausschnitt große Probleme, den Weg zum College zu finden und sich im Straßenverkehr angemessen zu verhalten. Bei der Einschreibung im College deuten sich seine sprachlichen Defizite an. Zudem weiß er wohl – entweder aus Berichten oder eigener Erfahrung –, dass die Gefahr besteht, die Aufenthaltsberechtigung zu verlieren und in das Heimatland zurückgeschickt zu werden. Aus dem kurzen Textabschnitts lässt sich nicht entnehmen,*

*wie Avtar die Probleme überwinden wird. Er ist zwar voller Tatendrang und Optimismus, ob er damit jedoch in der Wirklichkeit zurechtkommt, lässt sich nicht ohne Weiteres sagen.*
*In einer vergleichbaren Situation befindet sich die Hauptfigur des Films* Outsourced *von 2006. Der amerikanische Manager Todd Anderson wird nach Indien geschickt, um dort Personal für ein Callcenter zu schulen. Die Konfrontation mit einem völlig anderen Kulturkreis stellt ihn vor große Probleme, sowohl im täglichen Leben (Essen, Benehmen u. a.) als auch in seiner beruflichen Tätigkeit. Er muss Erfahrungen machen, die ihn sehr fordern und beinahe verzweifeln lassen. Anderson bewältigt diese Schwierigkeiten jedoch allmählich, indem er sich auf das Fremde einlässt und es zu verstehen versucht. Zuletzt zieht er positive Erfahrungen aus seinem Aufenthalt.*

In *The Year of the Runaways,* Avtar has just arrived from India and does not know very much about England. Some things are a positive surprise to him (trains, traffic, friendly people), while others present huge obstacles. For example, he has great difficulty finding his way to the college where he intends to enrol or crossing a main road. Used to the chaotic road traffic in his home country of India, which allows cars to drive where they want to and pedestrians to cross where they deem appropriate, he acts like he would have done at home. When he is almost hit by oncoming traffic, he realises that he will have to change and adapt his behaviour.
In the film *Outsourced,* the main character, Todd Anderson, faces a situation in a new country which is similar to Avtar's. Anderson works in Seattle as the manager of a company's call centre. The firm decides to outsource the call centre, and Todd has to go to India to train the staff there. Anderson's experiences are different from Avtar's inasmuch as he goes from the West to a relatively advanced developing country. Inexperienced in world affairs generally, like Avtar, and in Indian customs in particular, Anderson is thrown into a completely new and alien environment. The chaotic traffic, the exotic and polluted environment and the unfamiliar food take a heavy toll. Todd makes all the mistakes of a Western tourist to Asia: he buys a fruit drink with ice from a street vendor or eats with his left hand. Not surprisingly, he pays heavily for his errors (upset stomach) and feels completely exhausted and depressed.
Both characters face difficulties in their professional lives as well. At enrolment, it becomes obvious that Avtar does not speak English very well. Judging from what we know about him from this excerpt, it seems unlikely that Avtar will successfully complete the course he has indicated on his application form, "Computing with Security Systems". The girl in the registration office may have her doubts, too. The language barrier might be too great for Avtar.
For Todd Anderson it is not language barriers but cultural ones he has to cope with. As he does not know anything about the culture of India, he judges everything from his Western point of view. At work, the training sessions with his workers reveal the clash of cultures. Todd does not really understand Indian mentality and is dissatisfied with the performance of the people who work in the call centre. A young woman on the team eventually tells Todd, "You need to learn about India" to overcome misunderstandings and improve performance. An experienced American who knows the country advises Todd, not to resist India, but to give in to their way of life in order to

do much better. Anderson gradually adapts his perspective and learns that there is more to life than just making money.
To survive in London, Avtar will also have to adapt to the British culture. The Indian Students' Society the girl at the office mentions may help him with that.

3.3 *In dieser kreativen Aufgabe sollen Sie sich in die Rolle der jungen Dame versetzen, welche die Aufnahme Avtars vornimmt, und einen Artikel für die Indian Students' Society schreiben, in dem sie die Schwierigkeiten von Neuankömmlingen darstellt und Ratschläge gibt, wie man mit diesen fertig werden könnte. Entsprechend der Aufgabenstellung ergibt sich eine Zweiteilung für den Hauptteil. Beschreiben Sie zunächst die Probleme der Neuankömmlinge und formulieren Sie danach Ratschläge zur Lösung. Um den Artikel zu vervollständigen, sollten Sie nicht vergessen, eine Einleitung sowie einen Schlussteil zu verfassen. Den Artikel könnten Sie mit einer Vorstellung der Autorin beginnen oder allgemein auf das Interesse an einem Auslandsstudium eingehen. Der Schluss könnte eine Aufforderung enthalten, sich den Herausforderungen positiv gegenüberzustellen, denn nur so kann der Aufenthalt gelingen. Bei der Darstellung der Probleme beziehen Sie sich zunächst auf den Haupttext, in dem Orientierungsprobleme im Verkehr, sprachliche Schwierigkeiten und die Angst, wieder nach Hause geschickt zu werden, eine große Rolle spielen. Ergänzen Sie diese Herausforderungen im Abschnitt mit den Ratschlägen um weitere Bereiche.*

**The essential guide for international students**

Starting college or university in a foreign country is not easy. That is why we asked an expert, Jennifer MacMillan, the registration officer at North-West London College, to point out the most frequent difficulties foreign students are confronted with and give tips on how you will have fewer problems settling in.

*Jennifer MacMillan:* When you arrive in a new country, everything might seem strange to you at first, and you feel overwhelmed by all the new impressions. Let me begin with what would at first seem to be a triviality. Quite often, students arrive at my office rather confused because they had so much difficulty getting here. They had problems crossing the roads, using trains or the Underground, asking directions and understanding road signs. What made things worse was the fact that they also had language problems. Apart from these problems of settling in, many young people begin to feel disappointed because things aren't turning out as they had expected. Especially for those who haven't found accommodation at the college or university and lack personal contact. I'm also well aware that many new arrivals fear they might be sent back to their home country should they not succeed in passing their tests and exams. This is obviously a great worry.
I know there is no easy solution to all of these problems, but I would like to give you some advice which might help you to overcome the first obstacles. First of all, be realistic in your expectations. Do not expect everything to run smoothly. Starting college or university is difficult for all young people in any country when they first leave home. So, it is understandable that starting to study and live abroad is even more challenging! Secondly, be well prepared before you arrive. First and foremost, this refers

to your language skills. A language barrier will make life and studying extremely difficult. Therefore, it is essential that you learn English properly by attending courses in your home country, if you haven't learnt the language at school. In addition, search the Internet for information about the college and the city you have chosen. For example, download any orientation information, such as a map of the city and college or university, as well as Underground, train or bus timetables. Make yourself familiar with road and traffic signs plus transport facilities to the college or university. On your first day, make sure you have all the documents and papers required for enrolment and allow yourself enough time to arrive early. Most important of all, come to our country with an open mind. Be eager to learn new things, new customs and meet new people. Make things easier by joining a student society and taking part in events organised by student teams. You will realise that we welcome young people from abroad and try to do everything to make them feel at home. If you follow these basic recommendations, you will find that a new start is not so difficult. It is demanding, that is for sure, but it is also rewarding.

## Prüfungsteil 2: Sprachmittlung

### Aufgabenstellung 2.1

*In dieser Aufgabe sollen Sie einen Blogeintrag verfassen, also eine Art persönlichen Tagebucheintrag, der im Internet veröffentlicht wird. Im vorliegenden Text geht es um ein Experiment mit einem Roboter, das beim Sender RBB durchgeführt wurde. Verfassen Sie eine möglichst aussagekräftige Überschrift, die zum Weiterlesen einlädt. Wichtig, auch für einen Blogeintrag, ist eine sinnvolle und übersichtliche Gliederung. Diese könnte so aussehen: In der Einleitung geben Sie eine Überblicksinformation (wie beim* summary*), im Hauptteil beschreiben Sie das Aussehen und die Funktionen des Roboters sowie das Ziel des Experiments. Abschließend folgt die Einschätzung der Beteiligten, was Roboter können und was nicht.*

**Can robots replace humans?**

The German newspaper *Der Tagesspiegel* published an interesting article about an experiment carried out by the German TV and radio station RBB (Radio Berlin Brandenburg). The people used a robot to carry out tasks in various departments of the radio and TV station.

Robot Yolandi is 175 cm tall, its head is a computer display with a moving mouth and eyebrows, and there is a hole where the stomach should be. Yolandi speaks with the voice of a female radio reporter from the station and can read pre-recorded news or weather reports or assist the lighting technician with its long arms.

The experiment was part of a project week held by Germany's national TV network ARD on the future world of work. The main idea was to find out which jobs robots could carry out one day and if they could replace humans. The experiment was also meant to show what robots cannot do.

The official responsible for projects connecting radio, TV and online media says that computers have become indispensable work tools for certain editorial tasks, but that robots will not be able to produce a programme or show in the foreseeable future.
The radio reporter who lends Yolandi her voice adds that robots cannot replace a presenter, host or reporter. They cannot hold an interview because they are unable to sense what is said between the lines. She admits that one day a robot might perhaps read the TV news, but she is convinced that people prefer watching people.

**Aufgabenstellung 2.2**

*Sie sollen eine E-Mail an einen Freund/eine Freundin in England verfassen. Da es sich um eine Mail im privaten und nicht im geschäftlichen Bereich handelt, sind Sie zwar freier in der Gestaltung und der sprachlichen Formulierung, Sie sollten aber trotzdem auf sprachliche und formale Korrektheit Wert legen, d.h. überprüfen Sie Ihre Rechtschreibung und die formale Gestaltung des Textes. Inhaltlich geht es um eine Zusammenfassung des Interviews über Jugendherbergen in Deutschland, insbesondere wie diese sich verändert und auf die heutigen Erfordernisse umgestellt haben. In Bezug auf Verpflegung, Unterbringung und Unterhaltungsmöglichkeiten sind sie moderner und aufgeschlossener geworden. Geblieben ist jedoch, dass sie Wert auf das Erlebnis der Gemeinschaft legen, denn dadurch wollen sie sich von normalen Hotels unterscheiden.*

From: milofranor@gmx.de
To: leotaylor003@talk.net
Subject: youth hostel in Germany

Hi Leo,

I'm pleased that you're coming to Germany and will gladly answer your questions about youth hostels in my country. To begin with, there are 535 youth hostels all over the country, so you will easily find one wherever you go. At present, the German Youth Hostel Association has more than 2 million members. As to the image, many people, especially those who have never been to a youth hostel, still think of what they were like in the past, when only peppermint tea was served from a tin can and people had to be in bed by 10 p.m. Over the years, youth hostels have changed quite a lot and have become much more modern.
Today they are almost like hotels, with normal beds, although bunk beds still exist. The majority provide Internet, perhaps not in every single room, but at least in the community room. Although surfing is allowed and possible, the main idea of staying in a youth hostel is to meet other people, to come together in a group and feel as if you're part of a community. This makes the atmosphere in a youth hostel so special. Nobody sits at a table alone to eat their dinner. By the way, one old tradition has been preserved and is still alive: You are expected to lay the table and clear up.
All in all, Leo, I'm absolutely sure you will enjoy staying at one of the many youth hostels and I hope that you will come and visit me.

Happy planning – and see you soon
Milo

**Abiturprüfung Berlin/Brandenburg 2018**
**Englisch Leistungskurs/Erhöhtes Anforderungsniveau**

## Prüfungsteil 1: Leseverstehen und Schreiben (75 %)

Der Prüfungsteil 1 besteht aus zwei Aufgabenstellungen, von denen Sie eine zur Bearbeitung auswählen.

### Aufgabenstellung 1.1 – Tasks

**Themenschwerpunkte:** *Personal relations in their social context, Science and technology – visions of the future, The impact of the media on society*

1 Outline the information on chip implantation and the role it plays in the society described in the novel. (30 %)

2 Analyze the means the author uses to make the readers aware of the implications of "chipping". Give evidence from the text. (30 %)

3 Choose one of the following tasks:

3.1 "Although continuous government access to your exact location might have seemed an infringement of civil liberties, most Americans were long accustomed to having their movements tracked by commercial entities […]." (ll. 36–39)
Explain the quote and discuss the benefits and dangers of location tracking for commercial and political purposes. (40 %)

OR

3.2 Compare Nollie and her situation to that of a character in literature or film who refuses to conform to the mainstream. Comment on the reasons for their behavior.* (40 %)

OR

3.3 Write a speech for the 2018 Youth Mobile Festival Barcelona (YoMo) in which you comment on the oversharing of personal information online. Use ideas from the excerpt and your knowledge about the issue. (40 %)

* Dieser Aufgabentyp entfällt ab der Abiturprüfung 2021.

**Text** (excerpt from the novel)

**The Mandibles**
by Lionel Shriver

Note: *Willing is one of the protagonists in Lionel Shriver's novel, which is set in the near future. He has changed since he had a chip implanted in his neck. Other characters mentioned in the excerpt are Avery, Willing's aunt, and Nollie, his elderly great-aunt.*

[…] Ever since the chipping, the part of his head that perceived so clearly had gone dead.

Oh, it wasn't that he trusted the fringier theories on the net. He did not believe the federal government controlled his mind. He accepted that the chip performed the functions it was purported to. It registered direct deposits of his salary. It deducted the costs of any products he chose to buy. It debited his utility bills. Though Willing had no experience of either, it recorded investments and received state benefits. It subtracted local, state, and federal taxes, which totaled 77 percent of his pay. […] Any additional income, including gift coupons for a birthday, revenue from pawned possessions, bake-sale proceeds, and private-party poker winnings, would also register on the chip, and would also be taxed at 77 percent. Chipping solved the problem of the hackable, stealable, long dysfunctional credit card. Chipped, you *were* a credit card.

Parental protest over the chipping of newborns died down altogether when states began depositing a generous 2,000 "baby bond" in every infant's chip. To the population at large, chipping was promoted as the ultimate convenience, and the ultimate in financial security. No more having to carry a wallet or device that thieves could seize on the street. At self-checkout, the terminal simply scanned your head. No more PINs or unique twenty-five-digit passwords, with numbers and letters and signs. No more biometric verification – the fingerprints, facial recognition, and iris scans that hackers had learned to duplicate as fast as the novel authentications had been brought in, since anything digitized can be copied. Obviating the bank account, with its erosive fees, your chip had its own website, or *chipsite,* for arranging monetary transfers. Its calculation of GPS coordinates precise within a millimeter, your chip communed with your very DNA, thrummed to your very pulse. If anyone contacted your chipsite whose distinctive heartbeat didn't synchronize perfectly with the pounding in your chip, your funds went into lockdown. So no one could pretend to be you, and the account that went everywhere you went was safe from predators. […]

To Avery's delight, secure chipping had restored the online marketplace. Exhilarated by the prospect of once more buying a toaster without leaving the house, his aunt was an early adopter. (It was clever, making the first wave of guinea pigs pay for the privilege of implantation. Steep charges turned chips into status items.) Unfortunately for the likes of Willing and his cousins, the rousing return of internet shopping was largely theoretical. They commanded too little discretionary income to buy much. The economy was overwhelmingly powered by the whims of the retired.

Socially, Willing kept any reservations about chipping to himself. Detractors of the liberating fiscal protocol were pilloried as crackpots. Although continuous government access to your exact location might have seemed an infringement of civil liberties, most Americans were long accustomed to having their movements tracked by commercial entities like Google Maps. For decades, bicycles had been chipped. Pets had been chipped. People being chipped seemed inevitable. Buying goods with a mere tap at a terminal went back to smart phones, so the technological leap was minimal, while the security leap was huge. Now no one could appropriate the means of effortless purchase without chopping off your head, and nothing destroyed the functionality of a chip more instantaneously than its host being dead. Yet Willing felt not enough had been made of the chip's location. Its biological safeguards would have worked equally as well had it been embedded in an upper arm. The purpose of installing the thing right up against your spinal column was to keep you from digging it out. Employing shady surgeons, a few refuseniks had tried. They were recognizable for being paralyzed.

Nollie's disappointment that her grandnephew had freely become "their creature" was probably harsh. Nollie herself had an old-fashioned bank account, and made purchases with an ancient fleX. […] But the unchipped constituted a dwindling minority: the elderly, the far-flung and rural, a few expats abroad. Such anachronisms drew an accelerating suspicion and contempt. They couldn't buy a quart of milk without hauling out some *device*. Willing had noticed that customers behind Nollie in supermarket lines would fret. The unchipped inspired the widespread impatience that once greeted holdouts who spurned fleXes or their predecessor smart phones. In short order, the whole population would be chipped, and savings, checking, and investment accounts would be eliminated altogether – at which point it would be impossible to buy anything, sell anything, or possess any monetary wealth whatsoever in the absence of a pinhead-sized spy rammed into the back of your neck. That was certainly the plan, and Congress was unapologetic about this intention – a benevolence portrayed as akin to the nationwide polio vaccinations of the 1960s.

Naturally, the web bubbled with the feverish imaginings of paranoid kooks: chips would turn the American people into an army of hollowed-out robs that would do whatever a mad dictator in Washington commanded. True, research was under way to expand the implant's capacity by directly connecting the brain itself to the internet. […] Perhaps in the near future, then, you would be able to read webzines, play games, and watch cat videos in your very head. […] *(868 words)*



**Annotations**

l. 3 fringy: *here:* different from mainstream
l. 6 utility bill: request for payment for public services, e. g. telephone, electricity, water
l. 14 baby bond: *in this novel:* sum of state money given when a child has been chipped
l. 17 self-checkout: counter where customers themselves scan goods and pay for them
l. 21 to obviate: to make something unnecessary
l. 24 to thrum: to make a low sound like the sound of an engine
l. 31 steep: *here:* unusually expensive
l. 33 discretionary income: income that is left for spending or saving after paying all one's bills
ll. 35/36 detractors of … protocol: *here:* people criticizing the government for controlling taxes with the chip
l. 36 to pillory: to criticize someone strongly in public
l. 48 refusenik: *informal:* person who refuses to do something

l. 51 fleX: technological device similar to a tablet computer
l. 56 holdout: person who resists something or refuses to accept an offer
l. 61 unapologetic: not saying or feeling that you are sorry about something, even in situations in which other people might expect you to
l. 63 kooks: *informal:* insane people
l. 64 robs: *informal:* robots
l. 67 webzine: magazine published on the internet

## Aufgabenstellung 1.2 – Tasks*

**Themenschwerpunkte:** *Ethnic and cultural diversity, The impact of the media on society, Personal relations in their social context*

1 Summarize the information about Mohsin Hamid and his life. (30 %)

2 Analyze the means used to illustrate the importance of fantasy and imagination in the author's life. Give evidence from the article and the illustration published with it. (30 %)

3 Choose <u>one</u> of the following tasks:

3.1 "And I do spend many weeks in America and Britain each year, and many weeks in other places, and correspond on most days with friends and colleagues on multiple continents. My life might be peculiar, but it suits me." (ll. 43–45)
Using the quote as a starting point, comment on the potential of cross-cultural experiences for people's personal and professional development. (40 %)

OR

3.2 Compare Mohsin Hamid to a character from literature or film who moves from one country to another during his/her childhood. Assess how they cope with their experiences.** (40 %)

OR

3.3 Write a letter to the editor of *The Guardian*. In your letter, discuss Mohsin Hamid's views on the power of storytelling and the role writers play in envisioning "a brighter future." Address your letter to:
The Editors
guardian.letters@theguardian.com (40 %)

* Diese Aufgabenstellung entstammt der Prüfung aus dem Bundesland Berlin. Aufgabenstellung 1.1 wurde in beiden Bundesländern gestellt.
** Dieser Aufgabentyp entfällt ab der Abiturprüfung 2021.

**Text** (excerpt from the article)

**We need to imagine a brighter future**
by Mohsin Hamid

Note: *Mohsin Hamid is a male British-Pakistani novelist who lives with his family in Lahore, the second largest city and cultural centre of Pakistan.*

[…] When I was nine years old, my family moved back from California, where we had gone so my father could complete his PhD, to Lahore, where I had been born but had not visited since I was three. The jarringly total nature of this shift is perhaps difficult to imagine today. In 1980 there were no email accounts or social media or text messages. The post was slow and unreliable. International phone calls had to be booked in advance and cost a fortune. I never saw, or heard from, a single one of my friends again.

I had left one world and entered another. People looked different. The smells were different. Food tasted different. The languages were different, not just Urdu, which I had to relearn from scratch, but also English, where a Lahori form now presented itself as standard, and functioned often in sharp contrast to Californian. There was only one television channel, broadcast for only part of the day, with only one or two shows a week that I felt any desire to watch. And so I turned to books.

In particular I turned to fantasy. I read *The Chronicles of Narnia* by C.S. Lewis. The idea of children passing through a wardrobe into a strange and magical land seemed entirely plausible to me. I read the Middle-earth novels of J.R.R. Tolkien. [...]

I had always been a daydreamer, and I whiled away long hot summers in Lahore playing make-believe, by myself, or with my cousins. But I also began to do something strange. I became fascinated by atlases, with their gorgeous multicoloured maps, their different icons for settlements of different population sizes, their snaking, undulating contour lines. I became fascinated by almanacs, with their brief descriptions of countries: a snapshot of history, demographics, chief exports, climatic conditions. And I began to make countries of my own.

I would mark out their borders in pencil on my maps, sometimes claiming this peninsula and that island for my new nation state, sometimes that mountain range or valley. I would write out their histories in a few paragraphs, what goods originated there, what languages people spoke. [...]

These places were geographically unified but demographically varied. Lahoris and San Franciscans were often among the inhabitants, but equally often there were people from other places, from China, Kenya, Brazil or France. These islands sat in the middle of the Indian Ocean, or in the Pacific, but if one could travel to them and see their people, they might well look like the people of New York or London today.

The worlds I was creating, and the stories in them, were a starting point for what would become my present profession. I began my first novel 25 years ago, when I was not yet 22. I have been writing novels for more than half my lifetime. But I had already, before I began, been depending on storytelling to navigate an otherwise baffling world for more than half my lifetime before that.

Stories helped me unite parts of my existence that might otherwise have seemed irrevocably split by geography and time. And stories helped me find a future in which I, such a mongrel, could be comfortable. I do not inhabit an island in the Indian Ocean with a population as diverse as that of London, nor a nation composed of bits of Pakistan and California. But I have over the last three decades lived first in America, then in Britain, then in Pakistan. And I do spend many weeks in America and Britain each year, and many weeks in other places, and correspond on most days with friends and colleagues on multiple continents. My life might be peculiar, but it suits me. It flows directly from those first worlds I imagined as a child. Without my stories, without the journey and direction implicit in them, I might never have found it. Perhaps I would not even have looked.

Since well before the dawn of history, human beings have gathered together around flickering campfires to tell and listen to tales. We still do, even if the campfires are now more often glowing screens – in cinemas, on television sets, or in our hands. There are a great many reasons for this: fictional narratives offer us so many things. But in our present moment it is worth remembering one reason in particular: storytelling offers an antidote to nostalgia. By imagining, we create the potential for what might be. [...] Stories have the power to liberate us from the tyranny of what was and is.

We are all creators of fictions, and we all have a role to play in imagining our way out of the nostalgic traps strewn around us. But there are special opportunities open to those of us who create fiction for a living, and above all to those of us who are writers, because we are freer to create what we wish, without requiring funding for our projects, as a film-maker might. We are the startups of the storytelling world, the crazy solo inventors in the R & D department of humanity's narrative imagination.

We should be glad for these opportunities. The future is too important to be left to professional politicians. And it is too important to be left to technologists either. […]

*(875 words)*

*Source: Hamid, Mohsin. "We need to imagine a brighter future." The Guardian. Feb. 25, 2017. Accessed March 29, 2017. https://www.theguardian.com/books/2017/feb/25/mohsin-hamid-danger-nostalgia-brighter-future.*

**Annotations**

l. 3 jarring: disagreeable or unpleasant due to a sudden or shocking effect
l. 9 Urdu: national language of Pakistan
l. 14 *The Chronicles of Narnia:* classic set of fantasy novels by C.S. Lewis
l. 16 the Middle-earth novels: *The Lord of the Rings,* famous set of fantasy novels
l. 40 mongrel: *offensive:* person of mixed descent
l. 54 antidote: something that counteracts an unpleasant feeling or situation
l. 55 tyranny: cruel and unfair power over people
l. 61 R & D: Research and Development

## Prüfungsteil 2: Sprachmittlung (25 %)

Der Prüfungsteil 2 besteht aus zwei Aufgabenstellungen, von denen Sie eine zur Bearbeitung auswählen.

### Aufgabenstellung 2.1 – Tasks

**Themenschwerpunkte:** *Personal relations in their social context, Ethnic and cultural diversity*

Together with students from your American partner school, you are working on the issue of cultural identity.
For your project website, write a blog entry about the German concept of "Heimat", outlining its development as presented in the article.

**Text** (Auszug aus dem Artikel)

**Im Wohlfühl-Ort**
Von Christina Berndt

[…] Ganz offensichtlich erlebt der Begriff „Heimat" eine Renaissance. 88 Prozent der Bundesbürger stuften ihn einer Umfrage der Hamburger Sozialbehörde zufolge als „wichtig" oder „sehr wichtig" ein, nur zwei Prozent sagte er gar nichts. Dabei scheint der Begriff mit höherem Alter wichtiger zu werden. Aber auch junge Leute fühlen sich heute wieder stärker heimatverbunden als Ende des vergangenen Jahrtausends. Sie finden es schick, Jägermeister im Schrebergarten zu trinken, Volkslieder beim Bergwandern zu singen und in Dirndl oder Lederhose aufs Oktoberfest zu gehen. Und Deutschland-Wimpel am Auto sind während sportlicher Großereignisse schon fast ein Muss geworden. Auf der Suche nach dem schönsten deutschen Wort landete „Heimat" im Jahr 2004 auf einem der Spitzenplätze. Nur noch sieben Prozent der Deutschen verbinden mit diesem Begriff vor allem Enge oder Spießigkeit.

Was vor kurzem noch als abstoßend kitschig galt, scheint nun zum Zielort einer allgemeinen Sehnsucht nach bleibenden Werten zu werden. […] Sogar die großen Globalisierer haben diesen Trend erkannt und besinnen sich aufs Regionale, wie der Historiker Heinz Schilling betont, der bis vor kurzem an der Humboldt-Universität Berlin gelehrt hat. Bei McDonald's gibt es auf dem Burger neben Rinderhack deshalb auch mittlerweile Nürnberger Bratwürste.

„Heimat ist heute eine Sehnsuchtslandschaft der Gefühle", sagt Schilling. Dabei sei das Gefühlige zu dem Begriff erst spät gekommen. Bis ins 19. Jahrhundert hinein sei Heimat ein juristischer Begriff gewesen. Wer einer Heimatscholle zuzuordnen war, der besaß Bürgerrechte. Es ging also nicht um Emotionen, sondern um Ansprüche.

Heute ist nicht einmal mehr klar, wo die Heimat eigentlich liegt. Sie kann ein ganzes Land sein, aber auch eine Gegend oder ein kleines Dörfchen, das schon mit dem Nachbardörfchen in Feindschaft lebt. Und obwohl Großstädter mit ihrem direkten

Nachbarn oft nicht mehr als die gemeinsame Adresse verbindet, empfinden viele von ihnen doch ihren Straßenzug als Heimat. […]

Manche Menschen fühlen sich aufgehoben, wenn sie endlich einmal wieder den Kartoffelsalat genauso essen, wie ihn Muttern immer zubereitete. Anderen geht beim Blick übers weite Meer das Herz auf, wieder andere mochten am liebsten gleich jeden umarmen, dessen Dialekt an den ihrer Kindheit erinnert. […]

Dass die Kindheit das Heimatgefühl so sehr prägt und häufig sogar mit ihm verschmilzt, können Hirnforscher auch neurobiologisch erklären. Am stärksten brennen sich Ereignisse ins Gehirn ein, wenn sie mit starken Emotionen besetzt sind oder wenn sie häufig wiederholt werden. Auf das Erleben der Kindheit treffe oft beides zu, sagt Holger Schulze vom Leibniz-Institut für Neurobiologie in Magdeburg. Die Verknüpfungen im sich entwickelnden Gehirn werden dadurch so stark, dass verschiedene Bilder, Gerüche, Klänge oder Berührungen ein Leben lang Wohlgefühl auslösen.

Auch wenn sie eine Konstruktion aus Kindheitserinnerungen und subjektiven Deutungen ist: „Heimat ist super", sagt der Essener Sozialpsychologe Harald Welzer. Sie gebe in einer zunehmend komplizierter und unüberschaubar werdenden Welt Orientierung. Er glaube nicht an eine kosmopolitische Postmoderne, in der jeder überall und nirgendwo zu Hause sei. […]

Doch bei allem Positiven, das der Mensch des beginnenden 21. Jahrhunderts der Heimat abgewinnen kann: Es bleibt auch die andere, die dunkle Seite des Heimatgefühls, das verklärt, verkitscht und von Ideologen missbraucht wurde. Es gibt kaum ein Wort, das so zwischen Intimität und Weltpolitik zerrissen wird. Während Heimat vielen Geborgenheit vermittelt, erleben andere sie als finsteres Verlies, aus dem es kein Entkommen gibt. Und wieder andere spüren Heimat vor allem dann, wenn sie fehlt, und kranken unheilbar am Verlust dieses Wohlfühl-Ortes. […] *(544 Wörter)*

*„Im Wohlfühl-Ort", Christina Berndt, SZ.de vom 30.12.2010*

**Annotationen**

Z. 1 Renaissance: *hier:* Wiederaufleben
Z. 6 Jägermeister: Kräuterlikör
Z. 7 Dirndl: für Bayern, Österreich und die Schweiz typische Art von Trachtenkleid; aus buntem Stoff mit Rock, taillierter weißer Bluse und Schürze
Z. 11 Spießigkeit: Englisch: *narrow-mindedness/stuffiness*
Z. 20 Scholle: *hier:* Stück Erde
Z. 41 Postmoderne: Sammelbezeichnung für verschiedene Stilrichtungen der gegenwärtigen Kunst

## Aufgabenstellung 2.2 – Tasks

**Themenschwerpunkte:** *Ethnic and cultural diversity, Personal relations in their social context, The impact of the media on society*

Your school is taking part in an international media project on the integration of refugees into countries of the European Union.
Write an article for the project website in which you outline the information about Firas Alshater's background, his activities and experiences as a refugee in Germany.

**Text** (Auszug aus dem Interview)

**Interview mit Firas Alshater: „Es ist nicht mein Traumjob, Flüchtling zu sein"**
Von Ula Brunner

**„Wer sind diese Deutschen?" fragt Firas Alshater auf seinem Youtube-Kanal „Zukar". Ein Gespräch mit dem syrischen Filmemacher, der als Flüchtling in Berlin lebt, über Akzeptanz, Heimat und Humor.**

*Herr Alshater, seit Anfang 2016 haben Sie mit Ihrem Youtube-Kanal „Zukar" in den sozialen Netzwerken Furore gemacht. In den Medien werden Sie häufig als „Flüchtlings-Youtuber" kategorisiert. Wie würden Sie sich selbst bezeichnen?*
Ich bin einfach nur jemand, der versucht, Probleme darzustellen – für die deutsche Gesellschaft und für Flüchtlinge. Ich bekomme Feedback von Leuten, die meine Videos mögen, aber auch von Rechtsextremisten. Damit erreiche ich sehr unterschiedliche Zielgruppen. Aber es ist nicht mein Traumjob, Flüchtling in Deutschland zu sein, ich habe mir das nicht ausgesucht.

*In Ihrem ersten Video stellen Sie sich mit den Worten vor: „In Syrien habe ich Filme gemacht, wenn ich nicht gerade im Gefängnis war, weil ich Filme gemacht habe". Seit Mai 2013 sind Sie in Deutschland. Wie gehen solche unterschiedlichen Leben zusammen?*
Ich habe von Anfang an entschieden, dass ich – unabhängig davon, wie die Gesellschaft hier ist – die Menschen akzeptieren muss, damit sie auch mich akzeptieren. Ich muss weitermachen und tun, worauf ich Lust habe. Das ist mein Recht.

*In diesem Video, das Sie mit einem Schlag bekannt machte, stehen Sie mit verbundenen Augen auf dem Alexanderplatz, neben sich ein Schild: „Ich bin syrischer Flüchtling. Ich vertraue dir – vertraust du mir? Umarme mich". Wie ist die Idee dazu entstanden?*
Als im Herbst 2014 so viele Menschen bei den Pegida-Demonstrationen in Dresden „Ausländer raus" gerufen haben, habe ich mich gefragt: Sind alle Deutschen so? Um das herauszufinden, habe ich mich auf den Berliner Alexanderplatz gestellt und das Video gedreht.

*Zu welchem Fazit sind Sie denn gekommen?*
Die Deutschen – das sind 80 Millionen Menschen, eine große Gesellschaft. Man kann nicht sagen: Sie sind so oder sie sind anders. Genauso ist es mit den Flüchtlingen. Sie

kommen ebenfalls aus großen Gesellschaften mit ganz unterschiedlichen Menschen. Ich muss die Menschen akzeptieren, wie sie sind und umgekehrt. So läuft die Integration. Das will ich mit meinen Videos erzählen. [...]

*Gerade Vorurteile spielen in der gesellschaftlichen Debatte über die Flüchtlingsfrage aber eine große Rolle.*
Ich finde die Situation eigentlich gar nicht so kritisch. Doch die Medien zeigen vor allem die Problematiken. Momentan hören wir kaum von Leuten, die Flüchtlingen helfen, sondern mehr von Rechtsextremisten. Wir vergessen, dass es noch immer viele Menschen gibt, die Flüchtlinge willkommen heißen.

*Nach den Attentaten in Brüssel im März 2016 stellten Sie das Video „Brüssel, wir alle!" ins Netz. Darin heißt es: „Araber in Deutschland! Dies ist deine neue Heimat." Sie selbst leben im Berliner Stadtteil Prenzlauer Berg. Was bedeutet für Sie Heimat?*
Heimat ist ein Ort, wo ich mich wohlfühle, als ein Teil der Gesellschaft. Es ist der Ort, wo ich mich als Mensch wahrgenommen fühle und keine Angst haben muss, wenn ich meine Meinung sage. In Syrien genügt es schon, sich mit Posts oder Videos gegen Assad zu äußern, und man kommt ins Gefängnis.

*Nach Berlin sind alleine im Jahr 2015 fast 80.000 Menschen geflohen, viele davon aus Syrien. Sind Sie Anlaufstelle und Kontaktperson für Ihre Landsleute?*
Ich habe viele Kontakte zu Flüchtlingen, vor allem zu Leuten, die ich noch aus Syrien kenne. Viele wenden sich mit Fragen an mich, ich werde gebeten, zu helfen, zu übersetzen. Durch meine Youtube-Arbeit kennen mich mittlerweile sehr viele Menschen.

*Was sind Ihre weiteren Pläne?*
Wir wollen natürlich die nächste Zukar-Staffel produzieren, ich habe einen Studienplatz im Fach Montage an der Filmhochschule in Babelsberg, und im Herbst erscheint mein erstes Buch. Es gibt viele Möglichkeiten für mich zu arbeiten, viele Türen sind geöffnet. Jetzt muss ich schauen, was am besten für mich passt. *(601 Wörter)*

*Brunner, Ula. „Es ist nicht mein Traumjob, Flüchtling zu sein". August 2016. Entnommen am 10. September 2016. https://www.goethe.de/de/kul/med/20819516.html. (Ein sprachlicher Fehler in der Textvorlage wurde entsprechend der geltenden Norm korrigiert; Zwischenüberschriften des Originaltextes wurden weggelassen.)*

**Annotation**
Z. 1 Firas Alshater: syrischer Aktivist und Filmemacher

**Lösungsvorschläge**

## Prüfungsteil 1: Leseverstehen und Schreiben

### Aufgabenstellung 1.1

1 *Die Aufgabenstellung verlangt von Ihnen eine Zusammenfassung des Textes unter bestimmten Gesichtspunkten. In diesem Fall geht es um das Implantieren und die Rolle, die es in der Gesellschaft spielt. Halten Sie sich also zwei Textmarker bereit und unterstreichen Sie zunächst im Romanauszug die entsprechenden Textstellen. Zum Verfassen Ihrer* summary *können Sie dann ganz leicht die jeweiligen Punkte so anordnen, wie Sie es für Ihre Ausführungen brauchen.*

In the novel *The Mandibles* by Lionel Shiver, chips are being implanted in people's necks. They serve as a means of payment and replace cash and credit cards. All common financial transactions can be performed that way, from bill-paying to price checks and finally to taxes. Furthermore, your whereabouts can also be tracked at all times.
The chip comes along with its personal website, and as access is only granted when the owner's heartbeat and pulse synchronise with the pounding in the chip, it is practically unhackable.
In the beginning, having it implanted was very expensive, so it had become a status symbol. Later, when it was meant to be introduced nationwide, protests died down after the announcement of a 2,000 baby bond. First advertised as a logical consequence after pets and property chipping, it has become a convenient device which people have grown accustomed to and which is planned to directly connect the brain to the internet. Only a minority are still clinging to the old-fashioned gadgets.
However, rumours about the government planning to control everyone's mind have spread, and those who have already regretted their decision to have themselves chipped learn that trying to remove the chip leaves them paralysed.

2 *Da es sich bei* The Mandibles *um einen Romanauszug handelt, kommen für die Bearbeitung die folgenden vier Aspekte der Analyse fiktionaler Texte in Frage: Erzählstruktur, Charakterisierung, Atmosphäre und sprachliche Besonderheiten. In diesem Fall, wo es nur wenig szenische Beschreibung, aber viele Einzelinformationen gibt, bietet sich der Blick auf den Erzähler und die Sprache an. In Prosatexten findet man als sprachliche Besonderheiten häufig Aufzählungen, bildliche Beschreibungen (Personifizierungen, Vergleiche und Metaphern) und parallele Strukturen (Anapher etc.).*

Different means are used to make the readers aware of the implications of chipping.
First of all, the story is told by a third-person narrator who looks at the scene from Willing's point of view. We know Willings' thoughts, but we can only judge other characters' behaviour from what he knows about them. The third-person perspective

creates a certain distance to the protagonist which allows the readers to form their own opinion of him.

While it is not said explicitly, the reader can observe that Willing has a rather ambiguous view of the matter of chipping. On the one hand, we learn that "he [does] not believe the federal government control[s] his mind" (ll. 3/4) and even "accept[s] that the chip perform[s] [certain] functions" (ll. 4/5), but on the other hand he keeps "any reservations about chipping to himself" (l. 35). Thus, he obviously has his doubts but does not dare speak out about his personal opinion.

This characterises Willing as a puppet, who, like thousands of other critical people in the *Mandible* society, has been silenced by propaganda which portrays critics as "crackpots" (l. 36). His great-aunt Nollie even thinks that he "ha[s] freely become 'their creature' " (l. 49), expressing that the government has somehow 'brainwashed' him into accepting chipping as a necessary procedure.

Next to the narrative perspective, the language and the atmosphere created also play an important role in understanding the implications of chipping.

The description of the future world generates the image of a 'Big Brother' society. The space is limited. You allow the government "continuous […] access to your exact location" (ll. 36/37), which even "infringe[s] [your] civil liberties" (l. 37). The mere thought of it causes a feeling of claustrophobia.

When we find out about the chipping at the beginning of the excerpt, we first learn that it has left "the part of [Willing's] head that perceived so clearly […] dead" (ll. 1/2). Immediately afterwards we hear of "fringier theories" (l. 3) and rumours about "the federal government control[ling their] mind[s]" (ll. 3/4). This casts chipping in a strange light. It is followed by the extensive listing of all the advantages of chipping, such as "direct deposits of […] salar[ies], […] debit[ing] utility bills, […] receiv[ing] state benefits" (ll. 5–7) etc. This sounds like a mantra, like a part of a commercial which you cannot help learning by heart because you have continuously been showered with it. Maybe this is the reason why Willing has become "their creature" (l. 49). The advantages seemingly far outweigh the negative aspects, such as local tracking, the (theoretical) risk of turning into a "hollowed-out rob" (l. 64) or the high taxes. The repetition of phrases like "no more" (ll. 16–18) supports the idea of an advertising slogan.

Critics and technical devices, which are replaced by the new technology, are connected to words with negative connotations. People who oppose chipping are "refuseniks" (l. 48), "holdouts" (l. 56) or "paranoid kooks" (l. 63). Credit cards and technical devices count as "anachronisms" (l. 52), which are meant to be "hackable, stealable [and] long dysfunctional" (ll. 11/12). The fact that it "*might have seemed* an infringement of civil liberties" (l. 37) sounds like a true understatement, and even cynicism from our perspective.

Therefore, when reading between the lines it is easy to see that chipping represents more of a danger than a benefit to society.

3.1 *Wenn Sie diese Aufgabenstellung wählen, machen Sie sich sinnvollerweise zunächst einen Schreibplan. Erstens, Zitat erklären, dann Vorteile und Gefahren des* local trackings *mit Beispielen aus dem Text* ***und*** *mit Ihren eigenen Überlegungen darlegen, dann zusammenfassen und die persönliche Meinung zum Thema deutlich machen. Einfach so loszuschreiben endet oft in einem wenig strukturiert erscheinenden Text, der dann auch wenig überzeugen kann.*

We all hold our civil liberties high. Any kind of infringement of the freedom of the press or freedom of speech often provokes loud protest among people. However, when this process is executed from behind the scenes, it slowly establishes itself in our minds and we feel as if we have to take the bad with the good.
That is how the characters in Lionel Shriver's *The Mandibles* feel when the government has all the citizens chipped to be able to track them. They have been tracked by companies like Google for years and have experienced the convenient effects. Now it seems like a normal aspect of life and any reservations feel overly cautious.
The USA has a long tradition of granting civil rights. From the beginning, the First Amendment to the Constitution has granted the freedom of religion, press and speech. For years, the Americans have defended the right to keep and bear arms, as the Bill of Rights guarantees. However, when it comes to personal convenience, they – like the people in the novel – are more than willing to allow the big companies to access, store and sell their data or give their consent to location tracking.
It has become a huge market in our digital, globalised world. You are no longer snowed under by thousands of ads – no, the cookies on your computer place the products on your desktop that seem to be of interest to you judging from the websites you have visited, but also by finding out where you are. If you google the term "Tribeca" in Berlin, the search engine will offer you an ice cream shop as one of the first hits, in Munich it will be a coffee shop, and you will be shown other things in New York, where the neighbourhood is. This can of course be very useful, as can weather apps, public transport apps and apps that show you good restaurants that match your eating habits wherever you go. However, it is most often used for advertising, as we are more willing to click on offers we feel match our hobbies, life or leisure activities.
However, that is nothing compared to the risks of applying tracking to political purposes. The current debate on Russian hackers having manipulated elections in other countries gives us an idea of its proportions. You can customise not only ads, but also political statements or party platforms to meet or manipulate people's opinions!
Researchers have found out that social media like Facebook provide articles, newsflashes and reports about topics you or your friends would probably like, so you actually never get to know the other side of the story or the facts behind the news unless you read a "real" newspaper or a magazine. So even if we allow for its being unintended, our political decisions are influenced by cookies and algorithms. This is a rather spooky realisation.
Therefore, we should be much more careful about what we allow to be done with our data. Never should we grow accustomed to an infringement of our civil liberties!

3.2 *Zum Vergleich eignen sich eigentlich viele Klassiker, von* Fahrenheit 451*, über* Brave New World *bis zu* Nineteen Eighty-Four. *Es liegt in der Natur der typischen Sci-fi Werke, dass durch die Darstellung einer* dystopian society *mindestens einer zum Außenseiter wird. Wichtig ist hier in der Vorbereitung auf das Abitur die entsprechenden Fakten, d. h. Namen von Autoren, Regisseuren und Protagonisten zusammenzutragen, damit man sie dann in den Ausführungen verwenden kann.*

In a good dystopian novel there is always that one character that flies the flag of nonconformity. In Lionel Shriver's *The Mandibles,* it is Nollie, the great-aunt of Willing, the protagonist. Nearly everyone else in this society is chipped, i. e. they have a chip implanted in their neck that performs all necessary monetary transactions. When she does her shopping, people behind her in the queue grow impatient and start complaining about her old-fashioned method of using a device to settle her bill. Although the government heavily promotes chipping, she clings to her outdated fleX system, fearing that her personal data would not be safe with the modern technology. Her resistance has turned her into a kind of outsider, looked upon by others with contempt.
Usually, these characters are there to act as a warning to the readers of the current world that they should observe what happens to a society that blindly worships the god of consumption and technology. A very similar example is that of Mercer from Dave Egger's *The Circle*. His girlfriend Mae starts working for that company and is quickly drawn into the vortex of manipulation and loss of control. He tries to warn her by showing her how much she has changed and how she has given up privacy to a world of posting and public display, but she will not listen. Mercer withdraws to a hideout in the country where he cannot be found by cameras. When Mae is given the chance to test a new tracking system, she tries it on her former boyfriend, who sees no way out except suicide. Mae still seems to be unaware of her part in this development.
Like Nollie, Mercer is a nonconformist in his society, but he is more of an active fighter compared to Nollie. He is also a member of the target group that would be expected to embrace the new technology, whereas the elderly aunt seems to be a kind of dinosaur that will soon "die out" anyway. Willing, on the other hand, is not exactly like Mae. He *is* chipped, much to the disappointment of his aunt, but he keeps any reservations about chipping to himself, as the text reveals. Mercer's girlfriend is a complete believer in all the technology who never really expresses doubts.
Still, Mercer and Nollie stand for the traditional, old-fashioned way of life, whereas Mae and Willing go with the flow and have conformed to the mainstream.
In the end, both novels can teach us to be on the alert when it comes to an infringement of our civil rights.

3.3 *Diese Aufgabenstellung sollten Sie nur wählen, wenn es Ihnen auch im wahren Leben Freude macht, eine Rede zu halten, ansonsten bietet sich eher die Erörterung/Argumentation zu einem Zitat an. Erstellen Sie sich auch hier einen Schreibplan, überlegen Sie, wie Sie am Beginn der Rede Ihr Publikum für sich einnehmen und sein Interesse wecken können. Wählen Sie dann ein Argument aus dem Romanauszug aus und setzen*

*Sie es zu Ihren persönlichen Erfahrungen in Bezug. Appellieren Sie am Ende an Ihre Zuhörer, etwas zu ändern, zu verbessern etc.*

Dear fellow smartphone zombies, digital natives, peers and guests,

When I opened my email account this morning, I felt bombarded with ads of all kinds. They recommended the latest fashions, Parisian hotels, an ointment to cure a rash and a pizza delivery service. Why would the internet know that I am planning to go to Paris, that it's my friend's birthday at the weekend and that I needed something new to wear? And how could they know about the itchy rash? Well, it's easy, I'm afraid. I shared these pieces of information with them. Involuntarily, but I did. Didn't I search for a low-cost flight to Charles de Gaulle in July? And that beautiful dress I clicked on the other day? And, well, I typed in "red itchy spot" on Google yesterday. No wonder their cookies tracked me and the hidden algorithms directed personalised ads to my IP address.

We recklessly share our private life online without considering the consequences. But this scenario – although rather annoying – is nothing compared to the vision of a society in which our data are controlled by a government; when cookies are not there to recommend something or to attract our attention but to manipulate or punish us. At the moment, though, any step in that direction would provoke a public outcry, but when it comes to deciding on which personal information to post, we are more than willing to share it with thousands of others on different social media platforms. We take pictures of our meals, selfies from our holiday destinations and feel somehow naked when we leave our homes without our smartphones. Here is where danger is lurking in the dark world of servers and providers. Use your mobile phone to pay your bills! Download our app now, and you'll never have to carry cash around anymore, they say. Countries like Sweden or Denmark are on the verge of a cash-free society like that. From here it is not a very far cry from a government controlling our financial transactions. It would allow them an end-to-end tracking of our whereabouts, our purchases and our leisure activities etc., etc. And they would sell this to us as a big step forward: no more tax dodgers, no cash-related crimes, but instead an immediate tracking down of any wrongdoers. Perfect, isn't it? But wait, you may still risk being robbed of your mobile phone? Here is the answer: we turn you into your own mobile phone! It simply takes a tiny little chip implanted into your arm or your neck. Does this sound too far-fetched? I'm not sure. We all love having things done with easily, don't we?

There is a lot more to warn people against as far as the oversharing of data is concerned. But let me appeal to you all here to show more responsible and considerate behaviour when it comes to our personal data. Let us be aware of the electronic devices we have grown so used to.

Thank you.

## Aufgabenstellung 1.2

1 *Im Prinzip ist der gesamte Text eine Information zu dem Autor und seinem Leben. Hier gilt es also, die wichtigsten Fakten zu finden und Aspekte zu verallgemeinern, damit die Technik der Textzusammenfassung deutlich wird. Bei dieser Aufgabenstellung sollten Sie in etwa 200 Wörter schreiben.*

Mohsin Hamid is a British-Pakistani novelist who had to move from California back to his father's hometown of Lahore when he was only nine years old. Although he was born in Pakistan and had lived there for the first three years of his life, the culture clash hit him very hard. Literally stranded in a foreign country without his friends and confronted with unknown food, his only escape was his books.
Always having been a daydreamer, he started reading all kinds of fantasy novels and then, inspired by Tolkien and C.S. Lewis, also began to create his own worlds. His obsession with atlases and almanacs helped him imagine countries that sat in the middle of the oceans and whose population shared features of his homes but also of exotic places. This led to his profession as a writer when he was not yet 22. His stories somehow helped him cope with the world around him.
After having lived in the USA, Great Britain and Pakistan, he now spends time in so many different places with people from numerous ethnic backgrounds that he is constantly reminded of his childhood tales. He thinks that stories have great power because imagination helps us create a vision of our future.

2 *Die Analyse nicht-fiktionaler Texte beschränkt sich meist auf die Untersuchung der Sprache. Gibt es parallele Strukturen (Anaphern, Alliterationen etc.), Metaphern, Aufzählungen, detaillierte Beschreibungen, bestimmte Wortfelder, positive/negative Konnotationen? Wenn Sie dafür Beispiele gefunden haben, sind Sie schon auf der sicheren Seite. Denken Sie aber auch immer daran, die Funktion der von Ihnen gefundenen Stilmittel zu erklären.*
*In den letzten Jahren war die Analyse eines Textes oft mit der Beschreibung eines Bildes oder einer Karikatur verknüpft. In diesem Fall ist es sinnvoll, Ausführungen zu dem diskontinuierlichen Material zu machen und inhaltlichen Parallelen zum Text aufzuzeigen.*
*Das Bild lag in der Prüfung in Farbe vor. Farbige Illustrationen sind in der Prüfung keine Seltenheit. Bereiten Sie sich daher gedanklich darauf vor, auch farbliche Elemente in Ihre Interpretation einfließen zu lassen.*

According to the text, fantasy and imagination play a considerable role in Mohsin Hamid's life. At the beginning of the text, Hamid reports a personal example from his life. It is quite a detailed description of a lasting childhood memory. We feel for Hamid when he says he "never saw, or heard from, a single one of [his] friends again" (ll. 6/7). However, when he tells us about how he managed to get along in his new surroundings, we understand that he had found compensation for the loss of friends. All the enumerations of place names and people and also the positive connotations of the words he uses, like being "fascinated" (l. 21) or stories "unit[ing] parts of [his] existence" (l. 38) create the image of a little boy with his tongue between his teeth, with rosy cheeks, lying on his stomach using "contour lines" (l. 21) to mark borders and writing small texts for the new countries' profiles. The world outside, however, is referred to as "baffling" (l. 36), "peculiar" (l. 45) and "irrevocably split" (l. 39). It makes him feel like "a mongrel" (l. 40). These are all rather negative connotations, but because of his stories he is "comfortable" (l. 40). They are a kind of lighthouse that help him "navigate" (l. 36) his way.

However, the article is also meant to convince the readers of the power of fiction and thus its importance in *all* of our lives. This can clearly be seen in the headline, which reads "*We* need to imagine a brighter future" and obviously includes everyone else. Towards the end of the article he includes the readers again when he justifies his storytelling as an ancient, traditional character trait of all human beings that used to "gather […] around flickering campfires to tell and listen to tales" (ll. 49/50) and even now use "glowing screens" (l. 51) to do so. The metaphor of storytelling offering "an antidote to nostalgia" (l. 54), i. e. a cure for people stuck in the past, grants fantasy and imagination "the power to liberate us from the tyranny of what was and is" (l. 55). The rather formal style of this sentence sounds like a section from a legal document. This impression lingers on when in the final paragraph Hamid appeals to all writers worldwide to "play [a role] in imagining our way out of the nostalgic traps strewn around us" (ll. 56/57). The comparison that the "future is too important to be left to professional politicians [and] technologists" (ll. 62/63) sounds like a vow he takes to defend fantasy and imagination forever.

The illustration supports the cosmopolitan, visionary aspect of Hamid's life. It shows a young man whose eyes are lifted up and who is gazing off into the distance. He seems to be ready to face the future and all the challenges that are waiting for him there. He looks determined, self-confident and at one with himself. The pink glasses he is wearing symbolise a positive attitude towards what lies ahead. They also remind the readers of Hamid's first home in California. The illustration seems to be a graphic version of the title showing a man who "imagine[s] a brighter future" (title).

3.1 *Hier wird ein Kommentar von Ihnen verlangt. Formulieren Sie zunächst das Thema (hier bedeutet das, das Zitat mit eigenen Worten wiederzugeben), geben Sie dann mithilfe des Textes Argumente für Ihre Meinung wieder. Die Aufgabe lautet „comment on the potential of cross-cultural experiences", es ist also impliziert, dass Sie sich positiv über die interkulturellen Erfahrungen äußern sollen. Berücksichtigen Sie auch, dass sowohl nach „personal" als auch nach „professional development" gefragt wird, dass also sowohl private als auch berufliche Aspekte in Ihre Argumentation einfließen sollen. Am Schluss steht Ihre persönliche Meinung.*

Moshin Hamid thinks that his life is peculiar when he works in different places all around the world and communicates in various languages with friends and colleagues from near and far. But why so? I am quite sure that many people envy him. I certainly do.

Travelling broadens the mind. In an increasingly globalised world we can only learn to understand each other when cross-cultural experiences are the norm, not the exception to the rule. It does not necessarily need the uprooting Hamid went through at the age of nine when he moved from California back to Pakistan, but meeting people from other cultural or ethnic backgrounds can only enrich your own life. There would surely be less xenophobia in the world with more cross-cultural encounters in schools, work places and private lives. The famous German writer Johann Wolfgang von Goethe used to say that he who does not know a foreign language knows nothing about his own. It is language that determines thinking, not the other way round. Therefore, not only speaking your mother tongue offers you a wider range of stylistic structures, of literature and poetry. "O brave new world that has such people in't", to quote Shakespeare here.
The fact that you question your own traditions, habits and values when you compare them to those of others is another advantage of cross-cultural experiences. It happens when you work abroad, in international teams, corresponding in numerous languages. Admittedly, there are people who would say that such cosmopolitans do not know where they belong. They have no refuge, because the whole world is their home. However, crossing cultures does not mean abandoning yours for another; it means exchanging experiences and in that way also defining your own world.
Mohsin Hamid concludes that his world is peculiar, but it suits him, and I can only agree with that. We should not look down on people like him but embrace his concept of world citizenship.

3.2 *Obwohl die vergleichende Aufgabenstellung im Allgemeinen eine sehr dankbare ist, da man sich gut darauf vorbereiten kann, ist es hier deutlich schwieriger. Eine Kindheitserinnerung dieser Art spricht in erster Linie für einen Kinderfilm oder ein Kinderbuch. Die Tatsache, dass es ein Umzug in ein anderes Land sein soll (und nicht etwa lediglich eine Erfahrung in einem anderen Land oder das Aufwachsen mit zwei Kulturen, das man in vielen Geschichten zum Thema Migration findet), macht die Sache nicht einfacher. Nachfolgend finden Sie jeweils ein Buch und einen Film.*
*In anderen Jahren und auch mit anderer Textgrundlage bietet sich der Vergleich vor allem für Abiturienten an, die mit argumentativen Texten weniger gut zurechtkommen.*

At the age of nine, Mohsin Hamid experienced a decisive turning point in his life when he had to leave all his friends and his home and the well-known places of his childhood behind and move to another country. To make things worse, it was also a completely different culture which bore hardly any resemblance to his former life. It must have been very hard for him to find a way to cope with that situation. Luckily, he found comfort in reading fantasy novels, which also led to him writing his own stories of worlds that lived his dream of a multicultural society. Obviously, he had come to terms with his new life after some time, but only by creating a parallel dream world in which he felt comfortable. As an adult and well-known writer, he has turned into a cosmopolitan, who feels at home wherever he lays his hat.

Sabine Kuegler, who at the age of eight moved to West Papua, Indonesia with her parents, had a similar experience. In 1980, when her father, a linguist, discovered a new tribe in the jungle, he took his wife and their three children into a world of poisonous animals, militant warriors, blood feud and malaria. For the next eight years they lived with the Fayu. To Sabine this meant a childhood in which life teaches you, not school. She would not need any books to help her escape from reality; she simply used her imagination to make up new games, to communicate with the children of the Fayu or to develop strategies to survive in the jungle. Not knowing cars or TV or shops, it must have been a real culture shock when she returned to Europe in the late 1980s. At the age of 16, she had to start her life over again and she struggled hard to find her way around in her new home. As an adult, she also wrote a book about her experiences called *Jungle Child*, in which she admits that even today her soul is caught between the two worlds. She has actually undergone that process of being thrown into a new culture twice. When looking at Hamid and Kuegler, one cannot help thinking that writing is an appropriate way of coping with such experiences.

However, this topic has also been dealt with by film makers. One example is Andy DeEmmony's *West is West* (2010), the sequel to *East is East* (1999). The film is set in 1976, when Sajid, the youngest of the seven Khan children, faces constant bullying at school. In an argument with his father he calls him a "Paki", which makes George fear that now all his children have lost their ethnic heritage and so he plans to take his son to his home country, much to his British wife's disapproval.

Since one of his sons and also his first wife live in Pakistan, he hopes to show Sajid that life there is better than in Britain. At first Sajid opposes everything that has to do with his new home, but then he gets to know Zaid, a boy his age, and they slowly become friends. Another important person for him is Pir Naseem, who subtly teaches him how to cope with his ambiguous feeling of being torn between two cultures. When they return to Britain in the end, Sajid has learned to be proud of his Asian background. Compared to Hamid, Sajid is someone who does not want to integrate himself in his new surroundings. His escape is his misbehaviour. He knows that he can hurt his father's feelings by calling himself an English boy. Like Kuegler, he lives in two worlds, but is not really torn between them.

What we can learn from all three is surely that it is the unknown that creates prejudices and xenophobia. Cosmopolitan visionaries like Mohsin Hamid can serve as the best example of how to form a world where we are not sorted into different ethnicities but feel like human beings.

3.3 *Bei dieser Aufgabenstellung sollten Sie sich immer erinnern, was genau Ihre Lehrkraft zur Ausführung gesagt hat. Leserbriefe in Zeitungen haben oft nur Sir/Madam als Anrede und den Namen bzw. Ort als Schluss, sie sind sehr kurz und tragen einen neuen Aspekt zur jeweiligen Diskussion bei. Keine Zeitung der Welt druckt seitenlange Lesermeinungen.*

*Der Zwiespalt entsteht durch die Mindestforderung von 250 Wörtern, die im Allgemeinen für die Bearbeitung einer Aufgabenstellung angesetzt sind. Im Zweifel schreiben Sie lieber ein wenig mehr und verwenden die offiziellen Vorgaben für das Schreiben eines formellen Briefes.*

The Editors
guardian.letters@theguardian.com

**Please imagine a brighter future**

Sir

I read your article of 25 February, 2017, "We need to imagine a brighter future", with interest and would like to express my wholehearted approval of the author's ideas and visions. In times where the present is rather frightening, we need someone to light a torch like a spark of hope guiding the way out of the darkness.
But I am afraid he is the only one who lives up to those standards. A simple look at any common bestseller list quickly reveals that the big money is made with rather dystopian visions of the future on the one hand, like *The History of Bees* or *The Tyranny of the Butterfly*, and various genres of detective stories like those by Jussi Adler-Olsen on the other.
What we need instead is writers who can provide a kind of guideline showing us how to cope with current problems. I would love to know how Mohsin Hamid, for instance envisions a future society in which different ethnicities live together peacefully, in which war and hunger no longer play a role and in which our data are perfectly secure. With our professional politicians not being able to motivate people, with the interest in political involvement shrinking and democracy being labelled a system of government that is not appropriate to solve the problems of the 21st century, writers need to jump in to fill that gap. Their imaginary power can give us characters we can look up to. With their visions in our hearts we will roll up our sleeves and start making a change. So writers all around the world: heed the call and follow Mohsin's example!

Elisabeth Mustermann
Ludwigsfelde

## Prüfungsteil 2: Sprachmittlung

### Aufgabenstellung 2.1

*Der Texttyp* blog entry *hat den Vorteil, dass Sie durchaus ein wenig informell schreiben dürfen, da ja die Leserinnen und Leser in Ihrem Alter sein sollen. Von der Struktur her werden auf jeden Fall eine Überschrift und auch ein Hinweis auf die blog-typische Kommentarfunktion verlangt.*
*Auch hier gilt die dringende Empfehlung, zunächst im Text zu markieren, was genau Sie übertragen wollen. Der Aufbau des Textes und der Argumente kann dann beliebig angepasst werden. Es gibt keinen Grund, warum man seine eigenen Ausführungen als Schritt-für-Schritt-Mediation des Artikels darstellen sollte. Eine gedankliche Umstrukturierung zeigt der korrigierenden Lehrkraft auch, dass Sie sich intensiv mit dem Text auseinandergesetzt haben.*

**A truly German word – *Heimat***

Have you ever heard Germans talking about their *Heimat*? They most likely wore an enigmatic smile and had misty eyes and probably told you something about their childhood, right?
Okay, did this help you understand what their concept of *Heimat* is? Well, maybe not, but the thing is, there is no 1:1 expression for that word in English. The closest you can get to is *home*.
Today it is one of the most beautiful words in the German language according to a poll from 2004. An overwhelming 88 percent of all the people here think it is an important or even very important notion to them.
But the idea of *Heimat* has gone through a lot of changes and misinterpretations. It was a legal term until the 19th century, which granted people who owned land certain civil rights. Later, ideologists abused the concept of *Heimat* for nationalistic purposes and even today there are tendencies to use it for drawing a line between "them and us". People who feel caught in the set of traditions and unwritten rules of their *Heimat* might also see it as a prison from which you cannot escape.
But for the vast majority of Germans, their *Heimat* is a certain region like the seaside, hearing their local accent spoken or eating home-made food they used to have when they were young.
Today even young people have come back to loving their *Heimat*. The feeling of pride and belonging made up for the old-fashioned concept of *Heimat* equalizing narrow-mindedness and stuffiness.
Okay, some of you may know terms like *Dirndl* or *Oktoberfest*, and, yes, that is what Bavarians would understand as an aspect of that concept. So it's not too difficult to understand after all, right?
Well, I'm sure you have a similar concept in your country. Let me know what you'd call *Heimat* or home. Comment on my blog in the section below. I'm looking forward to it.

**Aufgabenstellung 2.2**

*Die Aufgabenstellung verlangt die Produktion eines Artikels von Ihnen, d. h., Ihr Text benötigt eine Überschrift, muss sprachlich neutral verfasst werden und hat in diesem Fall die Besonderheit, dass er ein Interview zusammenfasst. Die originale Struktur von Frage-Antwort muss also aufgelöst werden. Sie können allerdings an passenden Stellen den Interviewpartner zitieren.*

**A Syrian and his struggle for integration into Germany**
by LISA BLUME

Two and a half years after a huge number of immigrants were welcomed to Germany, the refugees have hopefully found their place in everyday life.
One who seems to have done so is Firas Alshater from Syria. A famous film maker in his home country, he had to flee the persecution of the Assad regime, which repeatedly threw him into prison for criticising the government in his films.
He arrived in Germany in May 2013. When more and more people joined the Pegida protests in Dresden in 2014, he felt he needed to find out whether the majority of Germans supported this xenophobic movement. He came up with a rather unorthodox idea. "I was standing in the heart of Berlin Alexanderplatz, […] blindfolded and carried a sign reading: I am a Syrian refugee. I trust you. Do you trust me? Then hug me," he told a reporter in 2016. When asked about the results of this performance, he said that Germans differ in their views of political issues like integration. He also concludes that the media often concentrate too much on the problems refugees cause.
In 2016 he started a YouTube channel called *Zukar* in which he focuses on the problems of refugees and German society alike. He says, "I get a lot of feedback from people who like my videos but also from the right-wing extremists".
Alshater admits that Germany has now become his new home and appreciates that he can freely express his opinion here. Through his videos on *Zukar* he stays in contact with a lot of Syrian refugees. They often ask him for help with questions and translations.
What does the future hold in store? He has a lot of projects under way, Alshater says. In autumn, his first book will be published, he will, of course, go on making YouTube videos and he is going to start studying film editing at the University of Film in Potsdam-Babelsberg. A lot of doors open to those who are willing to become integrated.
Let us hope that this accounts for all the other refugees of 2015.

## Abiturprüfung Berlin 2019
## Englisch Grundkurs

## Prüfungsteil 1: Leseverstehen und Schreiben (75 %)

Der Prüfungsteil 1 besteht aus zwei Aufgabenstellungen, von denen Sie eine zur Bearbeitung auswählen.

### Aufgabenstellung 1.1 – Tasks

**Themenschwerpunkte:** *Aims and ambitions, Ethnic and cultural diversity*

1 Sum up the information about Tony, his family, and his workmates. (30 %)

2 Analyze the way the author characterizes Tony. Give evidence from the text. (30 %)

3 Choose <u>one</u> of the following tasks:

3.1 "Tony himself worked every day of the week. [...] He and Pavel and his brother intended to set up their own building firm next year." (ll. 51/52)
Using the quote as a starting point, discuss the opportunities and challenges for immigrant workers in their new countries. Refer to the text and your knowledge of the issue. (40 %)

OR

3.2 Compare the relationships within Tony's family to those within another immigrant family in literature or film. Assess the way the protagonists deal with their situation.* (40 %)

OR

3.3 A few years later, Tony's daughter is giving a speech at her graduation. Write this speech, in which she comments on the importance of good language skills for successful integration. Use her experiences as a starting point. (40 %)

* Dieser Aufgabentyp entfällt ab der Abiturprüfung 2021.

**Text** (excerpt from the novel)

**Transit**
by Rachel Cusk

Note: *Divorced and making a new start in London, Faye, the narrator, becomes fascinated by the lives of the people she meets, for example, Tony, who helps her to renovate her newly-bought house.*

[…] We sat in the slow-moving traffic with the radio on. Tony said he kept it on to improve his English. His daughter spoke better English than him, and she was only five.

"Five years old!" he yelled, slapping the leather steering wheel. "Amazing!"

The grey roadside inched along beside us. Tony glanced out at it frequently, drawing himself up in his seat. He drove erect behind his mirrored sunglasses with a single finger resting on the leather steering wheel. His big hard thighs were splayed comfortably in a perfect V. He wore a tight red T-shirt that showed his powerful chest and bulging forearms.

"I love England," he said. "I love most the English cakes." He grinned. "Especially the hijack."

You mean flapjack, I said.*

"Flapjack!" he shouted deliriously, throwing back his head. "Yes, I love the flapjack!"

His daughter, he went on, enjoyed school – she talked about it all the time. In the mornings he would find her sitting fully dressed in her uniform on the stairs, waiting. Her teacher had told him she read better than some of the ten-year-olds.

"My daughter," he said, jabbing his own muscled chest, "reading English better than the English." The family had moved to England three years before. The only person they knew when they came was Tony's sister-in-law, who lived in Harlow. Since then Tony had persuaded his brother and cousin to come here too. He liked to have his family around him – he returned to Albania every couple of months, driving non-stop in the Audi until he got there – but he wasn't sure it was so good for his wife.

"It stops her getting used," he said.

Used to it, I said. It stops her getting used to it.

"Yes," Tony said, nodding his head approvingly. "It's good."

It stopped her getting used to it, he went on, having her family to depend on. She had made no friends and was frightened of going anywhere on her own. She wouldn't even go to their daughter's school: it was Tony who dropped her off and picked her up and went to the assembling.

Assembly, I said.

"I love," Tony said, grinning widely, "the assembly."

Unlike their daughter, his wife could speak no English at all.

"And my daughter," he said, "she don't speak Albanian."

She could understand a few things but English was the language she knew.

So effectively, I said, his wife and daughter couldn't speak to one another. Tony nodded his head slowly, his eyes on the road.

"In other words," he said.

At the depot I waited while Tony collected the builder's order. I paid the bill and we set off on the return journey. On the road a small battered truck loomed up right behind us, blaring its horn repeatedly, and then swerved out so that it drew level with Tony's Audi. The driver was waving his arms and leaning over to shout through the open window. […] Presently the truck accelerated away, the contents of its open bed – rubbish sacks, old furniture, broken planks and piles of rubble – jolting up and down under the madly flapping tarpaulin.

"That's Kaput," Tony said […].

Albanians knew how to work, he went on, not like people here. Kaput didn't even have a house: his truck was his house. He made more money that way. He sent all the money back to his village. Tony frowned.

"The village of Kaput a bad place," he said.

Tony himself worked every day of the week. […] He and Pavel and his brother intended to set up their own building firm next year. Tony grinned.

"Pavel always say he going home. […]

He's homestruck," Tony said.

Homesick, I said.

Pavel was the other man the builder had sent along with Tony to do the work. He was a small, quiet, melancholic person who I would sometimes see sitting on my doorstep in the grey dawn reading a book while he waited for Tony to arrive. On the first day, Tony had explained that he would be doing the demolition and ripping out, and Pavel would do the rebuilding and making good.

"Destruction –" Tony had grinned widely and placed his hands on his own chest, then pointed at Pavel – "construction!"

Pavel came out to help Tony unload the car. They stood and considered the bags of cement and Pavel asked a question.

"English!" Tony commanded. "Speak English!"

Tony told me that today they were going to be taking up the floor. I asked whether there would be a lot of noise. He grinned.

"Hundred per cent," he said. […] *(761 words)*

*Cusk, Rachel.* Transit. *London: Random House, 2016, 152–156.*

**Annotations**

* Throughout the text what the narrator says is not in quotation marks, quotation marks are used only for what other people say.

l. 5 to inch: to move very slowly
l. 12 flapjack: thick soft biscuit made from oats
l. 18 to jab: to push a finger into somebody/something, with a sudden strong movement
l. 20 Harlow: town situated about 50 km north of London
l. 31 assembly: *here:* meeting of teachers and parents of students at a school
l. 39 depot: store for building supplies
l. 40 battered: old, used a lot, and not in very good condition
l. 43 bed: *here:* loading space
l. 45 tarpaulin: sheet made of waterproof material, used to cover things with and to keep rain off

## Aufgabenstellung 1.2 – Tasks

**Themenschwerpunkte:** *Science and technology – visions of the future, Aims and ambitions, The impact of the media on society*

1 Outline the information about the new Atlas robot and reactions to it as presented in Text A. (30 %)

2 Analyze the cover (Text B) and show how it reflects ideas from Text A. Give evidence from both texts. (30 %)

3 Choose one of the following tasks:

3.1 "But a robot doing a backflip is really impressive. It's evidence that we're getting much closer to being able to design robots that are equivalent to or better than an average person." (Text A, ll. 44–46)

Explain the quote and discuss the potential and risks of developing humanoid robots. Refer to the text and your knowledge of the issue. (40 %)

OR

3.2 Compare the Atlas robot introduced in Text A with another humanoid robot in literature, film, or real life. Assess their usefulness.* (40 %)

OR

3.3 For the website of an international robotics competition, write an article in which you comment on the advantages of using modern media to publicize and to discuss new inventions. Use Atlas as one of your examples. (40 %)

* Dieser Aufgabentyp entfällt ab der Abiturprüfung 2021.

**Text A** (Article)

**Backflipping Robot Is A Giant Leap For Robot Kind**
by Rebecca Feldhaus Adams.

Thursday, Nov. 16, 2017, was a day filled with news. So much news, in fact, that you might have missed the announcement of a backflipping robot. In less than a minute, the video posted by Boston Dynamics inspired screaming emotions from all corners of the Internet. It's a revelation in robotics, some said. It's the beginning of humanity's end, chirped others.

> we dead pic.twitter.com/IUys7DptdZ
>
> – alex medina (@mrmedina) November 16, 2017

The Atlas robot is described by its creators as "the world's most dynamic humanoid." And its acrobatic success comes after multiple iterations and what may have been hundreds of thousands of human hours. Atlas is one of nine robots in the Boston Dynamics family.

Siblings include Spot, the four-legged model that's deerlike in its movements, and Handle, which has both arms and wheels and seemingly takes inspiration from the Wheelers in the 1985 film Return to Oz.

The robotics community met an older version of Atlas during a robot competition sponsored by DARPA, the Defense Advanced Research Projects Agency, which is an arm of the U.S. government. DARPA announced the competition in April 2012; its purpose was to inspire teams to use a humanoid robot to solve problems created in natural or man-made disasters. DARPA commissioned Boston Dynamics to create Atlas for the competition. Though DARPA sponsored it, Boston Dynamics owns the intellectual property rights. Competing robots had to complete seven tasks.

DARPA Competition Tasks For Robots

- Drive a vehicle
- Exit a vehicle
- Open and go through a doorway·
- Turn a valve
- Use a drill to cut a hole in a wall
- Climb a flight of stairs
- Mystery task (revealed): Plug or unplug something from an electrical wall socket

New Atlas, the backflipping version, is shorter and lighter than the version used in the DARPA competition. Instead of 6 feet, 2 inches, the new Atlas is just about 5 feet tall, and instead of 330 pounds, it's about 165. The video shows a model that is untethered, meaning that it runs on battery power rather than being plugged into a stationary power source.

Boston Dynamics did not respond to multiple requests for comment.

Douglas Stephen, a research associate at the Institute for Human and Machine Cognition in Florida, was on the IHMC's team for the competition. He said this new version of Atlas is incredibly impressive because of the way it's made. Atlas uses hydraulics, which is part of what makes it so powerful, Stephen said. Usually that means a lot of hoses to run hydraulic fluid. This version uses technology that integrates tubing in the fabric itself, making it lighter and more compact.

But let's get to the real question. In what natural disaster scenario would a robot need to do a backflip?

"A robot doesn't need to do a backflip," Stephen said. "But a robot doing a backflip is really impressive. It's evidence that we're getting much closer to being able to design robots that are equivalent to or better than an average person."

To get a robot closer to being "better than an average person," Stephen says a little tough love is required. There are numerous videos in which Boston Dynamics staff members are shown pushing, kicking and hitting the robots with hockey sticks. It's not cruel, Stephen said. There's no artificial intelligence. It's just a computer with legs. And often the easiest way to test the computer's balance, flexibility and recovery skills is to simply give it a good hard shove.

The point of building a robot to act like a human is not to scare humanity, Stephen said. The point is to make a machine that functions in a human world.

"If you can make a robot that's the same dimensions and shape, and same dexterity as a person," he said, "you open up the possibilities of what you can do with that robot." As for whether the machines are coming for us:

"No," Stephen said. "Not anytime soon." *(661 words)*



**Annotations**

heading leap: jump, big step
l. 9 iteration: repetition
l. 14 Wheelers: group of bizarre characters with wheels instead of hands and feet
l. 19 to commission: to officially ask somebody
l. 26 valve: device controlling the flow of liquid, gas or air
l. 48 tough love: treating somebody in a kind but strict way
l. 55 dexterity: skill and ease in doing something with your hands
l. 57 to come for somebody: *slang:* to threaten to do harm to or replace somebody

**Text B**
**Cover from *The New Yorker***

*R. Kikuo Johnson, New Yorker © Conde Nast*

## Prüfungsteil 2: Sprachmittlung (25 %)

Der Prüfungsteil 2 besteht aus zwei Aufgabenstellungen, von denen Sie eine zur Bearbeitung auswählen.

### Aufgabenstellung 2.1 – Tasks

**Themenschwerpunkte:** *Science and technology – visions of the future, The impact of the media on society, Aims and ambitions*

You are taking part in an international youth project about sustainable food consumption in different countries.
Write a blog entry for the project website, presenting Mealsaver.

**Text** (Artikel)

**Zum Wegwerfen zu schade**
**Wie Start-ups und Initiativen versuchen, mithilfe von Apps die Verschwendung von Essen zu reduzieren.**
Von Marvin Strathmann

Kurz vor Ladenschluss im Hamburger Café Philo. In einer weißen Box liegen ein Stück Quiche, zwei Scheiben Baguette und ein gemischter Salat mit Caesar-Dressing. Eigentlich müsste das Café diese Lebensmittel wegwerfen, morgen wären sie unverkäuflich. Das Brot wäre vertrocknet, der Salat nicht mehr frisch. Doch Rettung naht bereits – in Gestalt von Ilona Ardiuschkina.

Ein Mitarbeiter des Cafés sieht auf Ardiuschkinas Smartphone, tippt auf den Bildschirm, dann darf Ardiuschkina die Box mit dem Essen mitnehmen. Bezahlt hat sie vorab per Handy. Mealsaver heißt die App, die ihr eine Freundin empfohlen hat. Mit ihr soll Lebensmittelverschwendung bekämpft werden.

Über Mealsaver können Restaurants und Geschäfte am Ende des Tages übrig gebliebene Lebensmittel Nutzern der App billiger anbieten. Was es gibt und wie viel die Nutzer sparen können, hängt vom Restaurant und vom Tag ab. […]

Dahinter steckt ein Berliner Start-up mit 16 Mitarbeitern, die EatUp GmbH. Seit Oktober bieten etwa 150 Restaurants übrig gebliebene Lebensmittel in der Hauptstadt an. Hamburg ist seit Dezember dabei, dort sind es bisher etwa 25 Restaurants. Weitere Städte sollen folgen.

In Deutschland landen der Umweltorganisation WWF zufolge jedes Jahr mehr als 18 Millionen Tonnen Lebensmittel im Müll. Weil man sich beim Wocheneinkauf verschätzt hat, Gemüse zu klein oder zu krumm gewachsen ist oder im Supermarkt Joghurt aussortiert werden muss, der am Tag darauf abläuft. Und eben, weil Restaurants, Cafés und Bäckereien ihre Waren am nächsten Tag nicht mehr anbieten können oder wollen. Mealsaver soll helfen, das zu vermeiden, wenigstens im Kleinen. […]

Die Boxen kosten meist zwischen zwei und vier Euro. Das Geld geht nicht komplett an die Restaurants. Einen Euro erhält Mealsaver für die Vermittlung und die Gebühren an Paypal. Das Unternehmen stellt auch die biologisch abbaubaren Boxen bereit, die mit Essen gefüllt werden. Die App zeigt Restaurants, die die sogenannten Foodboxen anbieten, in einer Liste an und sortiert sie nach ihrer Nähe zum Standort des Nutzers.

Auch auf einer Karte können sie angezeigt werden. Die App erkennt allerdings immer wieder mal den Standort nicht und schlägt den Nutzern dann auch Restaurants in 250 Kilometern Entfernung vor. Außerdem dauert es manchmal recht lange, bis die Karte geladen hat. Ein Neustart der App löst meist die Ortungsprobleme.

Außer der Entfernung bietet Mealsaver weitere Informationen zu den Restaurants an: Welche Gerichte werden angeboten, wie viel kostet eine Foodbox, wann können Nutzer sie abholen. Tippen die Nutzer auf die Vorschau, zeigt die App eine kurze Beschreibung des Restaurants an, die genaue Adresse und wie viele Foodboxen es dort noch gibt. Über den „Auswählen“-Knopf können Nutzer schließlich die Zahl der Boxen bestimmen und bestellen. Allerdings können Nutzer nur mit einem Paypal-Konto bezahlen.

Nach dem Kauf erhält der Nutzer einen virtuellen Gutschein. Den kann er einlösen, wenn er das Essen abholt. Ein Nachteil: Viele Restaurants verkaufen ihre Foodboxen erst spät am Abend, kurz bevor sie schließen. So kann der Kunde das Essen beispielsweise erst um 21 Uhr oder noch später abholen. Bei Bäckereien und Cafés sieht es anders aus, sie können schon am Nachmittag übrig gebliebene belegte Brötchen in die Box packen. *(499 Wörter)*

*„Zum Wegwerfen zu schade“, Marvin Strathmann, SZ vom 25.01.2017*

**Annotationen**

Z. 17 WWF: Abkürzung für *World Wide Fund For Nature*

Z. 38 Paypal: Online-Bezahldienst

## Aufgabenstellung 2.2 – Tasks

**Themenschwerpunkte:** *The impact of the media on society, Aims and ambitions, Science and technology – visions of the future*

An American friend of yours has asked you to help her/him prepare a term paper about e-sport tournaments worldwide.
Write her/him an email outlining the information about e-sport tournaments and their appeal to young people as reported by Till Simon Nagel.

**Text** (Auszug aus dem Artikel)

**E-Sport-Turniere sind, wie Rockkonzerte früher waren**
Von Till Simon Nagel

1 […] Auf den ersten Blick sieht es aus wie bei einem Rockkonzert: Hunderte Zuschauer sitzen auf Tribünen, aus den Boxen dröhnt laute Musik, die Bässe wummern. Doch hier in Halle sieben auf der Gamescom treten keine Musiker auf, sondern E-Sportler. […]

Einige Profispieler sind durchaus so etwas wie Rockstars der Szene. Und E-Sport, wie er hier und an anderen Ständen gezeigt wird, ist ein Trendthema der Videospielemesse. Aber was ist das eigentlich?

„E-Sport ist der professionelle Wettstreit in Videospielen", erklärt Felix Falk, Geschäftsführer des Bundesverbands Interaktive Unterhaltungssoftware, knapp. Gut jeder zweite Deutsche (53 Prozent) hat laut einer aktuellen Deloitte-Studie schon einmal von E-Sport gehört.

Ein Großteil davon weiß allerdings nicht so recht, was dahintersteckt. 47 Prozent wissen nichts über dieses Phänomen, das Zehntausende Jugendliche und junge Erwachsene begeistert. […]

Dabei ist E-Sport kein neues Phänomen. Hervorgegangen unter anderem aus den Netzwerk-Partys der 90er-Jahre, ist E-Sport in den letzten 20 Jahren zu einem Massenphänomen geworden. Spieler in Teams kämpfen in populären Videospielen von Shootern über Strategie bis Sport-Games gegeneinander, spielen bei Turnieren mitunter um hohe Geldsummen.

Der Berliner „Dota 2"-Spieler Kuro Salehi Takhasomi gewann jüngst mit seinem Team Liquid beim Wettbewerb The International in den USA ein Preisgeld in Millionenhöhe. Zahllose Zuschauer verfolgten das Turnier in der Arena, online per Stream oder in sozialen Netzwerken.

Anderen beim Spielen zusehen, statt selber zu spielen. Was ist daran so faszinierend? „Die Stimmung", „die ganzen guten Spieler sehen" oder „Freunde treffen" sind nur einige der schnellen Antworten der Jugendlichen im Publikum. „Entertainment", nennt es Melek Balgün, Journalistin und E-Sport-Moderatorin.

Für sie haben die Turniere wie das diesjährige ESL One in Köln starken Festival-Charakter gewonnen. Menschen treffen sich, sehen gemeinsam, wie ihre Lieblingsspiele von den Profis gespielt werden.

Für Balgün, selbst ehemalige E-Sportlerin, macht diese geteilte Leidenschaft für die Sache den Reiz aus: „Die unterschiedlichsten Leute treffen sich, freuen sich über die gleichen Sachen, brennen für die gleichen Mannschaften."

Also alles wie bei anderen Sportarten auch? Nicht ganz. Zwar ist das Publikum vor den Gamescom-Bühnen relativ gemischt, ein genauer Blick offenbart aber eines: E-Sport- Fans sind überwiegend jung, tendenziell männlich und sehr technikaffin, so die Deloitte-Studie. Stärker als beim Breitensport handelt es sich beim E-Sport um eine Jugendkultur.

„Eine Form von Abgrenzungskultur", nennt es Prof. Jörg Müller-Lietzkow von der Universität Paderborn, der seit Jahren auch zum Thema E-Sport forscht. Jugendliche erleben die Turniere und Events als elternfreie Zone. Ein wenig wie früher Rockkonzerte.

[…] Im Gegensatz zum großen Sport oder der Musikkultur sind E-Sportler den Zuschauern auch näher. Jeder kann – zumindest theoretisch – einer der Athleten auf der Bühne werden – etwas Talent und Übung vorausgesetzt. Jeder kann sich selbst inszenieren – über eigene Webvideos oder Streamingplattformen.

Und E-Sport ist schneller, kurzlebiger und vor allem direkter. Viel Kommunikation zwischen Teams, Spielern oder Fans findet über soziale Netzwerke statt, Live-Übertragungen hierzulande fast nur über Internet-Plattformen. […] *(461 Wörter)*

*Quelle: Nagel, Till Simon. „E-Sport-Turniere sind, wie Rockkonzerte früher waren".* Welt. *04. Sept. 2017. Axel Springer SE – DIE WELT*

**Annotationen**

Z. 3 Gamescom: europäische Leitmesse für digitale Spielekultur in Köln

Z. 10 Deloitte: internationales Dienstleistungsnetzwerk für Unternehmen und Institutionen aus allen Wirtschaftszweigen

Z. 18 Shooter: Computerspiel, bei dem die Spielenden mit Schusswaffen agieren

Z. 20 Dota 2: Echtzeit-Strategiespiel

Z. 28 ESL One: Turnier organisiert durch den größten E-Sport Organisator ESL

Z. 36 technikaffin: eine Vorliebe für Technik habend

## Lösungsvorschläge

### Prüfungsteil 1: Leseverstehen und Schreiben

#### Aufgabenstellung 1.1

1 *Da Tony im Zentrum der Erzählung steht, ist es am einfachsten, wenn er auch in der Zusammenfassung im Zentrum steht (natürlich ist auch eine andere Strukturierung grundsätzlich möglich). Von ihm ausgehend, können Sie zunächst auf die Situation seiner Tochter und Frau eingehen und anschließend die beiden Arbeitskollegen Kaput und Pavel vorstellen.*

Tony, one of the main characters in the excerpt from the novel *Transit* by Rachel Cusk, migrated from Albania to Great Britain three years ago. He is married and proud of his 5-year-old daughter, who meanwhile speaks better English than he himself and who loves going to school where she achieves good results. His wife is rather shy. Socially isolated, she refuses to leave the house to take her daughter to school, and thus has not learned any English at all. Due to the fact that her daughter speaks English only, they can hardly communicate. Tony is keen on learning English and likes everything about England. But he is also still connected to Albania and visits his family back home regularly. However, he doubts that this is a good situation for his wife, because it prevents her from getting accustomed to her new homeland. Tony is a hard-working man and dreams of having his own building company with his brother and his colleague Pavel, who rebuilds what Tony demolishes. Pavel is sometimes homesick and thinks about returning to Albania. His other workmate Kaput seems harder-working than Tony. He lives in his truck to save money and sends all his earnings home to his village in Albania.

2 *Im Text sehen wir Tony durch die Augen der Erzählerin Faye. Diese ist fasziniert von seiner Körperlichkeit. Bei vielen Beschreibungen im Erzähltext ist nicht immer klar, ob sie der Einschätzung der Erzählerin entsprechen oder ob Faye nur wiedergibt, was Tony selbst über sich sagt. Dies betrifft etwa die Passage, in der es um die Familienbesuche geht und die inhaltlich nahtlos von Erzähltext in Dialog übergeht und wieder zu Erzähltext wechselt (vgl. Z. 19–27). Insgesamt wird Tony jedoch nicht nur durch diese Beschreibungen, sondern auch durch seine Handlungen als hart arbeitender Familienmensch charakterisiert, der sich Mühe gibt, sich in seiner neuen Heimat zu integrieren.*

Tony is described by Faye, the female narrator who obviously feels attracted to him. He is characterised implicitly when she focuses on his physical appearance: "His big, hard thighs were splayed comfortably in a perfect V. He wore a tight, red T-shirt that showed his powerful chest and bulging forearms." (ll. 7–9). Thus he is characterised as a strong, hard-working man. He tries to adapt to British society and desperately wants to make his dream of success come true. He is keen on learning English and

tries to improve his language skills. He appreciates it when his mistakes are corrected by Faye: "'[…] hijack.' 'you mean flapjack.' 'Flapjack' he shouted deliriously, throwing back his head." (ll. 11–13). Later he says it is good when she corrects him (cf. l. 26). He also keeps the radio on as long as possible to improve his language skills (cf. ll. 1/2). Additionally, he tries to motivate his future business partner, Pavel, to learn English "'English!' Tony commanded, 'Speak English!'" (l. 65).
Tony is definitely a family man. He is proud of his 5-year-old daughter, who has acquired the language quickly and has no problems adapting to her new environment. Furthermore he keeps contact with his family in Albania and even persuades his brother and cousin to come to Britain. (cf. l. 21). He is thoughtful and takes responsibility for his family. Thus he even questions his own decisions when he doubts that returning to his home country has a positive effect on his wife adapting to their new society (cf. ll. 22/23). To put it in a nutshell, Tony is a hard-working man who is trying to do everything to provide for his family and grasp the golden opportunities in Britain.

3.1 *Der Text selbst enthält bereits wesentliche Herausforderungen für Migranten: Tony hat Schwierigkeiten mit der englischen Sprache, seine Frau beherrscht diese gar nicht. Ihre Familie und Freunde sind weit weg und sie müssen neue Kontakte suchen, was im Fall von Tonys Frau nicht gelingt und zu sozialer Isolation führt. Zudem müssen alle drei Arbeiter im Text sehr hart arbeiten (vgl. Zitat in der Aufgabe) und leben unter teils schlechten Bedingungen. Umgekehrt enthält der Text auch viele Hinweise auf Möglichkeiten, die sich für Migranten ergeben. Die Albaner stammen aus einem Gebiet, in dem teils noch große Gefahren (Z. 50) und große Armut herrschen (Z. 48/49). England bietet Sicherheit und die Möglichkeit durch harte Arbeit Wohlstand zu erreichen (vgl. Zitat in der Aufgabe). Insbesondere Tony steht auch für weitere positive Aspekte. Er liebt England und seine Kultur (Z. 10–14), lernt begeistert die neue Sprache und ist offen für neue Kontakte, wie sich im Gespräch mit Faye zeigt. Beachten Sie, dass Sie in Ihrer Lösung das Zitat als Einstiegspunkt nehmen müssen, dass Ihr Aufsatz sich also zunächst mit den wirtschaftlichen Aspekten des Themas befassen muss.*

Tony not only works hard, he works harder than ordinary people. He never takes a day off to make his dream of having his own building company come true. Despite the fact that he is doing hard physical labour, he is proud of his job and is obviously quite successful. The obstacles he has to cope with are both the language and the new culture. But in contrast to his wife, he is open-minded and open to new experiences. In his job, Tony frequently comes into contact with English people and therefore learns a lot every day. In spite of the fact that he stays connected to his roots – he visits his relatives in Albania regularly – he does not simply assimilate to society, he really wants to integrate.
His wife, on the other hand, is an example of what immigrants should not do in a new country. She is trying to escape from the challenges of integration and avoids meeting different people. But being a housewife in a foreign country makes it a lot more difficult to integrate. This means no contact at work, and there might be neighbours who

try to avoid contact and may not always be friendly. Tony was obviously the one who decided to go to Britain with his family. Although he tries to support his wife, he is not really able to help her.
The people in the text are obviously legal immigrants. Illegal immigrants have far more difficulties to overcome. They often have to repay their debts to human traffickers, which can be considered a kind of modern slavery. They work in pubs and restaurants for almost no money at all. And their families are threatened if they do not pay, so they cannot escape the situation.
According to the concept of the salad bowl, integration leads to an enrichment of society. But due to xenophobic and neo-liberal tendencies which can be observed in Britain, integration is not always possible. A multicultural society requires acceptance and tolerance on both sides. When this is missing, subcultures are formed where immigrants feel accepted and have a sense of belonging.
Immigrants often have to work harder than the locals to be successful and accepted by society. Still it is important for immigrants not to give up in the face of difficulties, but to work hard and try to cope with the hurdles they often face.

3.2 *Viele der Texte und Filme, die im Unterricht behandelt werden, eignen sich hier für einen Vergleich. Der Film* East is East*, der Roman* Tortilla Curtain *von T. C. Boyle und die Kurzgeschichte „My son the fanatic" von Hanif Kureishi sind nur einige der bekanntesten Werke, die herangezogen werden können. Beachten Sie bei Ihrer Auswahl, dass es im Werk um eine Familie gehen muss, also mindestens zwei Personen einer Familie eingewandert sein müssen.*

Tony is proud of his daughter and wants her to become successful. He is proud of the fact that she is talented and learns the language very quickly. Similarly, in the movie *Bend it like Beckham*, Mr Bhamra also wants his daughter to succeed and integrate into society. When she gets her excellent A-level results, he is very proud and wants her to become a doctor or lawyer. Mr Bhamra works at the airport and owns a semi-detached house next to a park. This shows he has become a middle class citizen. He also sticks to his Indian roots and wears a turban at work. Likewise, Tony returns to his home country, Albania, regularly and in this way keeps the connection to his roots. Another similarity between the two stories is the narrow-mindedness of both Tony's wife and Mrs Bhamra. Tony's wife refuses to learn English or leave the house to integrate into the new culture. She even has difficulty communicating with her 5-year-old daughter, who primarily speaks English. Mrs Bhamra is quite traditional and totally disapproves of her daughter playing football because she would then be showing her bare legs to men. Instead, she wants her to learn to prepare Indian meals in order to become a good housewife. Both Tony's wife and Mrs Bhamra are housewives and therefore have difficulties integrating into British society.
In the beginning Mr Bhamra disapproves of his daughter playing football in a club, but only due to the fact that he does not want her to be disappointed or frustrated. He doubts that, as an Indian woman, she will ever be accepted by her teammates. He himself was not accepted by his fellow cricket team members, who made fun of his

turban and caused him to quit his favourite sport. But later he gives in and allows her to play football, which shows he is obviously a lot more tolerant than his wife.
Both Jessminder and Tony's daughter are talented, work hard at school and are willing to adapt to society. They are and will be far more integrated than their parents are.
I think both Tony and Mr Bhamra are open-minded and thoughtful people who try to cope with the situation adequately. But their wives should try to integrate into society. By learning to understand their environment better they would also become happier.

3.3 *„Graduation" bedeutet Abschluss. Da Tonys Tochter erst fünf Jahre alt ist, können Sie sich auf ihren Schulabschluss beziehen. Die Zeitangabe einige Jahre ist jedoch so vage, dass auch die Abschlussfeier an der Universität als Bezugspunkt denkbar ist. Beachten Sie aber in jedem Fall, dass es sich um eine formelle Veranstaltung handelt, dass Sie also auf einen entsprechenden Sprachstil achten müssen.*

Ladies and gentleman, as we come together today to celebrate our graduation from Oxford University, we should remember where we came from. People in the audience represent over 20 different nationalities and 15 different languages, but we have all worked hard to be sitting in this garden on this day. Despite the differences in background and culture, we have all achieved one common goal, which we are celebrating here today.
It's been a long journey for many of us. When I came to Britain 16 years ago from the dire situation in Albania, neither my parents nor I spoke a word of English. But we came here anyway and strove to adapt to this society and be successful contributing members. Despite my father only attending school for seven years, he was able to make his dream come true. By working hard every day, he succeeded in founding his own building company. He also worked hard to learn the language he needed by studying grammar books at night instead of watching TV. I took him as a role model and soon found my love for the English language. I have no doubt that this love opened many doors for me and that I would not be standing here today if my father had not shown me that you need communication to really live in a country and become one of its citizens.
If you're talented and willing to work hard, you can achieve almost anything in this country, but it is its language that is the key to success. I'm very grateful for having been given this excellent opportunity to study at one of the most prestigious schools in the world and for that I thank my teachers. May you all continue your success but not forget your roots.

## Aufgabenstellung 1.2

1 *Vergessen Sie bei dieser Aufgabe nicht, auf die Reaktionen der Menschen auf den Roboter einzugehen. Diese werden in der Aufgabenstellung explizit gefordert, dienen im Zeitungsartikel aber nur als Einstieg ins Thema, der das Interesse wecken soll. Der Text beschreibt, dass die Reaktionen im Internet in zwei Richtungen gingen. Ein Teil äußerte sich beeindruckt über diese revolutionäre Entwicklung im Bereich Robotik,*

*ein anderer äußerte (wohl nur teilweise scherzhaft), dass dies das Ende der Menschheit bedeutet. Im Text wird es nicht explizit erwähnt, aber die Filmreihe* Terminator *hat ein Szenario präsentiert, dass mittlerweile viele Wissenschaftler wie etwa Elon Musk und der verstorbene Stephen Hawking für möglich halten – dass Roboter und künstliche Intelligenzen sich eines Tages gegen die Menschheit stellen könnten.*

The article "Backflipping Robot Is A Giant Leap For Robot Kind" by Rebecca F. Adams is about a new humanoid robot called Atlas that can do more human-like tasks than previous robots. Developed by Boston Dynamics, it is shorter and lighter than former versions. It runs on battery power and its movement is driven by hydraulic tubes hidden in its fibre. Its predecessor had taken part in a competition sponsored by DARPA – an arm of the US government – where it had to fulfill several tasks. The fact that Atlas can do a backflip is not important, rather it shows how far we are in making human-like machines. The goal is to make robots that are as good as or even better than the average person and to get these robots to solve problems in disaster situations and other circumstances too difficult or dangerous for humans.
The presentation of the Atlas robot evoked strong and controversial emotions on the internet, however. Researchers consider Atlas to be a huge step towards designing robots comparable to humans. While many people are simply impressed, others fear that robots may one day turn on humankind and that this may lead to its end. As Atlas is not artificial intelligence this is not very likely at the moment.

2 *Teil Ihrer Lösung sollte eine Bildbeschreibung sein. Hierbei können Sie sich auf die Aspekte beschränken, die für den Vergleich mit dem Text von wesentlicher Bedeutung sind. Es ist dabei weniger wichtig, wie die Roboter genau aussehen, als ihre Menschlichkeit impliziert durch die dargestellten Handlungen hervorzuheben. Auch das Verhältnis zwischen Mensch und Robotern ist für den Vergleich mit dem Zeitungsartikel bedeutsam.*

The cover of the *The New Yorker* magazine, published on October 23, 2017 shows robots walking along a city street and engaging in activities only living entities perform. One robot is giving "coins" to a human beggar who is sitting on the floor with his dog. Another is holding a hot coffee in his hand while walking, implying he is drinking it. Yet another is checking his smartphone, while another is taking a robot dog for a walk. In text A, the researchers are getting robots to perform seemingly unnecessary human tasks which in themselves are not useful but which show the progress of humanoid behaviour in robots. According to text A, there is evidence that "we are getting closer to being able to design robots that are equivalent to or better than an average person." (cf. ll. 45/46). Thus robots might become more humanoid than they used to be, as exaggerated in the cartoon. According to Douglas Stephen, one research associate and participant in the robot competition, new possibilities of what you can do with a robot will be opened if it's more human-like. (cf. ll. 55–57). Both text A and the cartoon show the rapid developments in robotics.
But there is another aspect that can be found both in the article and on the cover. The only human on the cover is a beggar. This implies that in the scenario humans are

inferior to robots, which seem to rule the world. Similarly the article states that some people fear that Atlas is "the beginning of humanity's end" (ll. 4/5). While Atlas is not artificial intelligence, but simply a robot and thus not a real danger for humanity, the article still leaves this possibility open. It ends with the statement of a scientist who claims that "the machines are [not] coming for us [...] any time soon" (ll. 57/58). The reader might get the impression that robots will come for us eventually – in the long run.

3.1 *Beachten Sie, dass es in der Fragestellung explizit um die Entwicklung humanoider Roboter, also solcher Roboter, die in Form und Gestaltung an den Menschen angelehnt sind, geht. Zwar können Sie bei Ihren Beispielen auch auf Ihr Wissen zu anderen Robotern eingehen, der Unterschied sollte jedoch aus Ihrer Lösung klar hervorgehen.*

According to the quote, the Atlas robot shows that we might soon be able to develop robots that can perform any task humans can and even more.
This technological progress can be used for the benefit of mankind. Dangerous jobs can be performed by robots and in the long run, the working hours for humans can be reduced. Humanoid robots could also be used to take care of elderly people and in other jobs where we need more people.
On the other hand, humanoid robots would be able to do any job humans can do. In car manufacturing robots have already replaced many jobs. Welding robots for instance, are cheaper and more precise than humans, and if more companies pick up on this trend, it could cause massive unemployment. One could argue that new jobs are created by robotization because engineers are needed for their development, construction and maintenance. But whether this will create the same number of jobs is questionable.
Robots can also be misused. Already drones are used in war, which reduces the hesitance of politicians to enter war, because their own citizens are not being deployed. Humanoid robots could be used in a similar way. If a country is technologically advanced, the casualties will only be on the other side. Thus wars might become more likely.
To sum up, humanoid robots offer both opportunities and risks. It depends on human decisions how they will be used and how they will be built. If you combine a humanoid robot with the technology of artificial intelligence there are even more risks you have to be aware of. Although *Terminator* is just fiction, some believe the scenario presented is not that unlikely.

3.2 *Die Liste mit Filmen und Serien, die humanoide Roboter enthalten, ist quasi endlos:* Terminator, iRobot, Ghost in a Shell, Blade Runner, Stark Trek *(u.a. mit Data),* Star Wars *(mit C-3PO) und* Iron Man *sind nur einige der Produktionen, die grundsätzlichen für einen Vergleich in Frage kommen. Überlegen Sie sich daher, bevor Sie sich für ein Werk entscheiden, in welche Richtung Ihre Lösung gehen soll. Die Aufgabenstellung fragt explizit nach dem Nutzen der Roboter. Daher ist ein Vergleich mit* Terminator *schwieriger zu beschreiben als etwa mit* Iron Man, *da für Tony Stark der*

*Nutzen seiner Roboter (er hat nicht nur einen Iron Man-Anzug, sondern auch ferngesteuerte Roboter gebaut) überwiegt, während bei* Terminator *der eigentliche Nutzen der Roboter (Menschen als Teil eines Verteidigungssystems im Kriegsfall zu schützen) nicht mehr wirksam ist.*

*In der Aufgabenstellung wird nach humanoiden Robotern gefragt, d. h. Sie können sich für einen Vergleich mit einer künstlichen Intelligenz entscheiden, es muss sich jedoch nicht um eine sogenannte AI handeln. Umgekehrt eignet sich eine reine AI, wie etwa im Film* Her *dargestellt, nicht da Samantha nicht in Form eines Roboters existiert.*

One quality of Atlas built by Boston Dynamics is that he is a better version of older attempts to build humanoid robots, as displayed by his backflip ability. This brings to mind the movie *Ex-Machina*, in which Nathan Bateman creates several versions of a human-like robot, trying to reach the point where it is indiscernible from humans.

Nathan, the CEO of a Google-like company, is secretly building female robots in a high security area at his remote home. This process results in Ava, a robot that develops self-consciousness, but also a desire to escape and the cunning to manipulate its captors.

In contrast to Ava, Atlas has no artificial intelligence. That means it cannot develop its own programming. While it is more humanlike in form and it has physical abilities similar to those of a human, it can not think on its own. All its actions have to be programmed and it is not capable of "learning" or developing.

While Atlas is not AI, there is a lot of research that has been done on robots and computer programs that can learn and develop on their own. Even today things like welding robots in the auto industry already have AI and are thus able to learn from their mistakes and adapt accordingly. The more robots are able to adapt their programming, the more likely it is that we will lose control of them, as they might one day develop their own self-consciousness.

3.3 *Vergessen Sie nicht, Atlas in Ihren Artikel einzubeziehen. Diesen zeigten die Erfinder zunächst nur über Twitter und nur in einem verlinkten Video. Dennoch erhielten sie so eine große Aufmerksamkeit, da sich die Innovation rasend schnell über die sozialen Medien verbreitete. Lesen Sie sich bei den Aufgaben auch den Kontext immer genau durch. Dieser kann oft als Aufhänger oder im Schluss der Argumentation genutzt werden, um einen ansprechenden, überzeugenden Text zu verfassen. In dieser Aufgabe erscheint Ihr Beitrag auf der Seite eines internationalen Wettbewerb für Robotertechnologie.*

**Why you should post about science on the internet**

When the video of Atlas, a newly developed humanized robot, was posted on Twitter, the reactions on the internet were stark and emotional. Someone posted, "we dead", which suggests that the future of humans is being endangered by robots. But why does a scientific research company such as Boston Dynamics publish such a success on a common platform as Twitter? Wouldn't it make more sense to use a scientific platform such as a science journal?

One of the major advantages of spreading information via the internet is that you can reach a large audience quickly. The internet is quite democratic in that everybody has access to a wide variety of information from different sources. People can share their opinions via online posts to make up their minds on a certain issue which may be inspirational for the inventors. The internet can also accelerate the development of new devices because scientists can exchange information instantly.
Users of technological devices can overcome their fear of new inventions when they get a glimpse of their development. They get informed about new gadgets and find out how to use them, which is good advertisement. For more complex inventions like the humanoid robot Atlas the huge number of clicks may result in more investors as the company and its invention reach a large audience.
Thus it makes sense for you to post about your robot and about the competition on Twitter, Facebook, Instagram and any other channel you use. The official hashtag is #IRC2019.

## Prüfungsteil 2: Sprachmittlung

### Aufgabenstellung 2.1

*Diese Aufgabe erfordert von Ihrer Seite eine Textzusammenfassung. Der Text ist leicht verständlich – die größere Herausforderung ist jedoch eine sinnvolle Strukturierung Ihrer Lösung. Die Informationen zu Mealsaver sind im Originaltext recht verstreut. Markieren Sie sich daher beim ersten Lesen alle wichtigen Informationen zum Unternehmen und zur App. Überlegen Sie dann, wie man die einzelnen Aspekte strukturieren kann. Wichtig sind das Ziel des Unternehmens, die Funktionsweise der App, die Hintergründe zum Unternehmen und den teilnehmenden Restaurants und wie das Abholen und Bezahlen für den Nutzer funktioniert. Da Ihre Lösung in Form eines Blogeintrags geschrieben sein soll, kann Ihr Text auch Umgangssprache enthalten.*

**Too good to be thrown away – How food waste can be avoided**

In Germany more than 18 million tonnes of food are thrown away annually. Most of the nourishment that is destroyed is still edible, it is just disposed of because it won't be fresh the following day or it will soon expire.
The Berlin start-up company EatUp offers an app called Mealsaver to do something about this problem. People can choose between 150 restaurants, bakeries and cafés in Berlin, and 25 in Hamburg and the figures are still increasing (you probably can use it in other large cities soon). On the app users can see a list with all the participating shops and restaurants nearby, they get some information about the food that can be found in the boxes, they can order online and pay via PayPal. The customers receive a virtual voucher to collect their order. The average price of a meal is two to four Euros of which one Euro is transferred to EatUp. The packaging also contributes to the protection of the environment, because the meals are sold in biodegradable boxes offered to the restaurants by the start-up business.

The app sometimes still has trouble with loading the map and tracking where you are correctly. In that case just try closing the app. Another disadvantage is that most restaurants don't offer their leftovers before nine in the evening, which is quite late to eat dinner, but sandwiches and bakery products are available earlier.

**Aufgabenstellung 2.2**

*In dieser Aufgabe sollen Sie eine E-Mail verfassen. Dazu gehört eine passende Betreffzeile sowie Anrede und Schlussformel. Da Sie an eine Freundin oder einen Freund schreiben, sollte die Nachricht in Umgangssprache gehalten sein. Binden Sie in der Einleitung den Kontext in Ihre E-Mail mit ein.*

From: MichaM@gmx.de
To: JennyBaker@talk.net
Subject: e-sport tournaments

Hi Jenny,

How are you? I'm doing great. I just got back from an e-sport tournament in Lisbon so the topic is really front and centre now. You need to write a term paper about them? Let's see if I can help fill you in.

Well, video game parties started in the 90s, as you probably know. Today they've become massively popular and professional, with the best teams and players earning millions and gaining a large following. The audience has also become huge. The venues have the atmosphere of rock concerts, because young people love to see the players compete, both in person at the arena, and online. It's become a kind of social festival as well, as young people create parties around the events.

I think a lot of older people aren't really aware of the popularity of these tournaments. I only see young people attending, mostly male. In fact, my parents have never heard of them. That is also the appeal for many young people though. They can distance themselves from their parents' world and create a parent-free zone. There is also a close bond between the audience and the players, and it's a democratic activity. With a little talent and practice, anyone can become a player. People involved can also express themselves in web videos and social media.

So basically that's it. I hope this helps you with your term paper.

Good luck and talk to you soon,

Micha

**Abiturprüfung Berlin/Brandenburg 2019**
**Englisch Leistungskurs/Erhöhtes Anforderungsniveau**

## Prüfungsteil 1: Leseverstehen und Schreiben (75 %)

Der Prüfungsteil 1 besteht aus zwei Aufgabenstellungen, von denen Sie eine zur Bearbeitung auswählen.

### Aufgabenstellung 1.1 – Tasks*

**Themenschwerpunkte:** *Aims and ambitions; The impact of the media on society; Ethnic and cultural diversity*

1 Sum up the information the text provides on Albie's interests and ambitions and his mother's reaction to them. (30 %)

2 Analyze the means used to convey Albie's father's attitude towards his son's career choice. Give evidence from the text. (30 %)

3 Choose one of the following tasks:

3.1 "What would he actually *do* for three years, apart from smoke and sleep?" (ll. 59/60)
Explain Douglas's attitude towards artists and comment on reasons for stereotyping certain groups in society. Refer to the excerpt and your knowledge of the issue. (40 %)

OR

3.2 Compare Douglas's worries about his son's future with those of another character from literature or film who is concerned about his/her children's aims and ambitions. Assess the way they deal with the situation.** (40 %)

OR

3.3 Using Albie's concept of photography as a starting point, write an article for a youth magazine in which you discuss young people's obsession with taking and sharing photos. (40 %)

* Diese Aufgabenstellung entstammt der Prüfung aus dem Bundesland Brandenburg. Aufgabenstellung 1.2 wurde in beiden Bundesländern gestellt.
** Dieser Aufgabentyp entfällt ab der Abiturprüfung 2021.

**Text** (excerpt from the novel)

**Us**
by David Nicholls

Note: *Douglas, a scientist, and his wife Connie, an artist, are on a trip with their teenage son Albie.*

[…] But now the train had finally begun to move, and Albie had switched the fearless truth-telling eye of his camera lens from his untied laces to the walls of the tunnels under east London, because you can never have enough pictures of dirty concrete.

'I hope you're going to take lots of pictures of the Eiffel Tower, Egg,' I said, in an affectionate, teasing tone. 'Me and your mother standing in front with our thumbs up?' We demonstrated. 'Or – another tip – I can put my hand out flat like this, so it looks like I'm holding it …'

'That's not photography, that's *holiday snaps*.' It seemed the tendency to wilfully misinterpret jokes was contagious. Connie winked at me and squeezed my knee beneath the table.

My son was soon to study photography on a three-year course which we were financing and although my wife, who knew about these things, insisted that he had talent, an 'eye', the fact of it filled me with an anxiety that I fought daily to suppress. At one point he had been intending to study theatre – theatre! – and at least I had managed to nip that in the bud, but now it was photography, the latest of a long series of temporary passions – 'street art', skateboarding, DJ-ing, drumming – the abandoned detritus of which cluttered cellar, attic and garage, alongside the optimistic chemistry set that I had bought and he had tossed aside, the hopeful microscope that had never been unpacked, the dusty box that offered an opportunity to 'Grow Your Own Crystals!'.

But there was no denying his enthusiasm. Albie with a camera was something to see, crouching and contorting his long body into a question mark as if playing the role of 'photographer'. Sometimes he fired off frames at arm's length, in what I believe is called 'gangster style', sometimes on tiptoe, back arched like a toreador. Initially I made the mistake of standing and grinning when the camera was produced, but soon realised that he wouldn't actually press the shutter until I'd stepped out of the frame. In fact, in all the thousands of shots that he had taken, many of them loving portraits of his mother – her eyes, her smile – alongside his usual repertoire of wet cardboard boxes and badgers hit by cars, etc., there was not a single photograph of me. Not of my face, anyway, just an extreme close-up of the back of my hand, black and white in heavy contrast, part of a college project that I later discovered was called 'Waste/Decay'.

Albie's passion for photography had been the cause of tension in other ways. I had a printer in my office, a top-of-the-range colour model whose features included glacial speed and shocking running costs. Consequently, I was more than a little annoyed to return from work one day and hear the printer grinding away. Irritably, I examined the top print of a sizeable pile of 8x10s. […]

I called Connie in. 'Have you seen Albie?'

'He's in his room. Why?'

I held up the photographs […].

'Why can't he just photograph someone's *face* for once?'

'Because he's a seventeen-year-old boy, Douglas. This is what they do.'

'I didn't. I photographed wildlife. Birds and squirrels and iron-age forts.'

'Which is why you're a biochemist and he's a photographer.'

'I wouldn't mind so much, but does he have any idea how much the cartridges cost for this thing?' […]

Soon after, Albie announced his intention to devote his life to a hobby. Why, I asked Connie, could he not study a more practical subject and do the things he enjoyed at weekends and in the evenings, like the rest of us? Because that's not how an arts-based course works, said Connie; he needs to be challenged, to develop his famous 'eye', learn to use his tools. But wouldn't it be cheaper and quicker to just read the manual? I could understand if people still used darkrooms as I had as a young man, but all of that know-how was obsolete, and how could Albie hope to excel in a field where anyone with a phone and a laptop could be broadly proficient? It wasn't even as if he wanted to be a photojournalist or a commercial photographer, taking pictures for newspapers or advertisements or catalogues. He didn't want to photograph models or weddings, athletes or lions chasing gazelles, photographs that people might pay for, he wanted to be an *artist*, to photograph burnt-out cars and bark, taking pictures at such angles that they didn't look like anything at all. What would he actually *do* for three years, apart from smoke and sleep? And what professional job could he hope for at the end of it?

'Photographer!' said Connie. 'He's going to be a photographer. […] Even if it's hard, he has to try! If he loves it, we have to let him try. Why must you always have to stomp on his dreams?'

'I've got nothing against his dreams as long as they're attainable.'

'But if they're attainable then they're not dreams!'

'And that's why it's a waste of time!' I said. 'The problem with telling people that they can do anything they want to do is that it is objectively, factually inaccurate. Otherwise the whole world would just be ballet dancers and pop stars.'

'He doesn't want to be a pop star, he wants to take photographs.'

'My point still stands. It is simply not true that you can achieve anything if you love it enough – it just isn't. Life has limitations and the sooner he faces up to this fact then the better off he'll be!'

Well, that's what I said. I believed I had my son's best interests at heart. That was why I was so vocal, because I wanted him to have a secure professional life, a good life.

Listening up in his bedroom, no doubt he had caught all of my words and none of my intention. […] *(991 words)*

*Source: Nicholls, David.* Us. *London: Hodder & Stoughton, 2015, 49–53.*

**Annotations**

l. 4 Egg: Albie's nickname

l. 15 to nip sth in the bud: to stop sth before it has an opportunity to become established

l. 17 detritus: waste, discarded matter
l. 24 toreador: torero, bullfighter
l. 34 glacial: *here:* extremely slow
l. 37 8x10: photo format
l. 58 bark: outer covering of a tree

## Aufgabenstellung 1.2 – Tasks

**Themenschwerpunkte:** *The impact of the media on society; Science and technology – visions of the future; Aims and ambitions*

1 Outline the information about digital and analog media and how they affect their users. (Text A) (30 %)

2 Analyze the cartoon (Text B) and relate its message to the arguments that David Sax makes in his article (Text A). Give evidence from both texts. (30 %)

3 Choose <u>one</u> of the following tasks:

3.1 "In contrast with the virtual 'communities' we have built online, analog actually contributes to the real places where we live." (Text A, ll. 50/51) Explain the quote and discuss the advantages and disadvantages of participating in virtual vs. real communities. Refer to the article and your knowledge of the issue. (40 %)

OR

3.2 Compare David Sax's attitude towards technology with that of a character from literature or film who uses technology differently. Assess how their attitudes affect their quality of life.* (40 %)

OR

3.3 Write a letter to the editor of The New York Times, commenting on David Sax's position on analog and digital media. Address your letter to:
The New York Times Company
620 Eighth Avenue
New York
NY 10018 (40 %)

* Dieser Aufgabentyp entfällt ab der Abiturprüfung 2021.

**Text** (excerpt from the article)

**Our Love Affair With Digital Is Over**
by David Sax

A decade ago I bought my first smartphone, a clunky little BlackBerry 8830 that came in a sleek black leather sheath. I loved that phone. I loved the way it effortlessly slid in and out of its case, loved the soft purr it emitted when an email came in, loved the silent *whoosh* of its trackball as I played Brick Breaker on the subway and the feel of its baby keys clicking under my fat thumbs. It was the world in my hands, and when I had to turn it off, I felt anxious and alone.

Like most relationships we plunge into with hearts aflutter, our love affair with digital technology promised us the world: more friends, money and democracy! Free music, news and same-day shipping of paper towels! A laugh a minute, and a constant party at our fingertips.

Many of us bought into the fantasy that digital made everything better. We surrendered to this idea, and mistook our dependence for romance, until it was too late.

Today, when my phone is on, I feel anxious and count down the hours to when I am able to turn it off and truly relax. The love affair I once enjoyed with digital technology is over – and I know I'm not alone.

Ten years after the iPhone first swept us off our feet, the growing mistrust of computers in both our personal lives and the greater society we live in is inescapable. This publishing season is flush with books raising alarms about digital technology's pernicious effects on our lives: what smartphones are doing to our children; how Facebook and Twitter are eroding our democratic institutions; and the economic effects of tech monopolies.

A recent Pew Research Center survey noted that more than 70 percent of Americans were worried about automation's impact on jobs, while just 21 percent of respondents to a Quartz survey said they trust Facebook with their personal information. Nearly half of millennials worry about the negative effects of social media on their mental and physical health, according to the American Psychiatric Association.

So what now?

As much as we might fantasize about it, we probably won't delete our social media accounts and toss our phones in the nearest body of water. What we can do is to restore some sense of balance over our relationship with digital technology, and the best way to do that is with analog: the ying to digital's yang.

Thankfully, the analog world is still here, and not only is it surviving but, in many cases, it is thriving. Sales of old-fashioned print books are up for the third year in a row, according to the Association of American Publishers, while ebook sales have been declining. Independent bookstores have been steadily expanding for several years. Vinyl records have witnessed a decade-long boom in popularity (more than 200,000 newly pressed records are sold each week in the United States), while sales of instant-film cameras, paper notebooks, board games and Broadway tickets are all growing again.

This surprising reversal of fortune for these apparently "obsolete" analog technologies is too often written off as nostalgia for a predigital time. But younger consumers who never owned a turntable and have few memories of life before the internet drive most of the current interest in analog, and often include those who work in Silicon Valley's most powerful companies.

Analog, although more cumbersome and costly than its digital equivalents, provides a richness of experience that is unparalleled with anything delivered through a screen. People are buying books because a book engages nearly all of their senses, from the smell of the paper and glue to the sight of the cover design and weight of the pages read […].

In contrast with the virtual "communities" we have built online, analog actually contributes to the real places where we live. I have become friendly with Ian Cheung, the appropriately opinionated owner of June Records, up the street from my home in Toronto. I benefit not only from the tax revenues that June Records contributes as a local business (paving the roads, paying my daughter's teachers) but also from living nearby. Like the hardware store, Italian grocer and butcher on the same block, the brick and mortar presence of June adds to my neighborhood's sense of place […] and gives me a feeling of belonging. I also have no doubts that, unlike Twitter, Ian would immediately kick out any Nazi or raving misogynist who started ranting inside his store.

Analog excels particularly well at encouraging human interaction, which is crucial to our physical and mental well-being. The dynamic of a teacher working in a classroom full of students has not only proven resilient, but has outperformed digital learning experiments time and again. Digital may be extremely efficient in transferring pure information, but learning happens best when we build upon the relationships between students, teachers and their peers.

We do not face a simple choice of digital *or* analog. That is the false logic of the binary code that computers are programmed with, which ignores the complexity of life in the real world. Instead, we are faced with a decision of how to strike the right balance between the two. If we keep that in mind, we are taking the first step toward a healthy relationship with all technology, and, most important, one another. *(888 words)*

*Sax, David. "Our Love Affair With Digital Is Over." The New York Times. Nov. 18, 2017. From The New York Times* 

**Annotations**

| | |
|---|---|
| l. 4 | trackball: device consisting of a small ball that you roll with your fingers to control the movement of a pointer on a computer screen |
| l. 7 | aflutter: nervously excited |
| l. 11 | to buy into something: *here:* to believe something |
| ll. 18/19 | pernicious: causing great harm or damage often in a way that is not easily seen or noticed |
| l. 25 | millennials: name for the generation born in the 1980s and 1990s |
| l. 31 | ying … yang: *here:* seemingly opposite or contrary forces that may actually be complementary and interdependent |
| l. 42 | to drive: *here:* to be the moving force behind something |
| ll. 43/44 | Silicon Valley: center of high-tech industry and development near San Francisco |
| l. 45 | cumbersome: slow and complicated |
| l. 52 | June Records: shop that sells vinyl records |
| ll. 55/56 | brick and mortar: *here:* relating to a traditional business serving customers in a shop |
| l. 58 | misogynist: person who hates or humiliates women |
| l. 66 | binary: relating to a system that uses only 0 and 1 |

**Text B** (Cartoon)

**Vintage social networking**
By John Atkinson

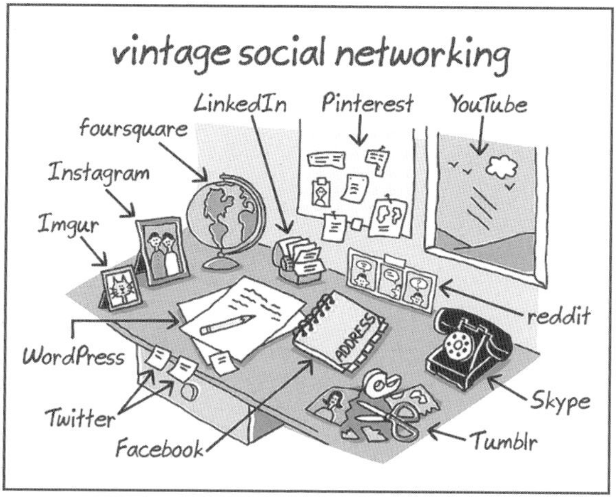


*© John Atkinson, Wrong Hands*

**Annotations**
**heading:**
vintage: *here:* classic, old-fashioned

**cartoon:**
foursquare: app that makes recommendations about nearby restaurants, bars, sights, etc.
Imgur: community site where pictures and humor are shared
LinkedIn: social network for professional contacts and exchange
reddit: website which collects and shares news, lists, ratings, etc.
Tumblr: blogging platform where you can post texts, pictures, etc.
WordPress: weblog where people exchange texts

## Prüfungsteil 2: Sprachmittlung (25 %)

Der Prüfungsteil 2 besteht aus zwei Aufgabenstellungen, von denen Sie eine zur Bearbeitung auswählen.

### Aufgabenstellung 2.1 – Tasks

**Themenschwerpunkte:** *Science and technology – visions of the future; The impact of the media on society; Aims and ambitions*

You are taking part in a European youth project on "Humans and Machines throughout the Centuries". You have come across the following article by Sven Stillich. Write an article for the project website, outlining the information on the development of the relationship between humans and computers provided in the text at hand.

**Text** (Auszug aus dem Artikel)

**Computerspiele nahmen uns die Angst vor Maschinen – Level 5**
**Von der Bedrohung zum täglichen Begleiter – wie uns Computerspiele die Angst vor den Maschinen nahmen.**
Von Sven Stillich

Im Oktober 1958 findet im Atomforschungszentrum Brookhaven National Laboratory auf Long Island ein Tag der offenen Tür statt. Vor einem Oszilloskop, auf dessen Bildschirm ein Punkt über eine Linie in der Mitte des Monitors hin- und herhüpft, bildet sich eine Schlange. Ganz vorn stehen zwei Besucher mit einem Metallkästchen in der Hand, über dessen Knopf und Knauf sie sich den Punkt gegenseitig zuspielen. Sie spielen auf dem Bildschirm einer Maschine gegeneinander Tennis – und damit in diesem Augenblick eines der ersten Videospiele überhaupt. Es ist einer der entscheidendsten Mensch-Maschinen-Momente der Geschichte.

Der Name des Spiels ist „Tennis for Two", und erfunden hat es der Physiker William Higinbotham, der früher in Los Alamos Zeitschaltkreise für die ersten Atombomben gebaut hat. Für seinen Erfinder ist es mehr als nur ein Spiel. Er hat es entworfen, um den Besuchern die Hemmungen vor den Maschinen des Labors zu nehmen. Immerhin geht es dort um die Zukunft der zivilen Atomenergie.

Ein Vierteljahrhundert später stehen Videospiele wie „Pong", „Pac-Man" oder „Donkey Kong" in vielen Kneipen und sind sogar in Wohnzimmern populär. Im Jahr 1981 wird Thomas Gottschalks erste Show in der ARD ausgestrahlt. Sie heißt Telespiele und führt ihre Zuschauer an die Spielmaschinen heran. […]

Damals, vor der Verbreitung des Personal Computers, gibt es Maschinen zum Spielen und Maschinen zum Arbeiten. Außerhalb der Universitäten sind diese beiden Welten strikt getrennt. Im Jahr 1985 kann man noch Games wie das gerade frisch erschienene „Tetris" gut finden und gleichzeitig den Computer am Arbeitsplatz verteufeln.

Genau das taten auch die meisten: „74 Prozent der erwachsenen Deutschen haben noch nie einen Computer bedient“, steht damals in der „Zeit“, und: „51 Prozent wollen das auch gar nicht.“ Bei der Frage, ob sie sich neue Techniken aneignen wollten, sagen 23 Prozent „auf keinen Fall“. Computer seien „Jobkiller“ auf „Vernichtungsfeldzug“, schreibt der „Stern“. Sie sind mächtig, nutzlos und böse. Als der Heimcomputer Commodore 64 zum Verkaufsschlager wird, urteilt die Stiftung Warentest: „Wir suchten verzweifelt nach sinnvollen Einsatzmöglichkeiten. Die Enttäuschung ist vorprogrammiert.“ Was da aber auch steht: 70 Prozent der Käufer nutzen den C64 zum Spielen. Genauer: Die Kinder der Käufer tun das. [...]

Es folgen zwei einschneidende Entwicklungen: Kinder, vor allem Jungs, schließen Freundschaft mit dem Computer, ihr nächster Rechner wird meist ein Amiga sein. Mit ihm haben sie ein Feld erschlossen, auf das ihre Eltern ihnen nicht folgen wollen. Denn auch 1994 – das ist erst gut 20 Jahre her – hat die Hälfte der erwachsenen Deutschen noch Angst vor dem Computer; ein Drittel von ihnen hat noch nie im Leben einen Rechner bedient.

Doch allmählich folgt der zweite Schritt: Die Grenze zwischen Spaß- und Arbeitsmaschine löst sich auf. Computer werden zugänglicher, und bald schon spielt sich beides auf demselben Bildschirm ab. Seitdem wird derselbe Rechner sowohl im Beruf als auch in der Freizeit eingesetzt [...].

Das Computerspiel passt blendend zum Lebensgefühl Ende der Neunzigerjahre und übernimmt ihre Ideologie: Sei schneller, sei kaltblütiger, sei dominant! Du bist „Need for Speed“, du bist „Doom“, du bist „Civilization“! [...]

Zehn Jahre später macht Nintendos Spielkonsole Wii den menschlichen Körper zum Eingabegerät und ringt auch dem letzten Joystickmuffel ein verschwitztes Lächeln ab. „Wir sind die Roboter“ ist angesagt, die Angst vor der Knechtschaft überwunden. Darauf folgt die Gehirnjogging-Mode. Computer sind nun gut und nützlich. Wenn man einer Maschine zutraut, die eigene Hirnleistung zu steigern, hat man keine Berührungsängste mehr. Die Maschine wird zum Trainer und Mentor. Das hatte sich William Higinbotham 1958 nicht träumen lassen. [...] *(563 Wörter)*

*Quelle: Wirtschaftsmagazin brand eins 07/2015, Text Sven Stillich*

**Annotationen**

Z. 2 Oszilloskop: elektronisches Messgerät, das elektrische Spannung auf einem Bildschirm sichtbar macht

Z. 16 Thomas Gottschalk: bekannter deutscher Radio- / Fernsehmoderator und Schauspieler

Z. 47 „Wir sind die Roboter“: Hit der Band Kraftwerk, Pioniere des Elektropop, vom Album „Die Mensch-Maschine“

## Aufgabenstellung 2.2 – Tasks

**Themenschwerpunkte:** *Aims and ambitions; The impact of the media on society*

An English-speaking friend of yours is doing research on artists in a digital world. Write her/him an email outlining the information about "Barbara" and her intentions.

**Text** (Auszug aus dem Artikel)

### Anonym erfolgreich: Streetart-Künstlerin „Barbara."

Ihre Werke werden ebenso gefeiert wie prämiert – aber kaum jemand weiß, wer sie ist. „Barbara." – so die offizielle Schreibweise – hat es in den vergangenen beiden Jahren zur vielleicht meistbeachteten Streetart-Künstlerin Deutschlands gebracht. Ihre Identität hält sie jedoch bewusst geheim. Und das soll so bleiben.

Ihr Spezialgebiet: Die Bearbeitung von Schildern – oder die Reaktion darauf. Bekannt wurde sie mit der Botschaft „Dieser Befehlston verletzt meine Gefühle". Diese hing unter einem Straßenschild mit der Aufschrift „Bekleben verboten". Das Typische für Barbaras Streetart: Weiße Schrift auf schwarzem Grund. Manchmal überklebt die Künstlerin auch offizielle Schilder. Statt mutmaßlich „Betreten verboten! Lebensgefahr!" ist dann etwa „Das Leben ist verboten! Lebensgefahr!" zu lesen.

Für Aufsehen sorgte jüngst eine Open-Air-Ausstellung mit rund 100 ihrer gesellschaftskritischen Werke am Boxhagener Platz in Berlin. Glaubt man ihrem Facebook-Auftritt, war sie sogar persönlich dort. Aber auch hinterher ist niemand schlauer, wer sich hinter dem Pseudonym denn nun verbirgt. Eine Frau, ein Mann? Oder doch ein Kollektiv? […]

Barbara sagt, sie wolle in der Anonymität bleiben, um sich weiterhin frei bewegen zu können. Interviews mit ihr sind selten – und wenn, dann nie persönlich, auch nicht am Telefon. Per Facebook-Chat macht sie Ausnahmen. Dem „Tagesspiegel" verriet sie, dass sie mittlerweile in Heidelberg lebe, sich aber immer wieder auch in Berlin aufhalte. Ihr Geschlecht gibt sie mit „Mensch" an. Ihr Alter? „Ich bin jünger als Angela Merkel, aber älter als Justin Bieber." Also zwischen 22 und 61. Mehr ist nicht zu erfahren.

Dass angeblich nicht einmal ihr Freundeskreis von ihrer geheimen Passion weiß, könnte ins Bild passen. „Ich muss darauf achten, mich nicht in widersprüchliche Angaben zu meinem Zeitvertreib zu verstricken", sagt die Künstlerin in der neuesten Ausgabe der „Grazia".

Als ihre Straßenkunst jüngst mit dem Grimme-Online-Award ausgezeichnet wurde, gab es Gerüchte: Kommt Barbara persönlich zur Preisverleihung? Die Künstlerin schickte eine Stellvertreterin.

Selbst beim Kölner Verlag Bastei Lübbe, der einen Sammelband ihrer Werke veröffentlichte, weiß niemand, wer Barbara wirklich ist. „Alles lief inkognito ab, sie wollte sich auch uns nicht offenbaren, um ihre Kunstfigur aufrechterhalten zu können", erzählt Referentin Sarah Fusshoeller. […]

Barbaras Erfolgsgeschichte hat ihren Ursprung in der Kindheit. Ihr (oder sein?) Opa habe ihr bei einem Spaziergang die Symbolik eines an die Wand geschmierten Hakenkreuzes erklärt, sagte sie (oder er). Als der Großvater es mit Spucke und Taschentuch nicht entfernen konnte, habe sie beim nächsten Spaziergang einfach einen Zettel mit einer lachenden Sonne über das Nazi-Symbol geklebt.

Mittlerweile ist Barbara ein Internet-Hit. Rund 460 000 Menschen folgen ihrem Facebook-Profil, auch auf Instagram ist Barbara aktiv. Ihre Themen sind grün und linksorientiert, ihre Werke richten sich gegen Homophobie und Hooligans, prangern Missstände etwa in der Agrarpolitik an.

Sie sollen aber vor allem ein Zeichen gegen Fremdenhass und Rechtspopulismus setzen. „Ich finde es erschreckend, dass so viele Menschen nicht aus der Geschichte gelernt haben und sich von rechten Hetzern mit plumpen ausländerfeindlichen Parolen vergiften lassen“, sagte Barbara der „Grazia“. […]

Für Katja Glaser, die sich in ihrer Dissertation an der Universität Siegen mit der Wechselwirkung von Streetart und sozialen Medien beschäftigt hat, ist klar, dass es das Phänomen „Barbara.“ ohne die sozialen Medien gar nicht geben würde. „Für ihre Art von Kunst ist sie auf die Straße ja eigentlich nicht angewiesen. Da ist das Internet der viel größere Resonanzraum und Multiplikator.“ Die Streetart-Szene an sich habe auch schon vor Barbara genügend Aufmerksamkeit erfahren. „Sie oder er spricht aber auch einen anderen Rezipientenkreis an […].“ […] *(562 Wörter)*

*Quelle: „Anonym erfolgreich: Streetart-Künstlerin ‚Barbara.‘“. 7. Juli 2016. Axel Springer SE – DIE WELT*

**Annotationen**

Z. 18 Tagesspiegel: überregionale Tageszeitung aus Berlin
Z. 21 Justin Bieber: populärer kanadischer Sänger
Z. 26 Grazia: Magazin mit kulturellen und Alltagsthemen
Z. 27 Grimme-Online-Award: Auszeichnung für publizistische Qualität im Internet
Z. 47 Dissertation: wissenschaftliche Arbeit zur Erlangung eines Doktortitels

# Lösungsvorschläge

## Prüfungsteil 1: Leseverstehen und Schreiben

### Aufgabenstellung 1.1

1 *Die Vorgehensweise bei der Textproduktion* summary *dürfte Ihnen bekannt sein. Wichtig ist bei dieser konkreten Aufgabenstellung, dass nicht der gesamte Auszug zusammengefasst wird, sondern nur die genannten Teilinformationen zu Albies Interessen und der Reaktion seiner Mutter gefordert werden. Sie müssen beim Lesen der Aufgabenstellung erfassen, dass die Position des Ich-Erzählers für diese Aufgabe keine Rolle spielt.*

Albie, a 17-year-old teenager, loves taking photos. He does not do holiday snaps or pictures of people or buildings, however, because he wants to be a real artist. That is why he has enrolled on a three-year course to study photography. He took up numerous interests like theatre, skateboarding, DJ-ing or drumming in the past, but did not pursue them further.
Nevertheless, Albie has already done a photography project at school called "Waste/Decay", so he seems rather determined to pursue this dream. He is so lost in his artistic self-expression that he is oblivious to any of the financial aspects of his hobby, since he used his father's cost-intensive printer for his photographs.
His mother, an artist herself, is sure that her son has got a talent for photography. That is why she defends Albie against his father's disapproval. She understands what drives him to take pictures of wet cardboard or dirty concrete walls. She also tries to convince her husband not to stomp on his dreams and allow him to pursue what is important to him.

2 *In der Analysefrage kommt nun die Position des Vaters zu den Karriereplänen seines Sohnes zum Tragen. Am besten beginnen Sie immer mit einer Deutungshypothese, die Sie dann mithilfe Ihrer Analyse überzeugend beweisen können. Diese Aufgabe kann nicht erschöpfend ohne die Betrachtung der Erzählperspektive und der Darstellungsform des inneren Monologs gelöst werden. Diese beziehen sich auf den gesamten Auszug und sind deshalb besonders aussagekräftig.*
*Durch die Ich-Erzählung stehen neben impliziten Mitteln, welche die Meinung des Vaters zu Albies Lebensweg ausdrücken (z. B. die Witze, die er über Albies Leidenschaft macht, Z. 4–7, oder seine Wut über die verbrauchte Druckertinte, Z. 33–46), auch explizite Aussagen dazu im Text. So spricht der Vater etwa konkret über seine Ängste (Z. 13) und Wünsche (Z. 74–76).*
*Anhand des inneren Monologs (Z. 47–61) wird deutlich, dass dem Vater schlicht das Verständnis für den Lebensstil eines Künstlers fehlt, aber auch, dass er seine Frau und seinen Sohn heimlich um ihr Verhältnis beneidet (Z. 21–32). Der Erzähler beschreibt in einem inneren Monolog, wie Albie seine Mutter regelmäßig in „loving*

*portraits" (Z. 27) festhält, während er selbst in den Bildern für gewöhnlich gar nicht auftaucht. Das Unverständnis für das Künstlerdasein zeigt sich unter anderem in den vielen (teils rhetorischen) Fragen, die der Ich-Erzähler im inneren Monolog stellt.*

Albie's father strongly disapproves of his son's future plans.
The choice of the first-person perspective is to help us understand why. As readers, we exclusively find out about Douglas's feelings and thoughts. He seems to be talking to us, and we serve as a kind of confidant to whom he lets on about his true motives. He wants the reader to side with him in his negative attitude towards art as a career choice.
Douglas feels helpless. He seems to believe that it is two – his wife and his son – against one – himself – in his family. He tries to convince us in his interior monologues, in which he is looking for a like-minded companion to share his opinion. He is "filled […] with an anxiety that [he fights] daily to suppress" (l. 13) – something that he tells neither his wife nor his son.
He also asks a lot of rhetorical questions, such as "What would he actually *do* for three years, apart from smoke and sleep?" (ll. 59/60) or "what professional job could he hope for at the end of it?" (ll. 60/61). These thoughts indirectly express his fear and uneasiness about his son's future. He also turns ironic when he states that "you can never have enough pictures of dirty concrete" (l. 3), a reaction commonly found amongst people who feel misunderstood and helpless.
His choice of words when talking about art and photography in particular also reveal that he does not understand his son's ambition to be an artist. To him, art is equivalent to self-inflicted poverty. It is Albie's parents who are "financing" the course (l. 12), the "cartridges cost" a lot (l. 45), it would "be cheaper […] to just read the manual" (ll. 51/52) and he wants his son to take "photographs that people might pay for" (l. 57). He also uses quite a lot of derogatory expressions regarding the arts or artists in general and contrasts them with what he believes to be a proper job. He wants his son to study "a more practical subject" (l. 48), as in photography "anyone […] could be broadly proficient" (l. 54). He thinks Albie is "devoting his life to a hobby" (l. 47) and would be better off with a "secure professional life" (l. 75). To him, his son's pictures do not "look like anything at all" (l. 59). Although he does not say this directly to his son, but only to his wife Connie, Albie is "listening up in his bedroom [and catches] all of [his] words" (l. 77). This must be very demotivating for him.
Douglas's disapproval is also expressed in the enumeration of Albie's former passions like DJ-ing, drumming and theatre (cf. ll. 14–16), which make photography seem to be another brief passion in a whole row of fleeting pastimes.
Yet Douglas does acknowledge Albie's "enthusiasm" (l. 21). He thinks that Albie with a camera is "something to see" (ll. 21/22) and envies Connie because she frequently shows up in Albie's pictures. He feels hurt that his son has "not a single photograph of" (l. 29) him.
Is Douglas also envious of his son? The excerpt does not allow any speculation here. However, despite Douglas's constant grumbling, which makes him rather charmless, it is quite likely that he will finally learn to accept his son's career choice.

3.1 *Die Vorgehensweise bei der Bearbeitung dieser Aufgabenstellung ist immer gleich: Geben Sie zunächst das Zitat mit eigenen Worten wieder. Suchen Sie sich dann gute Argumente im Text, die Sie erörtern können. Vergessen Sie nicht die außertextlichen Bezüge, die sich in der Formulierung „your knowledge of the issue" verbergen und zeigen sollen, dass Sie auch über den Auszug hinaus eigene Überzeugungen zum Thema formulieren können.*

Douglas boils all his disapproval of his son's career choice down to one argument: "What would he actually *do* for three years, apart from smoke and sleep?" (ll. 59/60). He is absolutely convinced that Albie studying photography would be equivalent to hanging around lazily, living for the moment and waiting for the monthly cheque paid by his parents. Sleep and smoke metaphorically stand for the pastimes associated with indolent students who do not want to study or work hard or strive for success, money or reputation. Douglas's mind obviously conjures up pictures of excessive parties late after midnight, smoke-filled bars and messy dormitories with would-be artists sleeping the day away. In a way, he might be right. There is no denying the fact that studying the arts is different from studying sciences. Douglas, as a biochemist, is most certainly a man of facts and figures. One plus one equals two. If you come up with another result, you have failed. But how can you measure failure or success in photography? It seems to be a matter of taste or of one's subjective point of view as to what is right and what is wrong. Douglas is, of course, also worried about his son's odds of making a living from exhibiting his photos. He sees photography as a hobby and he would not mind Albie doing that as such. However, he has a problem with accepting that his son would be on shaky ground for a long time and probably financially depenent on his parents for even longer.

But where do such clichés come from? Why are we so ready to stereotype people or certain groups in society?

One reason is very likely the fact that people reject what they do not know. It is much easier to say *I don't like it* or *I don't accept it* instead of *I need to find out more about it.* We probably also 'learn' from parents and family. They may pass certain clichés down to us and we do not question them because it provides us with a feeling of belonging.

Too many people also rely on hearsay. How often do we hear others say *I heard that on a TV programme* or *I read that in the paper.* We tend to jump to conclusions too quickly. Any stereotyped group in society could serve as an example here: refugees, homosexuals, you name it.

Douglas's wife Connie is an artist herself. Does this mean Douglas speaks from experience? Maybe he is the only breadwinner in the family and that is why he is so sure Albie will not be financially successful either. However, this does not give him the right to judge others by his own standards.

If we want to stop stereotyping people, we need to get to know them. Go out and meet people who are different. Ask them about their lives and learn to understand what drives them. It can also enrich your personal life and broaden your horizons.

3.2 *Zur Bearbeitung der Aufgabenstellung eignen sich viele ‚Klassiker', die im Englischunterricht eine Rolle spielen, angefangen bei Shakespeares* Romeo and Juliet, *deren Eltern andere Pläne mit ihren Kindern haben als deren gemeinsame Eheschließung, über* The Graduate, *in dem der Weg des jungen Benjamin exakt von seinen Eltern vorgezeichnet ist und in dem dieser für seine Pläne mit dem Elternhaus brechen muss, bis hin zu* Bend it like Beckham, *in dem die traditionellen Vorgaben der pakistanischen Eltern zunächst die Karriere der Tochter als Profifußballerin verhindern. Auch* East is East *und dessen Fortsetzung* West is West, My Big Fat Greek Wedding, Dead Poets' Society *und* The Hate U Give *wären zum Vergleich geeignet.*
*Beispielhaft soll hier an Stephen Daldrys Film* Billy Elliot *(2000) der Umgang mit der Aufgabe gezeigt werden.*

Douglas's son Albie wants to study photography. In his father's eyes, this is a waste of time, since he sees no future in being an artist. To him, it is a profession that means permanent financial struggle and raised eyebrows when you tell others about it.
Parents no doubt have a right to be worried about their children's career choices. They only want the best for their children, but, admittedly, there is also often a certain feeling of failure or shame which arises from the notorious thought of "what will neighbours, colleagues, grandparents etc. say?".
This is especially important when tradition or religion are involved. Think of *Billy Elliot*, for example. The 11-year-old main-character Billy from the north of England wants to be a ballet dancer. His father, a coal miner, actually sends him to boxing classes, but Billy discovers his passion for dancing when he watches the girls practising in the same gym. Like Douglas, Billy's father Jackie strongly disapproves of his son's hobby. The fact that Billy is much younger than Albie allows his father to simply forbid him to dance. He also sees this 'ballet whim' as something that will soon pass. Both fathers obviously try to force their children into the kind of hobby they feel is socially appropriate, with Douglas giving his son a microscope and a box to grow his own crystals, whereas Jackie wants his son to be a 'real man' who can defend himself. Albie seems to at least have the chance to try things out when we find out about all the equipment gathering dust in the attic of his parents' house. Billy only meets hostility, prejudice and ridicule when he tells his father or his brother about his passion. Both boys have an advocate to speak up for them, however. Albie's mother, Connie, an artist herself, sees her son's talent and defends it against her husband's disapproval. Billy, on the other hand, has his ballet teacher Mrs Wilkinson, who tries to convince his father of his son's talent.
The excerpt does not reveal whether Douglas finally gives in regarding Albie's career choice, but Billy's father does. When he sees his son dancing one day, he begins to understand. After overcoming a few more obstacles his emotional and financial support mean that Billy can attend a famous London ballet school. Since Douglas has also watched his son taking photos and finds that "he is something to see", he might learn to accept it, too.
Parents should certainly not jump on any bandwagon their children want to ride, but like Billy's and hopefully also Albie's father, they ought to listen to them and support them in their efforts to find their perfect career.

3.3 *Die Aufgabenstellung verlangt, dass Sie Albies Vorstellung eines guten Fotos miteinbeziehen. Da er eine fiktive Person ist, bietet es sich an, seinen Namen selbst gar nicht zu erwähnen, aber die Idee, nicht alles und jedes sofort ‚abzulichten', sondern auf den geeigneten Moment zu warten und den richtigen Winkel und Bildausschnitt zu finden, als sein Konzept zu verarbeiten. Für den weiteren Verlauf Ihres Kommentars können Sie sicher aus dem Vollen schöpfen, was Beispiele aus dem täglichen Leben angeht.*

**We have become image addicts**

'When did we last meet?' 'Can't remember, but wait, I'll have a look at my smartphone. I took a snap of the delicious pizza we had then. Ah, see, it was on February 27!'

Does this conversation sound familiar to you? Well, it probably does, since we have become obsessed with taking and sharing photos. Plus, we all feel like professional photographers because we have installed filters and apps that get the best out of our snapshots. What we ignore is the fact that a good photograph needs more than the right filter – it is also about finding the right moment, the right angle and the right perspective to give your picture meaning. You need to have an "eye" to create photographs rather than just take "snaps".

It is hardly a decade ago that you had to carry a real camera around when you wanted to take home memories of holidays, weddings or family gatherings, etc. Today, taking photos is easy, involves no effort at all and a camera is always at hand. When the big companies advertise their latest smartphone model they often emphasise the features of the camera installed rather than talking about the communicative functions of the gadget.

Our generation has grown up with having our pictures taken 24/7 – in an instant we can retrieve memories of our childhood and the years after. Now, as teenagers or young adults we use social networks like Instagram for self-promotion. With optimised images of ourselves rendered by apps like Photoshop, we tell the world how important, beautiful and successful we are. Pictures speak louder than words. Look where I'm spending my holidays! See how handsome my boyfriend is! Envy me for the awesome life I am leading! We are creating a fake world of superlatives where everything is positive. However, we have to be aware of that development because there is a dark side to it, too. No-one can trust pictures any longer, but they still show an illusion that is convincing enough to children and teenagers whose self-esteem is not strong enough to say "I am what I am".

We are flooding the Net with billions of pictures and still don't know who is going to see them. Our intention is to stay in touch with our friends and family, but are we always aware of who we are sharing our data with? Do we violate people's right to privacy?

Obsession is defined as something that you think too much about in a way that is not normal. Let us try to get back to normal. Next time you take or share a photo, think first before you click.

## Aufgabenstellung 1.2

1 *Diese Aufgabenstellung führt im Prinzip dazu, dass Sie den ganzen Text zusammenfassen. Trotzdem bietet es sich an, zunächst eine Tabelle mit „analog" und „digital" anzulegen, um nicht den Eindruck entstehen zu lassen, dass Sie kritiklos alles übernehmen. Sie können Ihre eigene Zusammenfassung gut strukturieren, indem Sie erst alles Analoge und dann alles Digitale aufzeigen. Das bricht mit der Struktur des Textes und unterstützt den Eigenanteil in Ihren Ausführungen.*

In his article "Our Love Affair With Digital Is Over" from *The New York Times,* David Sax calls on his readers to find a healthy balance between the digital and the analog world.
When smartphones came out, everyone loved the feeling of literally holding the world in their hands. They promised free access to nearly everything, from music and overnight delivery to more friends and unlimited information. Digital devices would make everything better.
However, people soon found out that they had become dependent on their smartphones. Studies now reveal that a growing number of Americans are acting quite reluctantly towards the digital world. They are concerned about harmful effects on their children, their country's economy and democratic institutions. They are afraid of automation threatening their jobs, and even Facebook has fallen out of favour, as they are suspected violating their customers' privacy.
Luckily, the analog world has not only survived but is still very popular, even among young digital natives, who cannot be blamed for being nostalgic.
The article reports that the sales figures of vinyl records, instant film cameras or print books have been rising in recent years. Customers appreciate the sensory potential of articles from the analog world. Sax himself is convinced that shops and local businesses contribute a great deal to the communities they are located in. As far as teaching is concerned, he explains that although digital media sometimes might be more efficient, the analog teacher-student relationship can contribute much more to effective learning.
The crux is always the balance between old and new, analog and digital.

2 *Wichtig ist hier das genaue Studium der Aufgabenstellung: Hier soll **erst** der Cartoon analysiert und **dann** der Text einbezogen werden. Oft wird die Aufgabe auch entgegengesetzt formuliert (d. h., die Cartoonanalyse folgt der Textanalyse).*
*Die Cartoonanalyse folgt im besten Fall der DIE-Regel. Das bedeutet **D**escription, **I**nterpretation, **E**valuation (Beurteilung; hier eventuell erst im Anschluss an die Textanalyse). Im Weiteren sucht man sich dann passende Textstellen, die die Aussage des Cartoons unterstreichen. Vergessen Sie nicht die Schlussfolgerung aus Analyse und Vergleich und eine begründete Wertung.*

The cartoon by John Atkinson taken from *Wrong Hands* pictures a desk underneath a window, which is cluttered with numerous items that usually used to be on a desk 10–15 years ago.

The title of the cartoon is "vintage social networking". There are a globe and some picture frames on the left-hand side, a landline telephone, scissors and a comic strip on the right-hand side, a pinboard with several notepads on the wall above the desk, and a pen, some sheets of paper, an address book, Post-its and a card index in the centre. All of the items are labelled as common social networking sites: seeing the world outside is like watching a video on YouTube, the telephone stands for Skype, the address book is the analog version of Facebook, for example.
It becomes obvious that all of our popular apps have an analog predecessor. They are not entirely new, but have simply undergone a certain development and are now available in a digital version. The cartoonist criticises our dependency on digital devices by showing that there used to be a (social) life before Facebook and Snapchat, but it also becomes evident that some of the new technologies have obvious advantages compared to their "vintage" predecessors.
The cartoon mirrors Sax's opinion that we need to find the right balance between digital and analog.
When Sax states that "analog actually contributes to the real places where we live" (ll. 50/51), we are reminded of the open window in the cartoon through wich we can see and experience the real world and nature around us. Although some of us might be guilty of a certain "nostalgia for a predigital time" (l. 41), it is also the "richness of experience that is unparalleled with anything delivered through a screen" (ll. 46/47). Cutting out photos and sticking them into an album is something that "engages nearly all of [our] senses" (l. 47), compared to moving an object around with your computer mouse to drop it on the page of a virtual photo album. There is a reason why people have their digital photo albums printed. You can leaf through the pages, you can easily "access", i.e. *open*, a book, and you can smell the paper and the ink. The same is true for other printed books and thus it is no wonder that independent bookstores "have been steadily expanding for several years" (l. 35).
On the other hand, social networks offer us completely new possibilities and a card index can hardly be compared to a complex career network like LinkedIn. Luckily, we "do not face a simple choice of digital *or* analog" (l. 65), but we can use both.
Both the text and the cartoon remind us not to forget that there was a life before digital and that there are devices and experiences in the real world that may be just as good or even better than recent technology.

3.1 *Einen Kommentar zu schreiben ist immer dann eine dankbare Aufgabenstellung, wenn Sie genügend Argumente pro und kontra aus Ihrem eigenen Wissen generieren können. Das Thema* virtual communities *dürfte dafür ein gutes Beispiel sein. Machen Sie sich einen Schreibplan, in dem Sie zunächst einmal Ihre stärksten Argumente und Beispiele notieren. Suchen Sie dann passende Anknüpfungspunkte im Text. Am Schluss müssen unbedingt eine überzeugende Schlussfolgerung und eine überzeugende Wertung stehen.*

Modern people like us feel at home in analog as well as virtual communities. Every morning we greet our neighbours on the way to school and we probably pass the little corner shop that sells newspapers and lottery tickets at 7 am. However, we explore virtual reality at the same time when we play computer games and we also appreciate the advantages of online shopping 24/7, of course.
In his article in *The New York Times*, David Sax claims that "analog actually contributes to the real places where we live" (ll. 50/51). The emphasis seems to be on the word '*contribute*'. Does that mean that analog communities are more valuable than their virtual counterparts? In my opinion, there are arguments for and against both aspects.
In an analog world like David Sax describes, you know everyone in your neighbourhood, you talk to real people and you see their immediate reactions. Any kind of change will be noticed, such as somebody moving in or out, or shops opening or closing. Sax says that he "ha[s] become friendly with" (l. 51) a shop owner who would "immediately kick out any Nazi or raving misogynist who started ranting inside his store" (ll. 57/58). In an analog community, the odds are high that moral and ethical standards will still be in use, as you have to insult someone face-to-face if you feel like that.
Additionally, small local businesses also have to pay taxes that the community benefits from (cf. ll. 53/54) and they contribute to a better environment as you do not have to send parcels around and wait for them to be delivered to you. You simply pop into a 'real' shop and buy the items you need. Imagine the amount of $CO_2$ nature is spared! There must also be a reason for all of that nostalgia regarding vinyl records and print books. I do not think people are made to use one sense only. They not only want to see, they need to smell, taste, hear and touch things. All this gets lost when analog disappears.
On the other hand, virtual communities have their advantages, too. They are cheap, easily accessible, 'open' 24/7 and global. You do not have to restrict yourself to the people in your neighbourhood, but can become friends with the whole world. Simply consider the access to information! It used to be difficult and strenuous to plough your way through piles of books and papers, contacting friends, colleagues or experts who could perhaps help you with your tasks. Now most of these documents are only a mouse click away. If you feel lonely – just go online and you will always find someone who feels like you. If you need anything – the virtual community is ready to help you out. 'Brave New World that has such people in it'!
This may well be true, but we all know the other side of the coin. In a digital store, the Nazi or the misogynist will be allowed to rant. Anyone who feels like bullying another person will do it. People who seem to be friends might turn out to be bots or fake profiles. Our data may be stolen and our privacy intruded.
All in all, there is no black or white but a great many grey areas. We have to learn to cope with new technologies in the form of virtual communities, for example, and be aware of the risks and dangers that lie there. On the other hand, I could not imagine analog dying out completely, otherwise we would all have to turn into avatars of some kind, and that will never happen.

3.2 *Die Aufgabenstellung ist ein wenig „tricky": Was bedeutet „using technology* ***differently***"*? Mit Blick auf den Text von David Sax scheint es darum zu gehen, dass man zwischen analog und digital hin- und hergerissen ist. Man kann sich auch darauf beziehen, dass Sax' Enthusiasmus gegenüber modernen Technologien langsam verblasst und er mittlerweile seine Geräte privat abschaltet.*
*Neben dem unten genannten Roman bietet sich* The Circle *von Dave Eggers (2013) zum Vergleich an.*

David Sax, a New York Times journalist, seems to be torn between the 'new' virtual and the 'old' analog world with a noticeable leaning towards the latter. He has found out for himself that his 'love affair with digital is over', as the headline of his article reads.

One example of a character from literature who feels like David Sax is Maddie Freeman from Katie Kacvinsky's *Awaken* (2011). The protagonist, a 15-year-old girl, lives in the dystopian world Sax conjures up in his article. In her world, everything is done by and on computers. Maddie practically lives in the virtual community Sax talks about. People do not go outside any longer. The whole world is artificial; there are no trees and no grass. Even school is done online. Maddie only meets her classmates' avatars in the lessons. Maddie knows what is expected of her with her dad being the headmaster of DS – Digital School. She has never really missed anything, although her mum, who still keeps some items from the analog world, has planted the seed of doubt in her brain.

Like Sax, Maddie has access to both worlds, although hers is much more digitalised than ours, but she would love to see a real tree and feel green grass under her feet, a fact which makes her prone to falling for the ideas of a young rebel. She accidentally gets into contact with Justin online. He suggests something that Maddie has never done before: a face-to-face meeting. She hesitates as to whether to do or not to do something so different, but finally gives in and agrees. Justin turns out to be a handsome, charismatic young man and Maddie falls in love with him. In their regular meetings he tells her about the analog world and Maddie learns to love real-life communication. Yet she is torn between the love for her mother, who supports her daughter, and loyalty to her father, who she knows is chasing Justin and all the other rebellious students. She slowly understands that her virtual world is not what makes any human happy. She has the will to stand up for her new beliefs and to tell other students about it. This fight changes her life forever, since she has to decide to go against her own father.

Like David Sax, Maddie strives to make people aware of the downsides of digitalisation.

All in all, *Awaken* shows us what will become of us if we go on digitising our world at the current speed. If we do not remain sufficiently aware, we will probably end up regretting it as Maddie does.

3.3 *Ein Leserbrief sollte sich deutlich von einem Kommentar unterscheiden. Konzentrieren Sie sich am besten auf ein Argument oder eine Aussage und geben Sie Ihre Ansicht wieder. Der Brief sollte neue Impulse bringen und so zur Diskussion beitragen. Zeigen Sie, dass Sie sich mit der Materie auskennen und einen eigenen Standpunkt verteidigen wollen.*
*Achten Sie auch auf die formelle Seite eines Leserbriefes, d. h. Adressen, Datum, Anrede usw.*

Lisa Blume
Anonymweg 23
12345 Musterstadt

The New York Times Company
620 Eighth Avenue
New York
NY 10018

10 April 2019

Sir/Madam

I am writing in reference to your article *Our Love Affair with Digital Is Over* from 18 November 2017. I am afraid I do not agree with the author's suggestion with regard to finding a balance between digital and analog.
I am a 17-year-old student and my peers and I are known for our addiction to the digital. We are often referred to as digital natives or the head-down generation and I am proud of it. How much more convenient has our world become since the launch of the internet?! How often in a day do you google anything that you surely would not look up in an encyclopaedia? I cannot see any sense in buying vinyl records either. They are too big to be carried around and you would need a clumsy device to play your songs, let alone listen to any playlists.
To me, David Sax seems like one of those men in their 40s or 50s, who do not want a part of their history to die because of some obsolete content. Nostalgia is for backward-looking people who do not want to face up to new technologies. We gave up horse riding and sending smoke signals in favour of cars and telephones, did we not? I know my mum is happy with her e-reader because it means she does not need her glasses to read her favourite novels. So why buy print books?
I am sure that we are now living in a period of transition. More and more people have grown up in digitalised surroundings. Soon, analog media, for example, will only be exhibited in museums around the world. What will remain, as always, is some nostalgics who cling to their old-fashioned devices, but I would say we need to fight for a Code of Conduct to make our digital world safer and fairer and punish all the wrongdoers who try to spoil our Brave New World!

Lisa Blume
Musterstadt

## Prüfungsteil 2: Sprachmittlung

### Aufgabenstellung 2.1

*Der Text gibt einen chronologischen Ablauf der Ereignisse vor, bei dem es relativ schwierig wird, zeitliche Eckpunkte wegzulassen oder andere zusammenzufassen. Achten Sie also darauf, dass Ihr Artikel insgesamt nicht zu lang wird. Wichtig ist auch, dass die Zielgruppe berücksichtigt wird.*

**From curse to blessing**

Where is my phone? I gather that most of us feel panicky for a second when our mobiles are unexpectedly out of reach. Our smart electronic helpers have become a vital part of our lives. But how did that start?

Let's go back to the year 1958. The Nuclear Research Center of the Brookhaven National Laboratory has invited people to their Open Day. Physicist William Higinbotham presents a game called *Tennis for Two*. What was originally meant to help people lose their inhibitions about machines became known as the birth of a new relationship between humans and machines.

Twenty-five years later, the first video games appeared in pubs and private living rooms. Everyone had heard of *Pac-Man, Pong* or *Donkey Kong*. German television decided to air the first game show based on computer games. But it was also the decade that strictly separated computers used for gaming and those for work. In figures, 74 % of all Germans had never used a computer and 51 % had no intention whatsoever of doing so. Computers were thought to be powerful, useless, evil job killers.

The release of the first PCs was sneered at as an attempt to find a practical use for computers. But it was children, the generation of our parents, who helped the machine to become popular beyond all measure. In the 1990s parents were still shying away from electronic gadgets while younger generations embraced them.

Finally, the worlds of work and gaming blended into each other and the same computer was used for work and leisure.

When Nintendo's Wii made joysticks obsolete and the human body took over their task, the motto became *We are the Robots* rather than *Slave to a Machine*.

Nowadays, with computers becoming reduced to the size of mobile phones, demonisation is no longer an issue. They have taken up the task of being our coaches or mentors when they allow us to improve our intellect by playing computer games.

I can literally see William Higinbotham smile down at us from cloud nine. Mission accomplished!

**Aufgabenstellung 2.2**

*Für die Ausgestaltung der Aufgabenstellung muss eine authentische E-Mail erstellt werden. Formulieren Sie also zunächst eine Betreffzeile und auch eine informelle Einleitung, in der Sie die Idee der Recherche thematisieren.*
*Da die Informationen über „Barbara." anscheinend nur für den Freund bestimmt sind, können Sie auf einer informellen Stilebene mit gelegentlichen Kommentaren die relevanten Fakten wiedergeben.*

To: Josh2001@gmail.com
Subject: Re: artists in a digital world

Hi Josh,

How's it going? I've been snowed under with work for weeks. Hope you're better off when it comes to homework.
Anyway, I've found some space to squeeze in a little research on artists in a digital world. Helping a friend out is top priority!
What I found is something amazing. I'd never heard of "Barbara." before, but she is said to be one of the most renowned street artists in Germany. The thing is: nobody knows who she really is. Although Barbara is a girl's name, it could be a man, a woman or even a group of artists! She insists on remaining anonymous. So an interview with her is a very rare occasion and when she grants one to a paper, then only via Facebook. In one of these chats she said that she now lived in Heidelberg, but would also visit Berlin from time to time. When asked about her gender, she said 'human', and the only thing we know about her age is that it's between 22 and 61.
Okay, but what does she do that makes her so famous? She edits road signs or reacts to the regulations they stand for by gluing messages onto them. She seems to hate restrictions of personal freedom and a sticker might read: 'This imperative tone hurts my feelings'. Her signature feature is white lettering on a black background. She speaks up against different social and environmental issues like homophobia, hooliganism or flaws in agrarian policy. When asked how all that started, she remembered a day when, on a walk with her granddad, they tried to remove a swastika from a wall. When they failed, she returned the following day to glue a smiley sticker over it.
"Barbara." has also been awarded several prizes and her works were published in an anthology. She lately had an exhibition in Berlin, where she appeared incognito, as her 460,000 followers learned from her Facebook account.
You're now probably asking yourself what "Barbara." has got to do with your topic. Well, the thing is that social scientists are sure that she would not be successful without social media. "Barbara." simply doesn't need public acknowledgement – the internet is the place where people like and share her works.
Well, Josh, do you think that's something you could use? Hope you like it too. Tell me what you think. Looking forward to your response.

Take care
Lisa

## Abiturprüfung Berlin 2020
## Englisch Grundkurs

### Prüfungsteil 1: Leseverstehen und Schreiben (75 %)

Der Prüfungsteil 1 besteht aus zwei Aufgabenstellungen, von denen Sie eine zur Bearbeitung auswählen.

### Aufgabenstellung 1.1 – Tasks

**Themenschwerpunkte:** *Ethnic and cultural diversity, Aims and ambitions*

1 Outline the information about Edison and his problem. (30 %)

2 Analyze the means used to illustrate the relationship between mother and son. Give evidence from the text. (30 %)

3 Choose <u>one</u> of the following tasks:

3.1 "I have worked so hard to keep Edison from feeling this line being drawn, it never occurred to me that when it happened – which, I guess, was inevitable – it would burn even more, because he had never seen it coming." (ll. 51–53)

Explain the quote and discuss to what extent parents can protect their children from negative experiences. Use Edison's mother as one of your examples. (40 %)

OR

3.2 Compare Edison's experience to that of another character from literature or film who is also rejected because he/she is different. Assess the way they cope.* (40 %)

OR

3.3 For the international youth conference "Celebrate Diversity" write a speech assessing ways to promote tolerance and celebrate diversity at school. Use Edison's experience as a starting point. (40 %)

* Dieser Aufgabentyp entfällt ab der Abiturprüfung 2021.

**Text** (excerpt from the novel)

**Small Great Things**
by Jodi Picoult

Note: *Edison lives with his mother, the narrator, in a rather affluent part of New Haven, Connecticut. They moved there because Edison's mother, who is a nurse, wanted him to attend a better high school.*

[…] Edison explodes. "Why does everything have to be my fault?" He shoves away from the table so fast that he nearly knocks over his chair. […]

After ten minutes pass, I knock softly on the door of Edison's room. It's been his since he was thirteen; I sleep on the pullout couch in the living room. I turn the knob and find him lying on his bed, his arms behind his head. With his T-shirt stretched over his shoulders and his chin tilted up, I see so much of his daddy in him that for a moment, I feel like I've fallen through time.

I sit down beside him on the mattress. "Are we gonna talk about it, or are we gonna pretend nothing's wrong?" I ask.

Edison's mouth twists. "Do I really get a choice?"

"No," I say, smiling a little. "Is this about the calculus test?"

He frowns. "The calc test? That was no big deal; I got a ninety-six. It's just that I got into it with Bryce today."

Bryce has been Edison's closest friend since fifth grade. His mother is a family court judge and his father is a Yale classics professor. […]

"Hey," I say. "Hey." I tug at the pillow and realize that there's one single streak, left by a tear, darkening the skin of his temple. "Baby," I murmur. "What happened?"

"I told him I was going to ask Whitney to homecoming."

"Whitney …" I repeat, trying to place the girl from the tangle of Edison's friends.

"Bryce's sister," he says.

I have a brief flash of a girl with strawberry-blond braids I met years ago when picking Edison up from a playdate. "The chubby one with braces?"

"Yeah. She doesn't have braces anymore. And she's definitely not chubby. She's got …" Edison's eyes soften, and I imagine what my son is seeing.

"You don't have to finish that sentence," I say quickly.

"Well, she's amazing. She's a sophomore now. I mean, I've known her forever, but lately when I look at her it's not just as Bryce's little sister, you know? I had this whole thing planned, where one of my buddies would be waiting outside her classroom after each period, holding a note. The first note was going to say WILL. The second was going to say YOU. Then GO, TO, HOMECOMING, and WITH. And then at the end of school, I'd be waiting with the ME sign, so she'd finally know who was asking."

"This is a thing now?" I interrupt. "You don't just ask a girl to the homecoming dance … you have to produce a whole Broadway event to make it happen?"

"What? Mama, that's not the point. The point is that I asked Bryce to be the one who brought her the HOMECOMING note and he freaked out."

I draw in my breath. “Well,” I say, carefully picking through my words, “it’s sometimes hard for a guy to see his little sister as anyone’s potential girlfriend, no matter how close he is to the person who wants to date her.”

Edison rolls his eyes. “That’s not it.”

“Bryce may just need time to get used to the idea. Maybe he was surprised that you’d think of his sister, you know, that way. Because you *are* like family.”

“The problem is … I’m *not*.” My son sits up, his long legs dangling over the edge of the bed. “Bryce laughed. He said, ‘Dude. It’s one thing for *us* to hang out. But you and Whit? My parents would shit a brick.’” His gaze slides away. “Sorry about the language.”

“That’s okay, baby,” I said. “Go on.”

“So I asked him why. It didn’t make any sense to me. I mean, I’ve been to *Greece* with his family. And he said, ‘No offense, but my parents would not be cool with my sister dating a Black guy.’ Like it’s okay to have a Black friend who comes on family vacations but it’s not okay for that friend to get involved with your daughter.”

I have worked so hard to keep Edison from feeling this line being drawn, it never occurred to me that when it happened – which, I guess, was inevitable – it would burn even more, because he had never seen it coming. […] *(708 words)*

*Picoult, Jodi.* Small Great Things. *New York: Random House, 2016, 56–60.*

**Annotations**

l. 11 calculus test, calc test: type of maths test
l. 15 Yale: renowned American university
l. 18 homecoming: *here:* traditional school dance event
l. 22 chubby: slightly fat
l. 26 sophomore: student in his/her second year at high school or college
l. 44 to shit a brick: *vulgar:* to be extremely surprised and unhappy about something
l. 52 to burn: *here:* to hurt

## Aufgabenstellung 1.2 – Tasks

**Themenschwerpunkte:** *Aims and ambitions, Science and technology – visions of the future*

1 Outline the steps necessary for preparing college students for future careers in the digital age. (30 %)

2 Analyze the cartoon (Text B) and show how its message relates to that of Text A. Give evidence from the article (Text A). (30 %)

3 Choose <u>one</u> of the following tasks:

3.1 “Students must also gain workplace experience before fully entering the workforce – to deepen their understanding beyond ‘what’ into ‘why’ and ‘how.’” (Text A, ll. 24–26)

Explain the quote and comment on the role work experience plays in shaping young people's aims and ambitions. Refer to Text A and your knowledge of the issue. (40 %)

OR

3.2 Compare the challenge of lifelong learning faced by students as depicted in Text A to that of a character from literature or film who has to adapt to a changing environment. Assess how he/she reacts to the challenges.* (40 %)

OR

3.3 For the science blog Popular Science (www.popsci.com), write a blog entry discussing whether or not it is necessary to make high school students robot-proof. Use ideas from the article (Text A) as your starting point. (40 %)

* Dieser Aufgabentyp entfällt ab der Abiturprüfung 2021.

**Text A** (article)

**How College Students Should Prepare for Our Automated Future**
by Joseph E. Aoun

Note: *Aoun is president of Northeastern University and the author of "Robot-Proof: Higher Education in the Age of Artificial Intelligence".*

Economists across the political spectrum agree that the single biggest threat to future job growth is neither immigration nor trade – it's the artificial intelligence revolution already underway. Studies by Oxford University, McKinsey and Pricewaterhouse-Coopers forecast that up to 50 % of current jobs could be replaced by smart machines within the next 20 years. Already, more than 5 million U.S. factory jobs have been lost to automation since 2000. It's become clear: If a job can be automated in the future, it will be.

What's less clear is how educational institutions – the incubators of human talent – will respond to this sea change in the future of work. Despite being the envy of the world, American universities have been slow to modernize – too often educating students for 20th century career fields that will be obsolete by the time they graduate. Beyond simply conferring degrees, the foundational purpose of colleges and universities must be to *educate* – and that means equipping people of all ages, at all stages of their careers, to build successful and fulfilling lives. This means we need to take several important steps to make our students robot-proof.

First, we must design and implement a curriculum that empowers humans to do those jobs only humans can do. Call it *humanics*. This curriculum provides students with three literacies: technical literacy, data literacy and human literacy (such as teamwork, entrepreneurship, creativity, ethics and cultural agility). Then it integrates them, allowing learners to develop a creative mindset and the mental elasticity to invent, discover and produce original ideas in the A.I. age. Even as smart machines become smarter, we will still need humans to launch new companies, engage in global diplomacy, and supervise diverse teams of other people.

But a modernized curriculum will not be enough. Students must also gain workplace experience before fully entering the workforce – to deepen their understanding beyond "what" into "why" and "how." For example, an engineering student might leverage her classroom studies in circuitry design during an internship at Waymo, Google's autonomous vehicle project. By integrating firsthand experience with intelligent machines with her academic work, she learns agility and adaptability, and, most important, she learns how to continue learning.

We must also recognize that technological progress doesn't come with a brake pedal. As machines get smarter, the shelf life of a human education gets shorter. It's time to end the fiction that four years of college, plus a smattering of graduate studies, is enough to last a lifetime.

For-profit educational providers were early adopters that recognized the growing demand for lifelong learning, as have many employers. Some, like General Electric, have adopted in-house bachelor-completion programs. Others, such as IBM, offer an extensive array of educational badges and credentials. Non-profit universities must embrace the opportunity to serve nontraditional students, who today comprise 85 % of all learners.

Lifelong learning must become a central facet of what universities do, not an ancillary endeavor. This means authentic, sustainable partnerships with industry to design courses that fill competency gaps employers actually need. It means going to where the learners are, providing them with an educational roadmap customized for every walk of life. And it likely means access to a multi-campus network, in which learners circulate among nodes across the country and around the globe – where they live and work.

The economic stakes are high. The well-being of societies has long been tethered to vibrant systems of higher education. By rising to the challenge of artificial intelligence, universities with the audacity to change represent humanity's best chance to win the jobs of the future. *(591 words)*

*Source: Aoun, Joseph E. "How College Students Should Prepare for Our Automated Future."* Time. *Sept. 26, 2017. Accessed Aug. 28, 2018. http://time.com/4957419/college-students-artificial-intelligence-preparation/.*

**Annotations**

ll. 3/4 McKinsey and PricewaterhouseCoopers: worldwide management consulting firms
l. 9 sea change: very big change in something
ll. 26/27 to leverage: to use something to maximum advantage
l. 27 circuitry: components of an electrical system
l. 32 shelf life: *here:* time in which the knowledge gained becomes obsolete
l. 33 a smattering of: a small number of
l. 35 for-profit educational provider: educational institutions run by private, profit-seeking businesses
l. 39 nontraditional student: student 25 years old and older
ll. 41/42 ancillary endeavor: *formal:* less important undertaking
l. 46 node: *here:* place of interest
l. 48 to tether: *here:* to tie or bind

**Text B** (Cartoon)

**Turing Test**
By Chris Madden

"The good news, Dave, is that the computer's passed the Turing test. The bad news is that you've failed."

*Chris Madden/cartoonstock*

**Annotations**

Turing test: Test for A.I. developed by Alan Turing in 1950. Test performed to determine whether a computer is as intelligent as a human: A human judge chats with a computer and another human being without seeing them. The machine passes the test if the judge cannot tell the difference between human and machine.

## Prüfungsteil 2: Sprachmittlung (25 %)

Der Prüfungsteil 2 besteht aus zwei Aufgabenstellungen, von denen Sie eine zur Bearbeitung auswählen.

### Aufgabenstellung 2.1 – Tasks

**Themenschwerpunkte:** *Aims and ambitions*

Your American friend is interested in recent changes in parent-child relations. She has asked you what the situation is like in Germany.
Based on the article, write an email to her outlining how and why the relationship between parents and their student children has changed in Germany.

**Text** (Auszug aus dem Artikel)

**Wenn Mama mit zur Uni kommt**
Von Simon Benne

[…] An diesem Tag wollte sie einfach dabei sein. Ihre Tochter hat den Bachelor gemacht, gerade holt sie sich ihr Zeugnis ab – und so lange wartet die Mutter im Lichthof der Leibniz Universität. Sie ist extra aus ihrem Heimatort bei Bremen nach Hannover gekommen, um Manuela an diesem Tag zur Uni zu begleiten […].

Eltern tauchen an der Uni seit einigen Jahren immer häufiger auf. Das Durchschnittsalter der Studenten ist nach Schulzeitverkürzung und Wegfall der Wehrpflicht deutlich gesunken. An der Leibniz-Uni hat sich die Zahl jener Studierenden, die erst 18 Jahre alt sind, seit 2009 etwa verzehnfacht. Je jünger die Studenten sind, umso willkommener sind ihnen ihre Eltern als Helfer bei der Wohnungssuche, beim Umzug und der Erledigung des Papierkrams. […]

Unter Dozenten kursieren mittlerweile Horrorgeschichten über „Helikopter-Eltern", die ihr Kind auch bei der akademischen Karriere gerne im Blick behalten wollen. Sie rufen schon mal bei Professoren an, um sich zu erkundigen, wie sich der Sohn so macht oder warum die Tochter kürzlich eine miese Note nach Hause gebracht hat.

„Die Anteilnahme der Eltern ist größer geworden", sagt Christiane Stolz, die seit mehr als zehn Jahren in der Studienberatung der Uni arbeitet. Sie kann von Müttern und Vätern berichten, die sich telefonisch nach Prüfungsergebnissen erkundigen oder wissen möchten, was ihr Sohn in der Beratung denn so gesagt hat. „Daraus spricht eine Form großer Fürsorge", sagt sie diplomatisch: „Manche Eltern sind sehr behütend, andere haben Schwierigkeiten, ihr Kind loszulassen." Zeitweise hat die Uni sogar Veranstaltungen für Mütter und Väter angeboten. Früher wäre ein Elternabend an der Uni so unvorstellbar gewesen wie eine Frauenbeauftragte in einer Bundeswehrkompanie.

„Wir wären seinerzeit nie auf die Idee gekommen, uns von unseren Eltern an die Uni begleiten zu lassen", sagt Sabine Kiel vom Studentenwerk. Heute würden Mütter und Väter ihren Sprösslingen hingegen ganz selbstverständlich bei Bafög-Anträgen oder Wohnungssuche unter die Arme greifen: „Sie machen sich mehr Sorgen als früher um ihre Kinder – und diese sind ihrerseits offener geworden.“

Für Generationen war das Studium samt Auszug daheim der entscheidende Schritt ins Erwachsenenleben. Die Immatrikulation kam einer Unabhängigkeitserklärung gleich.

Manchmal war der Einzug in eine versiffte WG in einer fernen Studentenstadt der endgültige Bruch mit den Eltern; fast immer war dieser Schritt in die Selbstständigkeit eine endgültige Abnabelung. Die Wörter „Bruch“ und „Abnabelung“ quittiert die 23-jährige Manuela, die von ihrer Mutter in der Leibniz-Uni empfangen wird, mit einem Lächeln: „Ich habe doch eine gute Beziehung zu meinen Eltern“, sagt sie. [...]

Der Germanistik-Professor Hans Bickes spricht gar von einer „grundsätzlichen Entkrampfung im Verhältnis der Generationen“: In Sprechstunden oder Seminaren würden Studierende inzwischen ganz ungeniert erwähnen, dass „Mama“ oder „Papa“ ihnen dieses oder jenes geraten hätten. „In meiner Generation war es in weiten Kreisen eher unüblich, dass die Eltern groß über den eigenen Studienverlauf Bescheid wussten“, sagt der 1953 geborene Germanist.

Bickes hält diese Entwicklung für durchaus erfreulich. „Das Verhältnis zwischen Eltern und Kindern ist entspannter und partnerschaftlicher geworden“, sagt er: „Die Meinung der Eltern ist gefragt und wird nicht grundsätzlich als Ballast bei der Gestaltung eigener Lebensentwürfe empfunden.“ [...] *(496 Wörter)*

*Quelle: Benne, Simon. „Wenn Mama mit zur Uni kommt.“ Hannoversche Allgemeine Zeitung. 8. Oktober 2016. Entnommen am 7. Juni 2017 von http://www.haz.de/Hannover/Aus-der-Stadt/Uebersicht/Helikopter-Eltern-an- der-Leibniz-Universitaet-Hannover. (Zwischenüberschriften des Originaltextes wurden weggelassen.)*

**Annotation**

Z. 25 BAföG: Bundesausbildungsförderungsgesetz: staatliche Unterstützung für Studierende

## Aufgabenstellung 2.2 – Tasks

**Themenschwerpunkte:** *Aims and ambitions, Ethnic and cultural diversity, The impact of the media on society,*

Your American friends are publishing success stories of second-generation immigrants in their school magazine.
Write an article summing up Elif Demirezer's personal and professional background for this magazine.

**Text** (Auszug aus dem Artikel)

**Born in Moabit**
Von Laura Hofmann

[…] Gerade noch war Elif im Süden Portugals, hat dort das Video für ihr Lied „High 5" gedreht, jetzt sitzt sie im Café Tirrée in der Birkenstraße in Moabit. Um die Ecke in der Stephanstraße wurde sie geboren, ist sie aufgewachsen. […]

„Gegenüber beim Kiosk habe ich früher immer meine Fahrkarten gekauft", erzählt sie, die eigentlich Elif Demirezer heißt, aber unter ihrem Künstlernamen Elif bekannt ist, und zeigt auf die andere Straßenseite, wo Gerüste vor Altbauhäusern daran erinnern, dass auch Moabit „kommt", und das schon ähnlich lange wie Wedding.

Damals ist sie an dieser U-Bahnstation mal beim Schwarzfahren erwischt worden. Das war in einem anderen Leben. Mit 19 zog sie von Zuhause aus, heute lebt die bald 25 Jahre junge Popsängerin in Friedrichshain und ist so bekannt, dass ihr nächstes Berlin-Konzert im Lido sofort ausverkauft war. […]

Um Beziehungsdramen geht es in ihrem Album „Doppelleben", das im Frühjahr erschienen ist. Der Titel ist auch der des Songs, in dem sie die schwierige Beziehung zu ihren Eltern besingt. „Ich will euch alles sagen können, damit ihr seht und versteht, wer ich bin […], den ganzen Fake aufgeben, Schluss mit diesem Doppelleben", heißt es darin.

Es sei notwendig gewesen, dieses Lied zu machen, sagt Elif an diesem Septembernachmittag. „Irgendwann haben wir nicht mehr richtig miteinander geredet, ich konnte mit meinen Eltern nicht in die Tiefe gehen." Als sie ihnen das Lied vorgespielt habe, seien sie in Tränen ausgebrochen, doch seitdem sei es zwischen ihnen besser geworden.

Ihre Eltern kamen 1987 aus der Türkei. Sie sind eher konservativ, und sie hätten sich sicher etwas anderes für ihre Tochter gewünscht als eine Karriere als Sängerin. […]

Die Sängerin hat das Café verlassen und läuft durch die Straßen Moabits, vorbei an der Bredowstraße. Dort rechts war früher die Bredowdisko, da war sie als 14-Jährige oft und hat „Capri-Sonne" getrunken. Zwei Jahre später nahm sie an der Castingshow Popstars teil, belegte mit ihrem Partner Niklas Dennin den zweiten Platz. Der Durchbruch kam mit 16 Jahren. 2012 nahm Tim Bendzko sie auf seine Clubtour mit. Im März 2013 erschien ihre erste Single „Unter meiner Haut". […]

Ob sie sich selbst als Deutsch-Türkin sieht? Sie fühle sich als Deutsche mit Migrationshintergrund, antwortet Elif. Obwohl sie findet, dass „Migrationshintergrund“ wie eine Krankheit klingt. „Im Urlaub bin ich einfach deutsch. Ich lege jetzt nicht mein Handtuch auf die Liege, aber ich bin sehr herzlich und umarme immer alle.“

Sie wirkt so emotional wie ihre Lieder, alle Texte haben einen autobiografischen Hintergrund. Und sie passen gut in ihre Generation, die oft als „Generation Y“ bezeichnet wird und sich unter anderem durch angebliche Beziehungsunfähigkeit und einen Drang zur Sinnstiftung durch Arbeit auszeichnet. „Wir gehören zu einer Generation, die immer ‚next‘ klickt. Das sieht man auf Dating-Apps wie Tinder und bei Läden wie H&M und Co. Du kannst alles jederzeit kaufen, alles ist ersetzbar“, stellt Elif fest. Doch dass sich nur scheinbar alles ersetzen lässt, auch davon handelt ihr Song „Umwege gehen“, in dem sie eine besonders schmerzhafte Trennung verarbeitet hat. […]

*(493 Wörter)*

*Quelle: Hofmann, Laura. „Born in Moabit.“ Der Tagesspiegel. 19. September 2017. Entnommen am 30. Mai 2018 von https://www.tagesspiegel.de/berlin/mit-popsaengerin-elif-durch-ihren-alten-kiez-born-in-moabit/20338076.html. (Ein sprachlicher Fehler in der Textvorlage wurde entsprechend der geltenden Norm korrigiert.)*

**Annotationen**

Z. 11 Lido: bekannter Veranstaltungsort für Konzerte und Partys in Berlin
Z. 27 Capri-Sonne: Softdrink
Z. 29 Tim Bendzko: deutscher Singer-Songwriter

## Lösungsvorschläge

## Prüfungsteil 1: Leseverstehen und Schreiben

### Aufgabenstellung 1.1

1 *Der Kern von Edisons Problem, die rassistische Behandlung durch seinen Freund Bryce, wird erst am Ende des Textausschnittes offenbart. In Ihrer Lösung sollte dieser Aspekt jedoch bereits zu Beginn genannt werden. Im Textausschnitt erzeugt die verzögerte Information darüber, warum Bryce nicht will, dass Edison mit seiner Schwester zum Ball geht, für besondere Spannung. Eine Zusammenfassung hat eine andere Funktion. Hier geht es darum Informationen zu vermitteln, nicht darum, zu unterhalten.*

Edison is a Black* high school student who lives with his mother in an affluent area. He comes into conflict with his best friend, Bryce, whom he has known for many years. Bryce is from a White family who has even invited Edison on holiday with them. When Edison admits that he fancies Bryce's sister and wants to take her to the homecoming dance, Bryce gets angry, saying that his parents wouldn't allow his sister to date a Black boy. Edison gets very upset at this racist comment and retreats to his room. It takes his mother some time to find out what the problem is.

2 *Der Arbeitsauftrag lautet „Analyze the means", das heißt, neben Textverweisen wird auch von Ihnen erwartet, darauf einzugehen, wie die Informationen präsentiert werden. Relevant ist hierbei, dass die meisten Informationen über die Beziehung indirekt über die Art und Weise dargestellt werden, wie Mutter und Sohn miteinander interagieren. Sprachliche Mittel, die Sie ansprechen können, sind die offenen und konkreten Fragen im Gespräch, die Wortwahl und der Sprachstil (teils informeller Sprachgebrauch; spielerischer aber sehr offener Umgang miteinander) und die Tatsache, dass viele wesentliche Hinweise auf die Beziehung in direkter Rede im Dialog offenbart werden, da das Gespräch sehr offen und einfühlsam stattfindet.*

Edison's mother is definitely a caring parent who is always trying to do her best. Despite her low income as a nurse, she moved to an affluent area to give her son a better chance at a good high school. She can only afford a one-bedroom flat, but she gives the bedroom to Edison and sleeps on the couch in the living room (cf. ll. 3/4).
When her son explodes and retreats to his room angrily, she remains calm and tries to find out what's wrong with him. She knocks "softly on the door of Edison's room", (l. 3). The choice of words here reveals that she is understanding and has a good relationship with her son. She tries to persuade him to talk about what happened, saying "Are we gonna talk about it, or are we gonna pretend nothing's wrong?" (ll. 8/9) This question shows that she is respectful and playful. However, when she sees that he is crying she softens up ("'Hey,' I say. 'Hey.' I tug at the pillow and realize that there's one single streak, left by a tear, darkening the skin of his temple. 'Baby,' I murmur.

'What happened?'", ll. 16/17). Edison is finally willing to talk to his mother about the problem.
Edison's mother tries to calm him down, trying to justify Bryce's attitude ("Bryce may just need time to get used to the idea. Maybe he was surprised that you'd think of his sister, you know, that way. Because you *are* like family", ll. 40/41).
Edison reveals the actual conflict when he quotes Bryce: "No offense, but my parents would not be cool with my sister dating a Black guy," (ll. 48/49). This also reveals that Edison trusts his mother and that he can talk to her frankly. Before that, he apologises for Bryce's informal choice of words ("'My parents would shit a brick.' [...] Sorry about the language," ll. 44/45), which shows that he is very respectful towards his mother.
During the whole time, the dialogue between Edison and his mother is very open and honest – much more open than you would expect from a teenage boy, which shows how close their relationship is.

3.1 *Lesen Sie den Arbeitsauftrag genau, bevor Sie zu schreiben beginnen. Das Zitat beschreibt, dass Edisons Mutter versucht hat, ihren Sohn zu beschützen, dadurch jedoch das Gegenteil erreicht hat. Da Edison unvorbereitet auf den versteckten Rassismus in seiner Umgebung war, traf ihn die negative Erfahrung umso härter. In Ihrer Lösung müssen Sie zeigen, inwieweit Eltern ihre Kinder vor negativen Erfahrungen schützen können. Dabei soll Edisons Mutter ein Beispiel – neben weiteren Beispielen – sein. Hier können Sie konkret auf Personen (aus Ihrer eigenen Lebenswelt oder auf prominente Figuren) oder auf allgemeine Situationen eingehen.*

Edison's mother wanted to protect him from racism and thought she would do so by moving to a "nice" neighbourhood. She did not prepare him for the experience of racism. However, it turns out that even well-educated people, who would never see themselves as racist, can show racist behaviour when their own family is involved. Edison did not expect his best friend to turn out to be racist when Edison wanted to date his sister. When looking back, Edison's mother realises that sooner or later an experience of this kind was "inevitable" (l. 52), as most Black people or people of colour will be confronted with racism like this at some point in their life. By trying to shield her son from this she leaves him unprepared and Bryce's racist behaviour hits Edison even harder.
Parents can never protect their children from negative experiences, but they can make them aware that these things exist and be there for them in times of trouble. On the other hand, you do not want to destroy your children's open-mindedness with worst-case scenarios. Nor do you want to overprotect your children. This issue is reflected in the story of Buddha, who, as a child, was sheltered from any kind of unpleasantness. It was only when he left his parents' house and went out into the world that he saw suffering, and was profoundly shocked. This experience caused him to reject his privileged life as a prince and become an ascetic, meditating on why man must suffer. Thus, he founded Buddhism.

Helicopter parents overprotect their children and thus show that they do not trust them, making them afraid of the outside world. However, young people need to have their own experiences and cannot be sheltered from bad ones.

3.2 *Der Fokus der Aufgabe liegt auf dem „Anderssein", das gewählte Beispiel kann, muss sich aber nicht mit dem Thema Rassismus beschäftigen. Weitere mögliche Aspekte, die hier für einen Vergleich passen würden, sind etwa LGBTQ-Themen oder Behinderungen. Die folgende Lösung zieht den Film* Monsieur Claude and his Daughters *zum Vergleich heran, der die Themen Rassismus und Antisemitismus aufgreift.*
*Diese Art der Aufgabenform entfällt ab dem Abitur 2021.*

Edison's experience is quite similar to the issues alluded to in the film *Monsieur Claude and his Daughters*. Monsieur Claude and his wife, who are quite traditional and conservative, have four daughters, three of whom are married to husbands from different ethnic groups: a Chinese man, an Israeli Jew and a Muslim. Despite the fact that they totally disapprove of these marriages, they try to grin and bear it. In family reunions, everyone is friendly, but there are often misunderstandings due to racial prejudice. All their hope lies on their youngest daughter, who is not yet married. When she announces that she intends to marry a French Catholic, they are quite relieved. However, when they see him they are shocked because he is Black. This comedy reveals hidden racism. In the extract from *Small Great Things,* Bryce's family also pretends that the colour of Edison's skin is not an issue for them. They take their son's friend with them when they go on holiday, but, as Bryce puts it, "[i]t's one thing for *[him and Edison]* to hang out. But [Edison] and Whit? [His] parents would shit a brick", (ll. 43/44). In both stories, people who try to be politically correct turn out to be racist when it comes to their daughters.
Although the daughters in *Monsieur Claude and his Daughters* have to cope with their father's prejudice, they try to mediate between their husbands and their families. Funnily enough, the husbands are also somewhat prejudiced towards each other. In the end, the father of the Black husband befriends the daughter's father and there is a happy ending, as in every comedy.
In my view, this comedy reveals that there is still a great deal of latent racism in most societies, even when everyone seems tolerant on the surface. It shows in a humoristic way that people are the same regardless of religion or ethnicity.

3.3 *Die Geschichte von Edison und Bryce dient für Ihre Rede als Ausgangspunkt. Darüber hinaus sollen Sie Möglichkeiten diskutieren, wie man mehr Toleranz erreichen und Verschiedenheit feiern kann. Wieder kann es darum gehen, Rassismus zu verhindern, es kann jedoch auf andere Formen der Vielfalt und Toleranz gegenüber Andersartigkeit eingegangen werden. So können beispielsweise die Themen Ableismus (Diskriminierung von Menschen mit Behinderungen), Antisemitismus oder Homo- und Transphobie aufgegriffen werden.*

Good afternoon, ladies and gentlemen, and welcome to the "Celebrate Diversity" international youth conference. Most people think the situation of tolerance and racial discrimination has subsided and even disappeared altogether. However, many of us know that this is far from the truth. There are indeed fewer people who are openly racist, but underneath the mask of tolerance latent racism is still lurking.
Let me tell you a story about Edison, an African American and his White best friend. Edison was raised by a single mother who works as a nurse, and his best friend's family is rather affluent. They supported Edison a lot, taking him with them on holiday. But everything changed when he considered dating his best friend's sister. It was then that their hidden racism came to the surface. His best friend admitted that his parents wouldn't approve of their daughter dating a Black boy.
How does this fit together? On the one hand they wanted to support and help Edison, and treated him like one of the family. Yet when it came to relationships, they were suddenly against him. I think there are many people who would react the same way. They pretend to be liberal, altruistic and non-racist, but are in fact subconsciously the opposite.
In my opinion, the only way to overcome this hidden racism is through education. And this is why we have to start here at this school – as well as every other school in this city, this country and this world. White people have to learn about racism. They have to understand that racism is not a thing of the past that disappeared when slavery was abolished or when Black people were given the right to vote or when segregation was abolished. Racism is very much alive today and to achieve true tolerance and diversity, everyone needs to learn how to detect it – through education. As a starting point we have put together a reading list that will teach every student, every teacher and, I hope, many parents about racism – but not only about racism, also about ableism, sexism and homo- and transphobia. We have to understand each other better and see the problems other people face to achieve a better world.

## Aufgabenstellung 1.2

1 *Für diese Aufgabe sollen Sie sich in der Lösung auf die Aspekte des Textes beschränken, die beschreiben, wie man Collegestudenten in Zukunft auf eine Karriere im digitalen Zeitalter vorbereiten kann. Da im Artikel viele unterschiedliche Aspekte angesprochen werden, ist eine wichtige Herausforderung, diese zu ordnen. Drei wesentliche Bereiche, zu denen sich die einzelnen Punkte bündeln lassen, sind wichtige Kompetenzen (z. B. technische und soziale Kompetenzen), praktische Erfahrungen in der Arbeitswelt und das lebenslange Lernen, das in der heutigen Zeit immer wesentlicher wird und Arbeitswelt und Colleges miteinander verzahnt. Führen Sie für eine gute Lösung alle drei Teilbereiche weiter aus.*

According to the article, lifelong learning is essential for workers to have a successful career. In the digital age, many jobs have been replaced by robots and even more will be so in the future.
First, universities have to adapt their curricula to meet the new challenges and thus enable their students to do tasks only humans can do. This means that they have to

teach a broad range of skills, such as technical, data and social skills, so that graduates become creative and can manage businesses and teams. Another important point is that students should not just study theory, but their studies need to be combined with internships at high-tech companies. By combining theoretical issues with practical work, students will adapt more readily to future challenges. However, even after the students finish their degrees, lifelong learning is vital for their continued success and therefore universities and industry need to work together to provide flexible education for the changing job markets of the future.

2 *Beginnen Sie Ihre Lösung mit einer Beschreibung des Cartoons. Erläutern Sie anschließend dessen Bedeutung. Um diese wie gefordert in Bezug zum Zeitungsartikel zu setzen, sollten Sie diesen erneut lesen und sich geeignete Textstellen markieren. Für Ihren Vergleich können Sie Gemeinsamkeiten und Unterschiede zwischen den Aussagen des Artikels und des Cartoons in eigenen Worten wiedergeben und diese anhand der markierten Textstellen belegen.*

In the cartoon by Chris Madden there is a man sitting at a desk with a laptop that is connected to a huge computer. He is turning his head towards a researcher standing behind him in a lab coat. The researcher says, “The good news, Dave, is that the computer’s passed the Turing test. The bad news is that you’ve failed.” The Turing test determines whether a human can tell if they are talking to a computer or a human. Thus, the man did not know he was talking to a computer and the computer did not realise it was talking to a human. This implies that the computer is getting better and better at imitating humans, whereas (some) humans do not evolve. As the computer surpasses the test candidate at social skills that determine whether an artificial intelligence can be detected as non-human, it is very likely that the machine will now be able to replace the man in his job no matter what he does.
According to the article, “up to 50 % of current jobs could be replaced by smart machines within the next 20 years,” (ll. 4/5), which infers that the employee’s job will most likely be replaced by a robot. “We must also recognize that technological progress doesn’t come with a brake pedal. As machines get smarter, the shelf life of a human education gets shorter,” (ll. 31/32). This means that employees who do not work hard at their jobs to keep up with the changing times will be made redundant. However, the author of the article believes that there are “jobs only humans can do” (l. 17). While AI is evolving, there are certain skills it cannot acquire to the same level as humans.

3.1 *Lesen Sie das Zitat mehrfach und stellen Sie sicher, dass Sie seine Bedeutung verstanden haben, bevor Sie diese dann in Ihrer Lösung in eigenen Worten wiedergeben. Natürlich geht es im Wesentlichen darum, dass die Studierenden praktische Erfahrungen sammeln müssen. Es geht jedoch auch darum, warum diese Erfahrungen wichtig sind: damit sie neben dem theoretischen Wissen auch lernen, wofür sie dieses brauchen und wie sie es praktisch anwenden können. Stellen Sie in Ihrer Lösung Textbezüge zum Zeitungsartikel her und bauen Sie zusätzlich weiteres Wissen zum Thema ein. Hier können Sie sich etwa auf eigene Praktika, Geschichten aus Ihrem Lebensumfeld oder auch auf allgemein bekannte Erfahrungen zum Thema beziehen.*

The quote refers to the fact that students need to gain practical experience in order to understand their field fully. On top of the theoretical knowledge they gain at college, they have to understand what they need this information for and how they can use it in their workplace.
Students also see what it is like on the job market and not just in a classroom. When students realise how much fun it is to do their job, they will work harder and bring new knowledge back into their studies. This is why universities and companies have to cooperate. Theoretical knowledge can never replace real experience. An engineering student who is able to work for Google and see how the theoretical knowledge is implemented in real projects, such as the autonomous vehicle project, will have new perspectives on her field when she is back at college. If students do internships, they gain more insight into the field they are studying.
Alternatively, they may find out that the job is unfulfilling and rethink their educational path. When I was a pupil at elementary school, all the children were afraid of a certain trainee teacher, who fortunately changed his career path. Obviously, he did not have that much contact with pupils during his studies at university. If he had had the opportunity to interact with pupils while still studying, he would not have wasted his time on an ill-fitting career path.

3.2 *Diese Aufgabenstellung ist vergleichsweise komplex. Zwar war der Vergleich zu einem literarischen Werk oder einem Film bis 2020 fester Bestandteil der Abiturprüfung, in dieser Aufgabe müssen Sie jedoch ein Transferleistung bringen. Ein Werk oder einen Film zu finden, der sich konkret auf die Arbeitswelt bezieht, ist mitunter nicht leicht. Da es jedoch allgemein um das Einstellen auf eine neue Lebenssituation geht („environment" bezieht sich hier allgemein auf die Lebensumstände), kommen viele Werke in Frage. Allerdings ist es dann nicht ganz leicht den Bezug zum „lebenslangen Lernen" herzustellen. Die folgende Lösung behandelt die Kurzgeschichte „The Unfortunate Fate of Kitty da Silva" von Alexander McCall Smith, in der sich die Hauptfigur auf eine neue kulturelle Lebensumgebung in einem anderen Land einstellen muss.*

In the age of globalisation, lifelong learning has become vital for anybody who wants to be successful in their job. Students not only have to adapt to new findings in science and keep pace with technological developments, it is also important to develop cultural awareness to cope with different situations abroad.
In Alexander McCall Smith's short story, "The Unfortunate Fate of Kitty da Silva", stem-cell researcher Dr John has difficulty coping with the local customs when he moves from India to Scotland. First, he becomes accustomed to nodding when he means yes, instead of shaking his head, as is the case in India. Later, however, he has problems coping with the fact that, unlike in India, people do not always mean what they say. For example, when someone invites him to visit their home, he does not know whether they are serious or just being polite.

Dr John thinks he is settling into his job and new environment, when he meets his neighbour, Jen. They invite each other over for dinner regularly, and then daily. However, Dr John is not sure about his feelings for her or her feelings for him and does not know how to talk to her about it. Instead, he places a picture of his cousin on his kitchen shelf. When Jen sees it, she asks him who it is, and he simply says, "Kitty da Silva", leading her to believe she is his girlfriend. After this incident, the relationship changes completely. They do not see each other any longer and when he rings the doorbell, Jen does not open the door, even though he knows she is at home.
A few weeks later, they meet again. When Jen asks him how Kitty da Silva is, he answers that she was eaten by a tiger and died. Jen bursts out laughing in relief, and that is the end of the story.
Thus, Dr John kept on trying, and finally succeeded in coping with his new life. Similarly, young students must always recognise the challenges confronting them and adjust to new situations if they want to make their dreams come true.

3.3 *Für Ihren Artikel sollten Sie zunächst einmal klarstellen, was mit „robot-proof" gemeint ist, da es sich sicher nicht um einen allgemein bekannten Begriff handelt. Hier kommt, wie in der Aufgabenstellung gefordert, der Artikel ins Spiel, dessen Autor (wie im Vorspann beschrieben) auch ein Buch geschrieben hat, das „Robot-Proof: Higher Education in the Age of Artificial Intelligence" heißt. Nutzen Sie den Artikel, um zum Thema hinzuführen und darzustellen, was man unter „robot-proof" verstehen kann. Beachten Sie, dass Sie Argumente dafür UND dagegen darstellen müssen, dass es notwendig ist, Schüler*innen auf die automatisierte Arbeitswelt vorzubereiten. Sie müssen also in Ihrer Argumentation über das hinausgehen, was sich im Artikel findet und auch Argumente finden, die für eine klassischere Schulausbildung sprechen könnten.*

**It's high time we got our high school students robot-proof!**

Lots of pensioners have worked in the same job their entire lives, and often even for the same company. But as Joseph E. Aoun, author of "Robot-Proof: Higher Education in the Age of Artificial Intelligence" describes it, it is becoming increasingly important to acquire new skills throughout life, due to the development of artificial intelligence.
High schools must respond to this challenge by teaching students not only to keep pace with technology, but also to become proficient in fields AI cannot replace – on other words, to get them robot proof.
Many jobs have already been replaced by robots. In car manufacturing for example, most welders have been made redundant. A welding robot can work faster, more cheaply and with more precision than a human. Similarly, the elderly may be cared for by "care-bots" instead of geriatric nurses in the future. Thus, there are fewer and fewer jobs that need to be done by humans. On the other hand, new jobs are being created, such as specialists for the maintenance of robots, computer scientists to develop the programmes, and of course engineers to build them. High schools must prepare students for a digital world in which our technical literacy and data literacy will most likely be a critical part of our career.

A major problem schools face is that it is impossible for them to always be up to date when it comes to the most recent technological developments. Technology is evolving so fast that schools cannot keep up with this development. They have, however, already found a way to deal with this problem: by teaching students human literacy – the ability to work in teams, make ethical judgements, be creative in fields such as music and art and use other cultural skills that a robot cannot perform. Students will be equipped to do the jobs computers and robots cannot do either developing technology, working together with robots and AIs or performing in job fields that are not affected by robotization. This could also be a golden opportunity. If robots replace the menial and repetitive jobs, people can concentrate on more creative endeavours. This can only benefit society.

It is important to keep in mind that high-school students must continue studying even after college if they want to keep up to date with innovations. While high school can equip them with skills such as agility and adaptability and a continuous effort to keep learning, the technology they will have to use in their future jobs has not been developed yet. It is all about lifelong learning!

## Prüfungsteil 2: Sprachmittlung

### Aufgabenstellung 2.1

*Ihre Lösung sollte drei Aspekte einbeziehen: wie war die Situation in der Vergangenheit, wie ist die Situation heute und welche Gründe zeigt der Artikel hierfür auf.*

**Re: Parent-child relations**

Hi Sarah,

You asked me about the situation regarding parent-child relations in Germany. I read an interesting article on that issue called "When Mommy accompanies you to university" ("Wenn Mama mit zur Uni kommt") by Simon Benne. Whereas in the past students were independent of their parents, who were not involved in university issues, nowadays parents are a lot more interested in their children's academic careers.

University lecturers are often shocked about helicopter parents who even phone the professors to ask them about their kids' results and participation. One reason is that in Germany students are younger these days because they don't have mandatory military service anymore and because in some places of Germany they spend fewer years at school. (German students are still older than Americans when they finish high school.) The younger the students are, the more the parents are willing to help them with issues like looking for an apartment, moving, or doing paperwork. Sometimes there are even parent evenings at universities, which was unthinkable 10 years ago. In the past, starting university was an important step toward becoming an adult, and students were more independent of their parents and shared apartments with friends. But, despite the fact that some parents are

overprotective, the parent-child relationships are more relaxed these days, with fewer conflicts between the generations. So, you could also see the development as a positive sign that shows that generations are growing together.
What are the relationships like in America?
Looking forward to hearing from you.

Best regards,
Laura

**Aufgabenstellung 2.2**

*Ihre (amerikanischen) Freunde veröffentlichen Erfolgsgeschichten von Einwanderern und Einwandererinnen in der zweiten Generation. Daher müssen Sie erwähnen, woher Elifs Eltern kommen, wenn Sie über ihren persönlichen Hintergrund sprechen. Wenn Sie auf ihren professionellen Hintergrund eingehen, können Sie ihre erfolgreiche Karriere beschreiben. Auch eine Verknüpfung der beiden Bereiche, in der Sie die autobiografischen Einflüsse in Elifs Liedtexten ansprechen, ist sinnvoll.*

**Elif – famous pop singer – between two cultures**

Elif Demirezer, or Elif to her fans, was born and raised in Moabit, a district of Berlin. Her parents came to Germany from Turkey in the 1980s and she sees herself as German with a migrant background, although she is not particularly fond of the term "migrant background".
In spite of her conservative upbringing, Elif became independent at an early age. When she was 14, she used to go to the disco frequently and two years later she took part in a talent show, where she tied for second place. This caught the attention of the famous pop singer Tim Bendzko, who took her on his tour and thus propelled her into the limelight.
Her first single came out in March 2013. Today her concerts are sold out immediately. Her latest album, called "Doppelleben" (Double Life), is about difficult relationships. Her lyrics are mostly autobiographical and fit with the so-called Generation Y, which is considered to have relationship problems and find meaning through work. "Doppelleben" is also the title of a song about her estranged relationship with her parents. When she played the song to them, they broke down in tears. Since then the relationship has become better.

* We have decided to capitalize "Black" and "White" to signal that they are not natural categories but social ones (for more background information on this topic see e. g. https://www.theatlantic.com/ideas/archive/2020/06/time-to-capitalize-blackand-white/613159/).

## Abiturprüfung Berlin/Brandenburg 2020
## Englisch Leistungskurs/Erhöhtes Anforderungsniveau

### Prüfungsteil 1: Leseverstehen und Schreiben (75 %)

Der Prüfungsteil 1 besteht aus zwei Aufgabenstellungen, von denen Sie eine zur Bearbeitung auswählen.

### Aufgabenstellung 1.1 – Tasks*

**Themenschwerpunkte:** *Ethnic and cultural diversity; Aims and ambitions*

1 Outline the information about Trevor Noah's first day at his new school. (30 %)

2 Analyze the means used to illustrate Trevor Noah's experiences with race and identity. Give evidence from the text. (30 %)

3 Choose <u>one</u> of the following tasks:

3.1 "I decided I'd rather be held back with people I liked than move ahead with people I didn't know." (ll. 71/72)
Explain the quote and discuss the impact a peer group may have on a person's development. (40 %)

OR

3.2 Compare Trevor Noah's decision with that of a character in literature or film who also makes an unexpected choice in life. Assess the reasons for their decisions.** (40 %)

OR

3.3 Write a blog entry for the website promoting the *International Day of Language,* in which you comment on the importance of knowing several languages. Take Trevor Noah's experience as one of your examples. (40 %)

* Diese Aufgabenstellung entstammt der Prüfung aus dem Bundesland Brandenburg. Aufgabenstellung 1.2 wurde in beiden Bundesländern gestellt.
** Dieser Aufgabentyp entfällt ab der Abiturprüfung 2021.

**Text** (excerpt from the autobiographical story)

**The Chameleon**
by Trevor Noah

Note: *Born to a South African mother and a Swiss father in South Africa in the 1980s, Trevor Noah was labeled a 'colored kid'. As a child he learned several languages spoken in South Africa.*

[…] At the end of grade six I left Maryvale to go to H. A. Jack Primary, a government school. I had to take an aptitude test before I started, and, based on the results of the test, the school counselor told me, "You're going to be in the smart classes, the A classes." I showed up for the first day of school and went to my classroom. Of the thirty or so kids in my class, almost all of them were white. There was one Indian kid, maybe one or two black kids, and me.

Then recess came. We went out on the playground, and black kids were *everywhere.* It was an ocean of black, like someone had opened a tap and all the black had come pouring out. I was like, *Where were they all hiding?* The white kids I'd met that morning, they went in one direction, the black kids went in another direction, and I was left standing in the middle, totally confused. Were we going to meet up later on? I did not understand what was happening.

I was eleven years old, and it was like I was seeing my country for the first time. In the townships you don't see segregation, because everyone is black. […] And at Maryvale, the kids were mixed up and hanging out together. Before that day, I had never seen people being together and yet not together, occupying the same space yet choosing not to associate with each other in any way. In an instant I could see, I could feel, how the boundaries were drawn. Groups moved in color patterns across the yard, up the stairs, down the hall. It was insane. I looked over at the white kids I'd met that morning. Ten minutes earlier I'd thought I was at a school where they were a majority. Now I realized how few of them there actually were compared to everyone else.

I stood there awkwardly by myself in this no-man's-land in the middle of the playground. Luckily, I was rescued by the Indian kid from my class, a guy named Theesan Pillay. Theesan was one of the few Indian kids in school, so he'd noticed me, another obvious outsider, right away. He ran over to introduce himself. "Hello, fellow anomaly! You're in my class. Who are you? What's your story?" We started talking and hit it off. He took me under his wing, the Artful Dodger to my bewildered Oliver.

Through our conversation it came up that I spoke several African languages, and Theesan thought a colored kid speaking black languages was the most amazing trick. He brought me over to a group of black kids. "Say something," he told them, "and he'll show you he understands you." One kid said something in Zulu, and I replied to him in Zulu. Everyone cheered. Another kid said something in Xhosa, and I replied to him in Xhosa. Everyone cheered. For the rest of recess Theesan took me around to different black kids on the playground. "Show them your trick. Do your language thing."

The black kids were fascinated. In South Africa back then, it wasn't common to find a white person or a colored person who spoke African languages; during apartheid white people were always taught that those languages were beneath them. So the fact that I did speak African languages immediately endeared me to the black kids.

"How come you speak our languages?" they asked.

"Because I'm black," I said, "like you."

"You're not black."

"Yes, I am."

"No, you're not. Have you not seen yourself?"

They were confused at first. Because of my color, they thought I was a colored person, but speaking the same languages meant that I belonged to their tribe. It just took them a moment to figure it out. It took me a moment, too.

At some point I turned to one of them and said, "Hey, how come I don't see you guys in any of my classes?" It turned out they were in the B classes, which also happened to be the black classes. That same afternoon, I went back to the A classes, and by the end of the day I realized that they weren't for me. Suddenly, I knew who my people were, and I wanted to be with them. I went to see the school counselor.

"I'd like to switch over," I told her. "I'd like to go to the B classes."

She was confused. "Oh, no," she said. "I don't think you want to do that."

"Why not?"

"Because those kids are … you know."

"No, I don't know. What do you mean?"

"Look," she said, "you're a smart kid. You don't want to be in that class."

"But aren't the classes the same? English is English. Math is math."

"Yeah, but that class is … those kids are gonna hold you back. You want to be in the smart class."

"But surely there must be some smart kids in the B class."

"No, there aren't."

"But all my friends are there."

"You don't want to be friends with those kids."

"Yes, I do."

We went back and forth. Finally she gave me a stern warning.

"You do realize the effect this will have on your future? You do understand what you're giving up? This will impact the opportunities you'll have open to you for the rest of your life."

"I'll take that chance."

I moved to the B classes with the black kids. I decided I'd rather be held back with people I liked than move ahead with people I didn't know.

Being at H. A. Jack made me realize I was black. Before that recess I'd never had to choose, but when I was forced to choose, I chose black. […] *(969 words)*

*Source: Noah, Trevor. "The Chameleon." In:* Born a crime – Stories from a South African Childhood. *New York: Spiegel & Grau International Edition. 2016, 57–59.*

**Annotations**

| | |
|---|---|
| Note | colored: *in South Africa:* a person of mixed European and African or Asian ancestry |
| l. 1 | Maryvale: Maryvale college, an expensive private Catholic school |
| ll. 26/27 | to hit it off: to get along well or to like one another at once |
| l. 27 | Artful Dodger, Oliver: allusion to Charles Dickens's novel *Oliver Twist:* Oliver, an orphan, gets help from the more experienced Jack, nicknamed the Artful Dodger |
| l. 32 | Zulu: name of an indigenous group in South Africa and their language |
| l. 33 | Xhosa: one of the official languages in South Africa and name of an indigenous group in Southern Africa |

## Aufgabenstellung 1.2 – Tasks

**Themenschwerpunkte:** *Science and technology – visions of the future; The impact of the media on society; Ethnic and cultural diversity; Aims and ambitions*

1 Summarize the information about DNA databases and the effect they have on users. (30 %)

2 Analyze how the article and the illustration published with it increase the readers' interest in the issue. Give evidence from the article and the illustration. (30 %)

3 Choose <u>one</u> of the following tasks:

3.1 "Are Genetic Testing Sites the New Social Networks? Like Facebook, but for fifth cousins, adoptive mothers and sperm-donor dads." (title) Explain the title and comment on how developments in science and technology affect the way we connect with other people. Refer to the article and your knowledge about the issue. (40 %)

OR

3.2 Compare Christine Carter's experience with that of a character from literature or film who makes surprising discoveries about who she/he really is. Assess the way they cope.* (40 %)

OR

3.3 For the 2020 "International Youth Conference on Genetic Research," you have been asked to write an introductory speech discussing the use and abuse of DNA research. Write this speech, referring to the article and your knowledge of the issue. (40 %)

* Dieser Aufgabentyp entfällt ab der Abiturprüfung 2021.

**Text** (excerpt from the article)

**Are Genetic Testing Sites the New Social Networks? – Like Facebook, but for fifth cousins, adoptive mothers and sperm-donor dads.**
by Alyson Krueger

Three years ago Dyan deNapoli, a 57-year-old author and TED speaker who specializes in penguins, was given a 23andMe genetic testing kit for her birthday. Intrigued, she spit in the tube and sent the results to a lab in Burlington, N.C.

About two months later she received a pie chart breaking down where her ancestors lived (99.4 percent of them were from Europe). What she was most giddy about, however, was a 41-page list of all the people who had done the test and were genetically related to her: 1,200 in all. (Customers can choose whether their information is shared with others.)

"I had the names of everyone from my immediate family members to my first cousins, second cousins, third. Once I got past fourth cousins, it went to my fifth cousins, and beyond," said Ms. deNapoli, who lives in Georgetown, Mass. "It started me down this genealogical rabbit hole."

Using the website's internal messaging system supplemented with Facebook, she connected with three second cousins, who were in neighboring towns. She met each one for breakfast in a local diner, where they spent hours drinking coffee and poring over family trees and photos, marveling at various resemblances. [...]

At-home genetic testing services have gained significant traction in the past few years. 23andMe, which costs $ 99, has over five million customers, according to the company; AncestryDNA (currently $ 69), over 10 million.

The companies use their large databases to match willing participants with others who share their DNA. In many cases, long-lost relatives are reuniting, becoming best friends, travel partners, genealogical resources or confidantes.

The result is a more layered version of what happened when Facebook first emerged and out-of-touch friends and family members found one another. Children of long-ago casual sperm donors are finding their fathers. Adoptees are bonding to biological family members they've been searching for their entire lives. [...]

Josh Broadwater, 44, a deputy sheriff in California, was abandoned when he was 1 day old in a gas station bathroom in California. When he was in his 30s, he implored the agency that placed him with adoptive parents to give him whatever information they had about his biological ones but ran into constant dead ends.

In July 2015 he sent a kit to AncestryDNA and found a cousin who shared DNA with him. That led to him discovering his biological father: a man who [...] never knew he existed. They connected over the phone, and soon Mr. Broadwater was driving 500 miles to go elk hunting on his father's farm in Kingston, Utah.

"He kind of sat there quiet for 10 to 15 seconds," said Mr. Broadwater about their first conversation. "And then in his cute little country voice he said, 'Well, if Gloria is your mom, and this thing says I'm your dad, there is a damn good chance I am your dad.' He is just the coolest person."

The two got along so well that they now talk on the phone once a week about the weather, what is going on with the children, about the hunting season. "I never thought finding my biological dad, he would be the one calling me," Mr. Broadwater said.

He also talks to a half brother who is eight months older than him. "I just got a text message from him that I'm going to be an uncle in October," Mr. Broadwater said. "I don't know how much I will be involved. This whole new family is new to me." […]

But other testers have found their results more alienating.

In February 2016 Christine Carter, a marketing strategist, was on a business trip to London when she decided to open her 23andMe dossier. She was in her hotel room, rushing to dinner. "I thought it would be a quick reveal," she said. "I was going to learn that I was Native American and black, and maybe learn a little bit more about the stories I heard as a child."

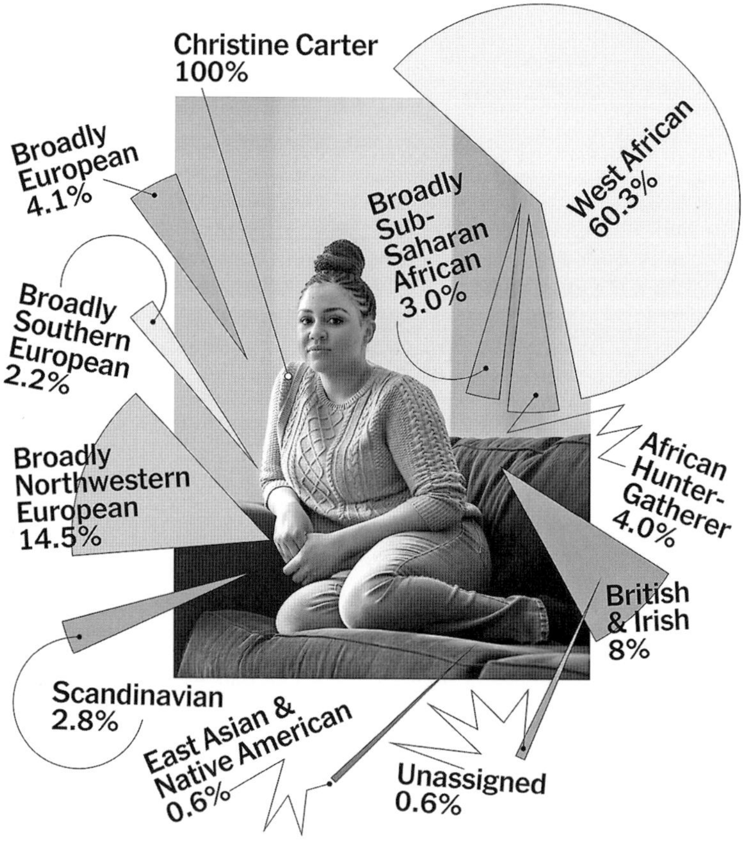


*Christine Carter was startled at her results, and found some solace in writing about them.*
*Credit: Justin T. Gellerson for The New York Times; illustration by the New York Times, https://www.nytimes.com/2018/06/16/style/23-and-me-ancestry-dna.html. From The New York Times.*

Ms. Carter was shocked when the results showed she was 31.5 percent white or European. She struggled through dinner, keeping this revelation mostly to herself, until she got back to her home in Baltimore and contended with her feelings.

She wrote a Huffington Post blog post, "I Celebrated Black History Month … By Finding Out I Was White" that went viral. It attracted thousands of comments, from white supremacists who berated her, to people who had a similar experience and shared her sentiments.

"It took me less than 30 minutes to write the post, it was like journaling, something to get it off my chest," said Ms. Carter, 32. "So to have that reaction was insane."

Perhaps the most frustrating reality is when users don't have any known connections at all. This can happen to people in certain ethnic groups, including Latinos and Asians, that thus far have fewer people using the services […]. *(863 words)*

*Krueger, Alyson. "Are Genetic Testing Sites the New Social Networks?" The New York Times. June 16, 2018. Accessed April 9, 2019. https://www.nytimes.com/2018/06/16/style/23-and-me-ancestry-dna.html. From The New York Times.*


**Annotations**

l. 1 TED: *abbr.:* Technology, Entertainment, Design; non-profit organization spreading ideas in the form of short powerful talks on the Internet covering almost any topic

l. 3 tube: thin piece of glassware used for laboratory testing

ll. 11/12 to start sb. down a … rabbit hole: *here:* to make somebody fall into a bizarre, surreal, or difficult situation

l. 51 31.5 percent: *The slight difference between this number and the total of the respectable numbers in the graph is caused by rounding.*

l. 55 to go viral: to spread quickly and widely, like a virus, on the Internet through social media

l. 56 white supremacist: racist who believes that white people are better than other ethnic groups

l. 58 journaling: writing in a journal, diary, or blog

## Prüfungsteil 2: Sprachmittlung (25 %)

Der Prüfungsteil 2 besteht aus zwei Aufgabenstellungen, von denen Sie eine zur Bearbeitung auswählen.

### Aufgabenstellung 2.1 – Tasks

**Themenschwerpunkte:** *Science and technology – visions of the future; Aims and ambitions; The impact of the media on society*

Your English class is taking part in the European school project "The Future of the World of Work".
Write an article for the project website, outlining the advantages and disadvantages of crowdworking as presented in the article below.

**Text** (Auszug aus dem Artikel)

**Tschüss Büro**
Von Corinna Budras

[…] Von einem „Heer digitaler Nomaden" ist seit einiger Zeit die Rede: Bemitleidenswerte Kreaturen, die sich mit vielen kleinen Aufträgen ohne soziale Absicherung nur mühsam über Wasser halten und deren einzige Freude darin liegt, dass sie ihre anspruchslose Arbeit vom thailändischen Strand aus erledigen können. Die Ungezwungenheit, das schwingt dabei mit, ist nur vorgetäuscht, auch hier ist die Kontrolle allgegenwärtig, über Screenshots oder die Messung der Tastenanschläge. Skeptiker warnen sogar vor einer „neuen Form des Taylorismus": Umfangreiche Tätigkeiten werden in viele kleine Aufgaben zerlegt und wie Brotkrumen an die Masse der Tagelöhner verteilt.

Doch Crowdsourcing ist längst mehr als das. Der durchschnittliche Crowdworker in Deutschland ist 36 Jahre alt und überdurchschnittlich gebildet. Etwa jeder zweite hat ein abgeschlossenes Hochschulstudium. Das heißt, die können was. Und viel wichtiger: Sie wollen sich nicht unterordnen.

Airbus, Adidas, Deutsche Bank, Deutsche Telekom, Volkswagen – es gibt kaum einen großen Konzern, der sich nicht Hilfe vom kreativen Mob da draußen holt. […]

Bisher erledigen viele Crowdworker vornehmlich Arbeiten, die auch früher oft nach außen gegeben wurden: Designer, Architekten oder Programmierer arbeiten seit jeher eigenständig. Nur kommen sie jetzt leichter an Projekte, für die sie sich bewerben können. Die Kehrseite allerdings ist: Auch alle anderen kommen an diese Angebote, der Wettbewerb ist härter geworden. Und Geld trägt […] nur der Sieger nach Hause.

Aber es sind auch ganz neue Tätigkeiten hinzugekommen. Viele „Microjobs" würde es ohne Digitalisierung nicht geben, sie waren früher viel zu aufwendig: Straßenschilder für den Navigationsgerätehersteller Tom Tom fotografieren, im Supermarkt um die Ecke für einen Schokoladenkonzern die aktuellen Werbeaktionen überprüfen – dafür gibt es Geld. Jeder, der ein Smartphone bei der Hand hat, kann das leicht übernehmen.

So unterschiedlich die Tätigkeiten, so unterschiedlich ist auch die Bezahlung: Sie reicht von deutlich unter 10 Euro die Stunde bis zu 70 Euro die Stunde für anspruchsvolle IT-Dienstleistungen, wie eine Studie der Hans-Böckler-Stiftung im vergangenen Jahr ergab. Ein einzelner Auftrag bringt mal drei, mal 2500 Euro. Den Spitzenverdienern unter den Crowdworkern gelingt es sogar, 10000 Euro im Monat zu verdienen. Doch für die allermeisten, rund 80 Prozent, geht es eher um einen Nebenverdienst.

Hinter diesen Zahlen könnte ein größerer gesellschaftlicher Trend liegen: die sanfte Befreiung aus der Umklammerung eines festen Arbeitsvertrags, den manche mit einem beschwerlichen Büroalltag verbinden. „Wir sehen gerade eine Verlagerung vom Angestellten zum Selbständigen“, sagt Jovoto-Gründer Unterberg. „Jovoto ist dafür der Katalysator.“ Und er fragt ganz unbedarft: „Kann diese neue Art zu arbeiten nicht auch ein Befreiungsschlag für die ganze Gesellschaft sein?“

Dafür müsste ein Problem allerdings noch gelöst werden: die fehlende Absicherung im Alter. In Deutschland gibt es mehr als zwei Millionen Solo-Selbständige. Viele von ihnen rutschen womöglich in die Altersarmut, weil sie nicht vorsorgen. Was passiert, wenn sich der Rest der Gesellschaft künftig auch um diese digitalen Freiberufler kümmern muss?

Stephan Gerhard, 54 Jahre alt, ist einer der wenigen, die ihren Lebensunterhalt komplett als Crowdworker bestreiten […]. Schon seit vier Jahren schreibt er Texte über Finanzen oder Versicherungen. Als Befreiungsschlag war das nicht gedacht, eher als Selbsttherapie nach einer persönlichen Krise. Für wen er die Texte schreibt, ob für einzelne Anbieter oder Vergleichsportale, davon hat Gerhard allenfalls eine leichte Ahnung.

Denn die Auftraggeber haben auf der Plattform keinen Namen, sondern einen Code. Gerhard stört das nicht. Die Plattform stellt für ihn sicher, dass er sein Honorar bekommen wird. 2000 Euro brutto im Monat verdient er so, bei einer geschätzten 40-Stunden-Woche.

Das ist nicht besonders viel, hat für ihn aber einen unschlagbaren Vorteil: die Freiheit, arbeiten zu können, wann er will, was er will und wie er will. „Selbstbestimmtes Arbeiten ist ein Wert an sich“, sagt Stephan Gerhard.

Sieht so die Zukunft der Arbeit aus? […] *(598 Wörter)*

*Budras, Corinna. „Tschüss Büro“. Frankfurter Allgemeine Zeitung. 13. Mai 2017. Entnommen am 17.08.2017 von http://www.faz.net/aktuell/wirtschaft/crowdworking-als-neue-arbeitsform-14993621.html?printPagedArticle=true#pageIndex_2. © Alle Rechte vorbehalten. Frankfurter Allgemeine Zeitung GmbH, Frankfurt. Zur Verfügung gestellt vom Frankfurter Allgemeine Archiv*

**Annotationen**

Z. 7 Taylorismus: nach dem US-Amerikaner Frederick Winslow Taylor (1856–1915) benanntes Rationalisierungsprinzip; Produktivitätssteigerung durch Aufteilung der Arbeit in kleinste Einheiten

Z. 8/9 Tagelöhner: jemand, der kein festes Arbeitsverhältnis hat und tageweise für einen Tageslohn arbeitet

Z. 10 Crowdsourcing: Synonym für Crowdworking

Z. 15 Mob: *hier:* große Menschenmenge

Z. 36 Jovoto: Internet-Plattform für Kreative in den Bereichen Design, Kunst und Markenbildung

## Aufgabenstellung 2.2 – Tasks

**Themenschwerpunkte:** *Aims and ambitions; The impact of the media on society*

For a school project, your Australian friends are examining changes in readership and reading habits in different countries as well as reasons for these changes.
Write them an email summing up the information provided in Sandra Kegel's article on the situation in Germany.

**Text** (Auszug aus dem Artikel)

**Leser auf der Flucht**
Von Sandra Kegel

[...] Zwischen 2013 und 2017 haben 6,4 Millionen Deutsche, die zuvor regelmäßig lasen, nicht mehr ein einziges Buch erworben, weder bei einer digitalen Plattform noch in der Buchhandlung um die Ecke. Das entspricht einem Rückgang von fast achtzehn Prozent.

Immerhin, könnte man einwenden, waren es im vergangenen Jahr immer noch dreißig Millionen hierzulande, die wenigstens ein Buch nach Hause getragen haben. Doch in Wahrheit markiert diese Zahl einen Einschnitt. Denn zum ersten Mal hat sich das Verhältnis zwischen Buchkäufern und -nichtkäufern umgekehrt: Weniger als die Hälfte, nur noch 44 Prozent aller Deutschen von zehn Jahren an, geben Geld für Bücher aus. Bis 2014 waren sie in der Mehrheit.

Das hat Folgen nicht nur für den Buchmarkt. Denn eine Gesellschaft, in der aufs Lesen mehrheitlich verzichtet wird, gibt einen Teil ihrer kulturellen Identität preis und lässt zudem eine gesellschaftliche Zweiteilung Realität werden: in diejenigen, die durch Lesen Kompetenz erwerben, und in jene, die den Tag womöglich am Bildschirm verbringen.

Die Ergebnisse der Studie „Buchkäufer – quo vadis?" [...] hat es in dieser Form bisher noch nicht gegeben. Erstmals wurden die sogenannten Buchabwanderer und ihre Motive ausführlich in den Blick genommen. Und klar wurde: Sie entstammen allen gesellschaftlichen Schichten und leben in der Stadt wie auf dem Land. Unterschiede hingegen sind in den Altersgruppen festzustellen. Am stärksten fällt der Rückgang bei den Vierzig- bis Neunundvierzigjährigen aus (minus 37 Prozent). Bei den Dreißig- bis Neununddreißigjährigen wie auch bei den Twens übt sich jeweils gut ein Viertel neuerdings in Kaufabstinenz. Nur Jung und Alt, Kinder und Leser über fünfzig, halten an ihrem bisherigen Kauf- und damit vermutlich auch Leseverhalten fest.

Auffällig ist dabei, dass diejenigen, die sich gegen Bücher entscheiden, immer häufiger im Netz anzutreffen sind. Diese Korrelation ergibt der Vergleich mit einer Studie von ARD und ZDF, wonach in nur zwölf Monaten, zwischen 2016 und 2017, die tägliche Internetnutzung bei den Vierzehn- bis Neunundzwanzigjährigen noch einmal um eine halbe Stunde zugenommen hat – auf jetzt mehr als viereinhalb Stunden. [...]

Die eigentlich spannende Frage bei all dem Zahlenmaterial aber ist, warum das Kulturgut Buch diesen Statusverlust erlebt, den der Börsenverein anhand der Befragungen durch die Gesellschaft für Konsumforschung ermittelt und in vielen bunten Tortendiagrammen und Balkenreihen veranschaulicht hat. Die Antworten der Exleser, die in der Studie zu Wort kamen und bei der gestrigen Pressekonferenz in Filmauszügen eingespielt wurden, fallen ernüchternd und wenig überraschend aus. Was diejenigen umtreibt, die nicht mehr lesen wollen, teilen sie mit sehr vielen anderen Menschen unserer Zeit: Sie fühlen sich von der Schnelllebigkeit des Alltags überfordert, wie die Befragten ein ums andere Mal sagten. Der chronische Mangel an Zeit und Energie, aber auch die ständige Reizüberflutung und der Druck, immer erreichbar zu sein, hält sie davon ab, zum Buch zu greifen. […]

Die Flut einstürzender Informationen, die blinkend und piepsend unentwegt Aufmerksamkeit einfordern, führe zu einem Gefühl der Abhängigkeit und des Ausgeliefertseins, sagen die Exleser, eben weil es ihnen kaum noch möglich sei, sich aus der digitalen Dauerbeschäftigung loszureißen. Die Folge: Es fällt ihnen zunehmend schwer, sich auf eine Sache zu konzentrieren und sich etwa in einen Text zu vertiefen so wie früher. […]

Viele geben aber auch an, statt zu lesen Fernsehserien zu schauen. Das mag auf den ersten Blick verwundern, denn gerade für Serien, die über Streaming-Dienste in Endlosschleife zu sehen sind und den Ergebnissen zufolge gern hintereinanderweg geschaut werden, braucht man Zeit. Doch das Seriensehen empfinden viele der Befragten als Entspannung. Dafür sei keine große Eigenenergie nötig. Serien sind verfügbar, angesagt und bequem. Auch weil sie oft gemeinsam geschaut werden, in der Familie oder mit Freunden.

Wer liest, wendet sich hingegen ab von aller Gesellschaft. […] *(592 Wörter)*

*Kegel, Sandra. „Leser auf der Flucht". Frankfurter Allgemeine Zeitung. 8. Juni 2018, 9*


**Annotationen**

Z. 16 Buchkäufer – quo vadis?: Studie des Deutschen Börsenvereins, auf die sich die hier dargestellten Angaben beziehen

Z. 22 Twens: Personen im Alter von 20 bis 29 Jahren

Z. 23 Kaufabstinenz: Verzicht auf Kauf

Z. 32 Börsenverein: Börsenverein des deutschen Buchhandels, vertritt die Interessen des deutschen Buchhandels
*Englisch:* German Publishers and Booksellers Association

Z. 36/37 jemanden umtreiben: jemanden stark beschäftigen

## Lösungsvorschläge

### Prüfungsteil 1: Leseverstehen und Schreiben

### Aufgabenstellung 1.1

1 *Beim Operator „outline" markieren Sie sich im Originaltext die Stellen, die die Erlebnisse des ersten Schultags widerspiegeln und „hangeln" sich beim Verfassen der Zusammenfassung daran entlang. Ein fiktionaler Text gibt oft schon eine zeitliche Abfolge der Ereignisse vor, so dass man hier kaum Gefahr läuft, etwas Wichtiges zu vergessen. Achten Sie darauf, dass hier wirklich nur die Ereignisse des ersten Schultages erfragt werden und Informationen aus dem Text zu Südafrika nur dann wiedergegeben werden müssen, wenn sie in direktem Zusammenhang zu den Ereignissen stehen.*

Trevor Noah, a South African with a Swiss father and a Black mother, experiences some unexpected behaviour on his first day in a government primary school.
An aptitude test places him in the A – the smart – classes where nearly everyone is White. At break time he is surprisingly surrounded by a large crowd of Black kids, but he feels lost since Black and White children do not seem to mix. He makes friends with an Indian boy from his class who finds out that Trevor can speak several African languages. This makes him rather extraordinary and he is shown around the schoolyard to have his language skills tested.
As Trevor notices that he feels more at home among the Black students he turns to the counsellor to ask her permission for him to switch over to the B classes, where all his new friends are.
After a long discussion that reveals the teacher's rather pejorative attitude towards her Black students, his wish is finally granted, which seems to make him happy.

2 *Der Text weist eine Reihe von Stilmitteln auf. Konzentrieren Sie sich auf ca. drei bis vier wichtige Mittel, die sich im besten Fall auch durch den gesamten Text ziehen. Von besonderer Bedeutung ist der* first-person narrator. *Der Text beschreibt das Geschehen aus Sicht eines elfjährigen Jungen, der zum ersten Mal die Gespaltenheit seines Landes wahrnimmt. Trevor, der einen* weißen* *Vater und eine Schwarze* Mutter hat, wird in seiner neuen Schule zum ersten Mal mit der Rassentrennung in seinem Heimatland Südafrika konfrontiert. Obwohl er der vermeintlich besseren Gruppe zugeteilt wird, da er mit den überwiegend* weißen *Kindern in den* A classes *landet, erkennt er für sich, dass er sich selbst stärker mit der* Black community *identifiziert. Die Leser*innen erleben das rassistische System aus Sicht eines Kindes, das zum ersten Mal mit der vorherrschenden Rassentrennung in Berührung kommt.*

Trevor Noah's experiences are best illustrated by viewing the scene through the eyes of the first-person narrator, an eleven-year-old boy. The naivety of the descriptions reveals a soul that has never been touched by the problems of identity crisis or racial segregation. He seems to be completely unaware of big political issues when he first enters his new school building. He is left alone, so the only one he can turn to is he himself when he asks: "*Where were they all hiding?* [...] Were we going to meet up later on?" (ll. 9–12) with reference to his fellow Black students.

When he sees them at break he compares their appearance to "a tap [being opened, where] all the black [come] pouring out" (ll. 8/9) to form an "ocean of black." (l. 8) In contrast to this metaphorical flood he considers himself in "a no-man's-land" (l. 22), something that is actually impossible among so many people. This paradox is strengthened when he says that "people [are] together and yet not together" (l. 16), which can only be understood when you sense the concept of segregation.

The whole scene creates an image of a little boy "left standing in the middle" (l. 11) as if he was indecisive of which side to lean to. This feeling shows again that seeing kids being segregated seems to be relatively new to him. From one day to the next he learns about the politics of his country. His informal, childlike language is exceeded by some 'learned words', i. e. segregation, or labels like Black, White, 'Coloured', etc.

Then, for the first time ever, someone addresses Trevor as an "anomaly" (ll. 25/26), and it is someone who is also an 'anomaly' because he is Indian and thus neither Black nor White. The adjective "fellow" (l. 25) added to the metaphor helps him not to feel lonely. All the direct speech is now spoken by the Black or 'Coloured' side. There are lots of positively connoted words to describe this group: Theesan, the Indian, "rescue[s]" (l. 23) him, they "hit it off" (ll. 26/27), "he [takes him] under his wing" (l. 27). Trevor gets help from an 'insider', which is illustrated by the allusion to Charles Dickens' novel *Oliver Twist*, in which an orphan is supported by an 'insider' too (cf. l. 27). His "language thing" (l. 34) or "trick" (ll. 29, 34), a synonym for his knowledge of different African languages like Zulu and Xhosa, "endear[s him] to the black kids." (l. 38) Trevor says that he's Black like them (cf. l. 40) and "belong[s] to their tribe" (l. 45). He later uses the personal pronoun "my" (l. 50) to express that he has realized who his "people" (l. 51) are. All in all, a very warm, comfortable atmosphere is created and the reader feels happy for the little boy having made friends on his first day at a new school.

In contrast to that, his dialogue with the school counsellor, most likely a White person, clearly shows her debasing of the majority of her students. Her answer to Trevor's request of switching over to the B classes insinuates a feeling of superiority ("I don't think you want to do that", l. 53). She is sure that Trevor is on her side "because those kids are ... you know" (l. 55) and is quite astonished when he insists: "No, I don't" (l. 56).

Whenever the counsellor refers to the Black students we get a wide range of negatively connoted words and phrases, e. g. "those kids are gonna hold you back," (l. 59), "there aren't" (l. 62) any smart kids in the B classes, they would have a negative "effect on [Tevor's] future" (l. 67), Trevor was "giving up [...] opportunities" (l. 68) and he would be missing out "for the rest of [his] life" (ll. 68/69).

After his first day at the new school, Trevor sees himself as a Black child. He has never had to choose, but now, being forced to do so, he notices that for him a true feeling of belonging can only be found in the Black community.

3.1 *Diese Aufgabenstellung bereitet schon ein wenig auf das Abitur ab 2021 vor. Bisher war es in den Aufgaben in Berlin und Brandenburg üblich, einen Zusatz wie „use Trevor Noah's story as one of your examples" zu ergänzen. Das fällt ab 2021 weg. Sie müssen aber auch ohne explizite Aufforderung den Bezug zum Ausgangstext herstellen.*
*Dieser Teil gestaltet sich hier etwas schwierig, da wir wenig Informationen dazu haben, wie sich Trevor Noah in dieser* peer group *zurechtfindet, und keine Informationen dazu, wie sich seine Situation entwickeln wird. Zunächst erfahren wir lediglich, dass Trevor Noah bei den Schwarzen* Kindern aufgrund seiner Sprachkenntnisse positiv aufgenommen wird, dass die Beratungslehrerin jedoch davon ausgeht, dass der Wechsel in die* B classes *und der Kontakt zu den Schwarzen* Kindern seine Zukunft negativ beeinflussen wird. Denkt man jedoch etwas weiter, fällt auf, dass der Text einer autobiographischen Geschichte entstammt, die international Aufmerksamkeit erlangt hat – ein Indiz für die positive Entwicklung von Trevor Noahs Werdegang. Trevor Noah ist ein südafrikanischer Comedian, politischer Aktivist und Moderator. Im Bezug zum Text ist es möglich, zu diskutieren, dass Trevor Noah die Entscheidung, in die* B classes *zu wechseln, unabhängig von den anderen Kindern an der Schule trifft, dass es sich also um eine Entscheidung handelt, die losgelöst von der* peer group *und möglichem Gruppenzwang getroffen wird.*

Trevor Noah is a 'Coloured' child, i. e. in the eyes of the South African authorities he is neither Black nor White. When he feels forced to decide for one side, he says that he'd "rather be held back with people [he likes] than move ahead with people [he doesn't] know" (ll. 71/72).
Trevor puts friendship and well-being over education or striving for improvement. He may have had a successful academic career ahead of him, but lacking friends or living outside your comfort zone would not make up for it. He would rather risk knowledge gaps or lower academic achievement than lack social connection and support.
I can understand his decision up to a certain point. What good is being able to solve every problem when you have no one to share your triumph with? If you haven't got anyone to help you through the ups and downs in life? And, how do you know for sure that your peers will hold you back?
Take Trevor Noah for an example. He felt lost and probably like an outsider in the schoolyard on his first day at H. A. Jack Primary. But he quickly made friends with the Black students from B classes and also with Theesan Pillay, the Indian boy. They found out they share something, in this case a common language and the fact that they belong to a different ethnicity, and this is what plays a major role in a peer group. You feel or think or believe the same and that gives you the feeling of belonging. We are social beings, we need to interact with other people and we want to be loved and accepted.
But this exact longing can also turn out to be the flipside of peer groups. Often teenagers want to belong to a certain group which they feel is cool. In their wish to become a part of it they might fall for the wrong people. It is common knowledge that this could lead to drug abuse, crime or anti-social behaviour. 13–19-year-olds in particular often do not want to see that their 'friends' do them no good; and parents and educators

will have a hard time trying to make them see the truth. In *Born a Crime* the school counsellor predicts such an outcome when she warns Trevor, "You do realize the effect this will have on your future? You do understand what you're giving up?" (ll. 67/68) and claims, "You don't want to be friends with those kids," (l. 64). In Trevor Noah's case the counsellor's (racist) prediction is wrong. He will become a famous TV host, have a successful career and achieve more than most people do in their lives. All in all, being among peers is an important step in the development of every young adult. While the wrong friends might pull you down, on the positive side the right ones will encourage and support you, comfort you and finally turn into friends for life.

3.2 *Ab 2021 entfällt die Aufgabe mit dem Vergleich zu einem weiteren Film oder literarischen Werk.*

3.3 *Obwohl der Internationale Tag der Sprachen nicht nur für das Erlernen von Fremdsprachen wirbt, sondern wohl auch mit Blick auf das Aussterben vieler Regionalsprachen und Dialekte ins Leben gerufen wurde, denkt man aufgrund der Aufgabenstellung bei der Bearbeitung doch in erster Linie nicht an die Muttersprache. Beide Aspekte sind aber möglich und lassen sich auch mit Trevor Noahs Geschichte vereinbaren. Wählen Sie also selbst. Der Vorschlag hier konzentriert sich auf die Fremdsprachen-Variante.*

¡Hola! Salut! Hello! Nǐ hǎo!
Nǐ – what?! Nǐ hǎo! This is 'hello' in Chinese! When I tore off a leaf from my calendar today I found it's the International Day of Language!
Did you know that?
Why do we need a special day to celebrate languages? Well, it's obvious: because it is a bare necessity to speak one! We all speak our mother tongues, but most of us have also learnt at least one foreign language at school, haven't we? It always makes me proud when I travel around the world and I can communicate with the local people there, either in global English or even with a few basic words in Spanish, Italian, Russian, etc. Let me tell you a little story:
Only last year, on our holiday in Tuscany, we got lost on a road in the middle of nowhere. Darkness was falling and we felt rather helpless. When an old man appeared suddenly we asked him in English for "the ferry terminal", knowing that it was just around the corner of our hotel. He didn't understand and we saw our hopes dashed when the word 'barca' and then 'port' popped up in my head. His face beamed and he showered us with a cascade of Italian sentences. Then he gestured to us to follow him and we found out we had been relatively close to our hotel! If we couldn't have made ourselves understood, he might as well have walked on, leaving it to us to find our way home.
This is just one example that shows how language is a powerful tool. Indeed, people often say that language is the key, and it's certainly the key to their hearts. In an autobiographical story I read lately Trevor Noah, a child with a White father and a Black mother in South Africa, felt rather lost on his first day at a new school in his class with

mainly White children. At break he found out that there were loads of Black kids in the other classes and they warmed up to him immediately when they learnt that he spoke their native languages, i. e. Zulu and Xhosa. Wouldn't he still be the lonely kid in the yard were it not for his language skills?

In our globalised world everyone should speak at least two languages other than their own. I think it was the great German poet J. W. Goethe, who once said that if you don't speak any foreign language, you know nothing about your own.

In the comment section below, feel free to share your experiences with using a language in any place around the world.

I'm looking forward to your contributions to International Language Day 2020!

## Aufgabenstellung 1.2

1 *Für die Aufgabe im AFB I gibt es zwei Operatoren:* summarize/sum up *und* outline. *Im Allgemeinen besteht der Unterschied darin, dass beim ersteren der Einleitungssatz zu Texttyp, Autor*in, Titel etc. steht. Da hier aber die Zusammenfassung auf Datenbanken und Auswirkungen auf die Nutzer*innen beschränkt ist, könnte Ihre Bearbeitung auch gleich mit den verlangten Fakten beginnen.*

The article "Are Genetic Testing Sites the New Social Networks?" by Alyson Krueger, published in *The New York Times* of June 16, 2018, deals with the trend of discovering your ethnic heritage.

At-home-testing-kits have become really popular in the USA. Since they were made available, millions of people have tried to find out about their genetic code at manageable cost, a lot of them rather out of curiosity.

It is easy to handle: you send a sample of your saliva to a lab and you receive a pie chart showing your ethnic heritage and a list of people related to you. Customers can also choose whether the testing sites are allowed to share their genetic information with the other testers.

The effect companies like 23andMe have is that of Facebook's early years. Long-lost relatives can reunite, friendships are established and the question of who you are and where you are from will be answered. Groups of people like sperm-donor-kids or adoptees now stand a realistic chance of tracing down their families, a chance they could never have dreamt of before.

Some customers report negative experiences, though. One says that she was shocked when she found out she was 31.5 % White when she was sure she was Native American and Black. She felt very much like sharing this shock with the net and her post went viral. She learnt that many more had had similar experiences.

Another frustrating experience is when people get no connections at all. For example, Latinx and Asians are not represented in larger numbers among the customers of genetic testing sites and thus sometimes find no people genetically connected to them.

2 *Bei der Analyse eines nicht-fiktionalen Textes kann sich die Bearbeitung auf einige wenige Stilmittel beschränken. Sehen Sie sich dazu z. B. die Struktur des Textes, das Verhältnis zwischen Autorenmeinung und Zitaten, die Sprache und die Stilebene des Artikels an. Oft werden die Untersuchung von sprachlichen Bildern (Metaphern, Vergleiche etc.) und ein allgemeines Mittel wie „choice of words" erwartet. Das reicht meistens schon für eine gute Leistung im AFB II aus.*
*Die Illustration gibt nicht viel Neues her, muss aber unbedingt berücksichtigt werden.* Give evidence *bedeutet auch zwingend, dass Sie aus dem Text (und der Illustration) zitieren.*

The author uses different means to attract the readers' interest. The rhetorical question in the headline is the first: "Are Genetic Testing Sites the New Social Networks?" (headline) At first it seems unusual: what do genetic testing sites and social networks have in common? The sub-heading "Like Facebook, but for fifth cousins, adoptive mothers and sperm-donor dads," may allow a first glimpse but still leaves some food for thought.
The article itself is presented as a feature story. Alyson Krueger does not simply write it from a scientific point of view but introduces the topic to the readers through the eyes of several real-life customers. We get names like "Dyan deNapoli" (l. 1) or "Christine Carter" (l. 46), places such as "Georgetown, Mass." (l. 11) and results "99.4 percent of them were from Europe" (l. 5), which help the reader relate to the topic and suggest reliability.
When reading about the personal experiences of the people who had their DNA tested you cannot escape the emotional side of their stories. The author quotes Josh Broadwater, who says that he "was abandoned when he was 1 day old" (ll. 27/28) and who through genetic testing met his father who to him "is just the coolest person" (l. 38). Reading this we secretly cry a silent tear in sympathy. Lucky him, he gets "along so well [with his father] that they now talk on the phone once a week" (l. 39). As for the success stories we read a lot about positive emotions. Dyan deNapoli, another customer of the testing sites, says that "she was most giddy about […] a 41-page list of all the people […] related to her" (ll. 5–7).
But Krueger not only refers to one side of the coin. She also reports about Christine Carter, who thought she was Native American and Black. When the list came, she was confronted with unexpected results. She is 31.5 % White. Her negative emotions are mirrored in the author's choice of words. Carter was "shocked" (l. 51) and "struggled through dinner" (l. 52), she kept this "revelation mostly to herself" (l. 52) and she wrote a post that allowed her "to get it off [her] chest" (l. 59). For Latinx and Asians the search may also be "frustrating" (l. 60), since not enough of them take the test to allow tracing down their ancestry.
When Alyson Krueger does not refer to her interviewees she focusses on the scientific background. Her language then changes. We get to know about "databases" (l. 20), "sperm donors" (l. 25), "[a]doptees" (l. 25) and "biological family members" (ll. 25/26).
The illustration that comes along with the article combines the personal approach with the scientific background. It shows a photograph of Christine Carter. Around her we

can see the scattered pieces of the pie chart that is to show her ethnic heritage. The slices show an astonishing variety of ethnicities. But it is still "100 % percent Christine Carter", as the caption says. This illustration automatically raises the question of what the reader's chart would look like. The statistics support the information provided in the article and strengthen the objectivity of Krueger's view due to the facts and figures mentioned.
All in all, that is how an objective image of the topic is created, while appealing to the reader's emotions at the same time. The sophisticated readership of the *New York Times* will surely appreciate it.

3.1 *Diese Aufgabe enthält zwei Teilaufgaben. Zunächst sollen Sie den Titel erklären und herausstellen, inwiefern Anbieter von Gentests eine ähnliche Funktion erfüllen wie soziale Medien. Anschließend sollen Sie darüber hinaus weitere Bereiche kommentieren, in denen technologische Entwicklungen Einfluss auf unsere Kommunikation haben. Während beide Aufgaben für sich genommen gut zu meistern sind, besteht die Herausforderung darin, die beiden Bereiche sinnvoll miteinander zu verknüpfen. Auch ist es nicht so leicht, über die erste Teilaufgabe hinaus Anknüpfungspunkte zum Zeitungsartikel herzustellen. Die folgende Lösung nimmt Bezug auf die Erlebnisse von Josh Broadwater. Alternativ könnten Sie auch darauf eingehen, wie Christine Carter ihre Erlebnisse in einem Blogpost verarbeitet und darüber sowohl positives Feedback von Leuten bekommt, die Ähnliches erlebt haben, als auch Opfer von Hass im Netz wird, wenn* White supremacists *sie beschimpfen.*

By definition, a social network is a website which enables users to communicate with each other by posting info, comments, images, etc. At first genetic testing does not seem to have this purpose. But as the title of the article suggests, when taking a closer look at the matter, 23andMe and other similar sites are also about connecting people. It is not their priority, but definitely intended that once you make your personal data known, you get into contact with long-lost relatives or family members you did not know existed – just as Facebook made people get in contact with long-lost friends and acquaintances.
This is just one aspect of how science and technology have affected the way we communicate today.
Let's take availability for a start. My grandma used to say, never phone anybody before 9 am and after 9 pm. This rule has long been obsolete. When you send a message via WhatsApp or Facebook, you don't care about time anymore. If the recipient reads it any time later it's okay. On the other hand, it creates a feeling of expecting a 24/7 availability, which is the reason for a lot of stress in my opinion.
Another aspect is the frequency of contact. Fortunately, you communicate more often with friends and relatives because it is easier to send a text message than to phone somebody. You may have lost contact, but once you have found each other again on social networks, you are more likely to share info, images and videos.

The contact between different generations has also improved. Grandparents who own a smartphone can keep in touch with their grandchildren via messaging services. This might lead to rarer visits, though.
The definition of 'friend' or 'family' is also affected by social networks. Nowadays everyone whom we contact on Facebook and similar sites is called a friend. We often do not know the people that read our posts or follow us on Instagram. And when you write to someone anonymously, it might be understood as intrusion into their privacy. In Josh Broadwater's case, he and his biological father found each other via AncestryDNA, and they were lucky enough that they both wanted to get to know each other. Wishing for contact with somebody could be a one-way feeling.
One last important point is the way we communicate. Social networks make it much easier to send hate mail or to bully someone. We are also more likely to open up our personal lives to anybody. Our personal data have become a product, so we need to be careful about giving them away too generously. Also, often conversations lack depth: we are limited to a certain number of signs to express what we feel. Emojis and abbreviations have taken the place of words and phrases. Unfortunately, short texts make it much harder to understand the tone of a message. How often do we add an emoji to a text simply because we fear the other will not get the hidden irony or might get irritated by our comment, etc.
In conclusion, social networks do affect the way we contact people. Only the future will show how positive or negative this effect ultimately is. Perhaps genetic testing sites will become so common that their databases will not only be used to match relatives but also potential partners or friends? Scientific development can be both: part of a utopian or a dystopian reality. It all depends on how we use it.

3.2 *Ab 2021 entfällt die Aufgabe mit dem Vergleich zu einem weiteren Film oder literarischen Werk.*

3.2 *Die Rede findet sich als geforderte Zieltextsorte vergleichsweise häufig in der Abiturprüfung. Denken Sie beim Formulieren Ihrer Lösung daran, Ihr Publikum nicht nur zu Beginn, sondern auch im Verlauf des Textes immer wieder anzusprechen und am Ende einen Dank für die Aufmerksamkeit auszusprechen. Auch sollten Sie den Kontext, in dem die Rede gehalten wird, nicht vernachlässigen, hier eine Jugendkonferenz zum Thema Genforschung. Beliebte Stilmittel in Reden sind rhetorische Fragen, Ausrufe und Einschübe. Versuchen Sie Ihre Sätze nicht zu komplex zu gestalten. Kurze Sätze mit Parallelismen, Anaphern und Alliterationen erleichtern den Zuhörenden das Verständnis und lenken ihre Aufmerksamkeit.*

Dear cousins,
You must be wondering why I am calling you that? I do so because everyone on Earth is at most 50th cousin to everybody else! How do we know? Well, that's easy. DNA research has taught us. So, I'd like to welcome you all here to our 'family reunion', our youth conference today!

Since the double-helix structure was first discovered in the 1950s, DNA research has revealed hundreds of hidden secrets about human nature. We can now have our unborn babies tested for hereditary diseases and react accordingly. DNA testing may also show whether we are more likely to suffer from heart conditions or different forms of cancer, for instance. Genetic 'scissors' can cut off flawed genes and 'repair' them. One of the latest developments are at-home DNA testing kits. You send a sample of your saliva to a lab and they will come up with detailed info about your ethnic heritage. Additionally, you can trace your cousins, as long as they have agreed to sharing their data, of course. But, remember, on the way you will somewhere find my name!

Well, joking aside, adoptees, sperm-donor kids who would never have stood a chance of meeting their birth parents may now be able to find out who they are and where they are from. This can be a great relief for those affected. This is especially so with people from traditional immigration countries like the USA who would love to learn of their ethnic backgrounds. Just consult the huge databases of the genetic testing sites, they will know!

Genetic engineering has also helped and will help in future to fight hunger and death. Plants' DNA has been altered to be more resilient to droughts, for example.

Oh brave new world! How I wish there were only positive sides to this! Have you ever heard of human enhancement? It can be described as the natural, artificial, or technological alteration of the human body in order to enhance physical or mental capabilities. 'Improving' the human body could also mean 'improving' our genes. If you want to know what life will be like when parents can choose their child's 'physical and mental capabilities', I recommend a novel by Andreas Elsberg, *Helix*, to you. This dystopian story conjures an alarming image of what impact DNA research can have when abused by scientists.

With all the blessings that progress holds we mustn't forget about the curse. If information about someone's genome falls into the wrong hands, their future is at risk. What if, in future, you can't get a job unless your employer has checked your genetic information in the database? Or you'll have to pay twice as much for your health insurance because your genes show you may often be ill?

Well, all that has to be considered when discussing the pros and cons of DNA research. Let's hope that our conference can provide food for thought to the scientists in the labs around the world. My dear cousins, I declare this conference open, thank you.

## Prüfungsteil 2: Sprachmittlung

### Aufgabenstellung 2.1

*Die folgende Lösung wurde während der Corona-Kontaktbeschränkungen im Mai 2020 geschrieben. In diesem Zeitraum arbeiteten etwa 50 % der Deutschen im Homeoffice, was dem Thema des Ausgangstextes eine besondere Aktualität bescherte. Auf dieses Ereignis bezieht sich auch die Einleitung der folgenden Beispiellösung. Generell eignen sich aktuelle Ereignisse für Blogposts, Reden oder Kommentare hervorragend als Einstieg.*

**Bye-bye office**

At the moment, the whole world seems to be working from home and we feel as if this is a rather new idea of how to organize work. Guess what? It is not. Doing your job from anywhere else but your office desk has quite a history already.
It's called crowdworking and means that people are working independently from every corner of the world, adding small fractures of work to a whole. Those digital nomads simply need a laptop or a smartphone with internet access and off they go!
Take Stephan Gerhard, 54, for example. He can even make a living from his job for Jovoto, a platform working in design, architecture and branding. A 40-hour-week generates a monthly income of € 2000 which he finds very satisfying. "Self-employment is what makes it worth it", he says. The average freelancer is about 36 and highly educated. A lot of the big global players like Airbus or Adidas, for example, offer these forms of 'micro-jobs'. They have been outsourcing design, architecture or programming for a long time. Today they upload their offers and so it's easy for any crowdworker to apply for jobs like photographing road signs for tom-tom or checking out marketing campaigns in their local supermarkets.
But not all that glitters is gold. Fulfilling your work contract slaving in an office cube includes at least some social security. You needn't care about pension or retirement plans. Truth be told, most of these freelancing jobs are not very demanding either. Payment also varies from € 3 to € 2500. The competition is very tough and the winner takes it all. Often jobs are broken down to such small tasks that you can't make a living from them anymore, even if you are frugal. That is why 80 % of all the crowdworkers use these jobs as an additional income only. Even fewer working hours cannot be guaranteed with bosses being able to check on your screen time by constant surveillance.
So, now you decide – is this the future of the world of work?

## Aufgabenstellung 2.2

*Sie schreiben eine E-Mail an Freundinnen und Freunde in Australien. Vermeiden Sie es im Rahmen der Abiturprüfung dennoch, zu stark ins Umgangssprachliche zu verfallen. Die folgende Lösung schließt auch Prozentangaben und viele Daten mit ein. Eine andere Variante wäre es, die Informationen zu abstrahieren und stärker auf die Gesamttendenzen einzugehen, als genaue Zahlen zu nennen.*

Antonia.blume@net.com
to: amy.stuart@australia.org

Hi Amy,

How is it going? Hope you are doing fine. I saw your pictures of Bondi Beach on your account the other day – amazing!
I'm quite busy with work, you know, with all the exams coming up. But don't worry, I haven't forgotten about your project. I did a bit of research and found an interesting article in one of Germany's most influential quality papers. The author Sandra Kegel dealt with

exactly the same topic you asked me about, so, luckily, I can summarize the facts and figures for you.
Here we go: between 2013 and 2017, 6.4 m Germans who used to read regularly, didn't buy a single book, neither online nor from their local bookshop. The positive thing about it is that there are 30m book lovers who still order them, but this sounds better than it actually is. For the first time ever the people who do no longer care about books outnumber those who appreciate a good read.
This has some serious consequences and not only for the book market. A society that does not read gives up on their cultural identity. Avid readers will gain knowledge and acquire social and cognitive competence the others will never have and, by that, a two-class-society that nobody really wants is created.
But what are the reasons why so many people have stopped reading? Well, a study of the German Publishers and Booksellers Association has revealed that, quite surprisingly, all social classes are affected. There is no difference between people living in cities or in the country either. But age plays a major role. Practically everyone between 20 and 49 has gone off reading. This seems to be especially significant among the 40-somethings. The study found a 37 percent decrease here! The good news is that children and the generation 50+ show no change in their reading habits.
What do people do instead? Well, that's easy to guess: they can be found online. 14–29-year-olds now spend an average of four and a half hours surfing the net. When asked, a lot of the non-readers say that they feel overwhelmed by their daily chores, by the lack of time and energy on the one hand and the pressure to be available 24/7 on the other. A constant blinking and beeping distracts them and does not allow them to concentrate or dive into a good read as it used to be.
It sounds rather paradoxical when they state that they often watch (TV) series on streaming platforms instead, since this seems to be a really time-consuming habit. But most people feel it's relaxing, it's passive and entertaining. You can also do it together with friends and family.
Well, I'm not quite sure what to make of it. I love reading, I buy books regularly. Am I the odd one out? How about you and Australian youngsters in general? Have they also given up on books?
I'd love to hear from you and your project.
Keep me informed, will you?

Take care
Antonia

* Schwarz wird in unseren neueren Publikationen großgeschrieben (und *weiß* wird durch die Schriftlage, also kursiv oder normal, gekennzeichnet), um deutlich zu machen, dass es sich nicht um Farbbezeichnungen handelt, sondern um Begriffe, die beschreiben, ob Menschen von Rassismuserfahrungen betroffen sind oder nicht.

**Abiturprüfung Berlin/Brandenburg 2021**
**Grundkurs/Leistungskurs**

Das Corona-Virus hat auch im vergangenen Schuljahr die Prüfungsabläufe beeinflusst. Um Ihnen die Prüfung 2021 schnellstmöglich zur Verfügung stellen zu können, bringen wir sie in digitaler Form heraus.

Sobald die Original-Prüfungsaufgaben 2021 zur Veröffentlichung freigegeben sind, können sie als PDF auf der Plattform **MyStark** heruntergeladen werden (Zugangscode vgl. Farbseiten vorne im Buch).

**Prüfung 2021**

**www.stark-verlag.de/mystark**